The SEVEN PEARLS *of* FINANCIAL WISDOM

ALSO BY CAROL PEPPER

Beyond Blood: A Novel

The

SEVEN PEARLS

of FINANCIAL

WISDOM

A Woman's Guide to Enjoying
Wealth and Power

CAROL PEPPER AND CAMILLA WEBSTER

St. Martin's Press ✖ New York

www.stmartins.com

Design by Patrice Sheridan

ISBN 978-0-312-64166-5 (hardcover)
ISBN 978-1-250-00832-9 (e-book)

First Edition: May 2012

10 9 8 7 6 5 4 3 2 1

FOR YOU—

may our pearls be your touchstones

CONTENTS

The SEVEN PEARLS *of* FINANCIAL WISDOM

Introduction

WHAT IS A PEARL?

A pearl is a treasured gift from the sea, created when a grain of sand accidentally finds its way into an oyster's shell. This natural gem is formed over months or even years as the oyster surrounds the sand with its lustrous nacre. In its final form, the pearl is a natural result of an organism's instinct for self-protection. Lifted from the sea by pearl divers, who risk the dangers of perilous waters so that others can enjoy the treasures they gather from the deep, this shimmering prize is a timeless, precious asset in the home and in the marketplace. Celebrated in classic novels, old master paintings, and passed from mother to daughter through the generations, the pearl is synonymous with lasting emotional and financial value.

We decided to call this book *The Seven Pearls of Financial Wisdom* because, just as an oyster produces layers of nacre to form its masterpiece, we as financial professionals have accumulated many layers of rich experience that have strengthened, beautified, and protected our financial lives and those of the many women we have counseled—resulting in the jewels we are now sharing with you. Like the pearl, our wisdom developed as a result of unexpected circumstances. Each pearl of wisdom is formed around a challenge, or grain of sand, that enters our lives; but like the oyster, we learned how to create layers of value out of obstructions and uncertainties. Over the course of months and even years, we hardened our own brilliantly reflective surfaces to transform challenging and even harmful situations into coveted assets and a deep store of what we recognize today as understanding. Now *our* pearls can be *your* touchstones.

Our hope for you is that you will make these pearls of wisdom your own. Take these lessons in, assimilate them deeply, and experience what it means to be truly happy with your money and the power it brings you. Your pearls will help you with financial decisions, no matter what you are facing.

WHY NOW?

This is not just another book about money. We are sharing a unique approach that will change your life forever and for the better, at a time when women are increasing their wealth and position in society. It is time for a new ideal.

We discovered that women face financial issues in seven areas of their lives. We identified the seven areas as wealth building, romance and marriage, motherhood, gathering power, crisis and loss, retirement, and legacy building. We also discovered that women may cycle through these areas repeatedly throughout their increasingly long lives.

We women are no longer following a traditional pathway from high school to retirement, but rather entering a new era that requires a fresh philosophy to support our relationship with money. We may sell our first business and set up a foundation at twenty-five, go back to school at forty, and remarry at seventy. Statistics tell us that women in the twenty-first century are going to live to be at least eighty-five and will often live to be one hundred or more. The year 2010 marked the first time that women constituted the majority of breadwinners and were projected to obtain more advanced degrees than men. Women now exert a tremendous amount of economic influence on all aspects of life; for example, women now control 85 percent of brand purchases.[1] This new world and the potential for even greater prosperity require new approaches from us.

The straight path from college to husbands to babies to homes and families, and from college to work and retirement—in that order—is crumbling. As a result, women may be feeling confused and uncertain—as if we are outside the norm, even when we are making traditional choices with our money and lifestyles. We have also noticed that changing economic trends are now making traditional choices increasingly unworkable or disappointing. For example, the "mancession" in 2009, during which more men lost their jobs than women, thwarted many women's desires to stay home and raise children full-time.[2]

It's been a long time since women wore a bustle, couldn't own a piece of real property, and had to be chaperoned about town. Yet some of our financial-planning decisions seem stuck in that long-ago era. It's time to acknowledge the power that women have to generate large incomes, and to celebrate our new financial clout. We need new ways to protect and grow our money. With this money comes the ability to influence our communities, societies, and the planet for the better.

Women now have the most freedom we've ever enjoyed in the history of humankind. Nothing is holding us back, other than the fact that our minds have not caught up to the variety of options we have today. We have heard from women over and over again that they really don't enjoy their money or their power, and in fact are very uncomfortable with the choices that living at this time in history presents. But now is the time to embrace financial freedom, and to build the amazing life that each of us has the potential to create.

WHY ARE WE QUALIFIED TO WRITE THIS BOOK?

Carol and Camilla met on the set of Forbes.com in 2009, when Camilla was interviewing Carol about the outlook for the world financial markets. We enjoyed the interview and later met for lunch on Manhattan's Upper East Side to learn more about each other. We quickly realized that the difference in our ages, and the difference in our careers, gave us a unique perspective on the questions that women face with their money. We got very excited about writing a book together in which we could combine our knowledge, expertise, and opinions.

Carol has worked in financial services for more than twenty-five years. Carol started her career at Salomon Brothers in 1984. She was the only female in the mergers group of the two-year analyst training program during the era of *Liar's Poker*. Carol then joined J.P. Morgan, earned an MBA at Columbia University, and went on to forge a career as a top private banker. She later managed more than $1 billion in assets at the Rockefeller family office. In 2001, she started her own family office called Pepper International. Carol offers top financial services with a focus on socially responsible investing, empowering female clients, and international issues. Carol is a highly sought-after global speaker and has won numerous awards in her field. Her firm was named a top family office by *Barron's* in 2009. She has been a writer for the Forbes Intelligent Investing Team. One of her main career goals is to teach women how to use their wealth effectively to create exciting and meaningful lives.

Camilla has been a top news and business journalist for nearly a decade. She has covered assignments for Forbes, *The Wall Street Journal*, MarketWatch, CBS News, and Fox News. She is a returning on-air guest covering business highlights to real estate opportunities to women's issues for leading TV and radio networks in the United States, including WABC and MSNBC. She also has appeared on Fox News Channel, Fox Business, and CNBC. As a broadcast news editor for *The Wall Street Journal*, Camilla handpicked business stories for TV audiences. She's interviewed celebrity entrepreneurs and leaders like Richard Branson, T. Boone Pickens, Sergey Brin, Sarah Jessica Parker, and Christine Lagarde, and has been one of the few invited journalists at the world-famous World Economic Forum in Davos. Early in her career, during Campaign 2000, Camilla produced coverage of the New Hampshire Primary for CBS News stations. She completed the historic and controversial election year at Fox News as a special projects producer, managing coverage of the Republican and Democratic conventions, election night, the Florida vote recount, and the presidential inauguration for hundreds of Fox News stations across the United States and Sky News in the U.K. Camilla was the coordinating producer for one of the first Fox News teams into Baghdad in 2003 during Operation Iraqi Freedom. She was one of the initial Western journalists to reach Saddam Hussein's "Palace of the Four Heads" and launched coverage of the U.S. Administration. Her intrepid style has put her in the midst of breaking news all over the world. Starting her career as a young intern at *60 Minutes*, Camilla has always searched for the truth in journalism, finding ways to make sense out of confusing or sensational headlines for her audience.

WHAT DO WE HOPE TO ACHIEVE WITH THIS BOOK?

Our seven pearls of financial wisdom do not come only from our combined experience; they also come from the expertise of the many prominent, successful women—women at the top of their various fields—whom we handpicked to share their expertise and experiences with you in this book. One of the things we hope to show is that as women talk with one another, they create the wisdom that takes care of the world. Another one of our goals is to guide you along the path that lies ahead of you, so you can begin to relax and actually enjoy your own wealth and power. Finally, we hope you will use the seven pearls to string yourself a necklace that will reflect your newfound radiance, a glow that comes from being a financially successful woman who lives her life to the fullest.

CHAPTER 1

WEALTH BUILDING

THE FIRST PEARL OF FINANCIAL WISDOM:
A Woman Must Build Her Own Wealth

THE FIRST PEARL OF WISDOM we want to offer you is that a woman must build her own wealth. Traditionally, we have been raised to think that somehow, magically, our financial well-being will be taken care of by others, either by family inheritance or, more likely, by marrying a man who earns a lot of money.

It is understandable that most of us have never really considered the idea of building our own wealth; only in the last few years has it even been a realistic possibility. Women couldn't get a business loan on their own until the 1970s in America. As Ana Harvey, the assistant administrator for women's business ownership at the U.S. Small Business Administration (SBA) explains,

> Congress passed the Equal Credit Opportunity Act in 1974, which, among other things, made it illegal for creditors to discriminate against anyone on the basis of race, color, religion, national origin, sex, marital status, age, or whether or not a person is receiving public assistance. Suddenly women, who had always been required to have a male cosigner, could secure loans on their own, at least in theory. In fact, women continued to face significant discrimination for a number of years.

It wasn't until 1988 and the passage of the Women's Business Ownership Act that the needs of women in business—such as access to resources and the elimination of discriminatory lending practices by banks that favored male business owners—were addressed. It was a move that Julie Weeks, the head of Womenable, a research, program, and policy-development consultancy whose mission is to improve the environment for women-owned businesses worldwide, calls "the big bang in women's entrepreneurship." According to the American Express OPEN State of Women-Owned Businesses report, in 2011 there were an estimated 8.1 million women-owned businesses in the United States, generating $1.3 trillion in revenues and employing nearly 7.7 million people.[1]

Here is the grain of sand that first enters our snug shell—the unfortunate reality of what happens to a woman who does not assume responsibility for building her own wealth: She develops an unspoken terror that one day *she* will be the little old homeless bag lady she sees on the street. A report from the Center for Progress called *Straight Facts on Women and Poverty* reveals that 13.8 percent of women are poor in the United States versus 11.1 percent of men. Over the age of seventy-five, 13 percent of women are poor versus 6 percent of men. This gap is bigger here than in any other developed country in the world.[2] Three quarters of the women with incomes below the poverty line are single women. We say a woman "must" build her own wealth to avoid becoming an unfortunate statistic. We really must take care of ourselves!

THE GRAIN OF SAND IN THE OYSTER SHELL

Do you know a woman who . . .

- Works in a low-paying, service-oriented job?
- Has a great corporate job but still earns less than the men in her field?
- Has been divorced and has had to lower her standard of living?
- Has been divorced and has to pay alimony to her husband?

- Has to shoulder the entire burden of child support because of an ex-husband who won't pay?
- Has a wonderful husband who lost his job and can't find another one?
- Has a husband who became ill and can no longer work?
- Has been widowed and whose late husband left insufficient funds for her retirement years?
- Has no money saved for retirement and no idea what she will do to support herself in her old age?
- Is one of the 13 percent of American women who are poor in their old age (versus only 6 percent of men)?

If you do know any women like this—or if any of these situations apply to you—then it's a perfect opportunity to turn a grain of sand into a pearl of great price. The good news is that today, by following our first pearl of wisdom and by realizing that you must build your own wealth—for your own sake and for the sake of your family—you can avoid the heartbreak of poverty in your later years. When you have money, you have security, you have choices, and you can make plans. Whether you are a mother planning your children's education, a new wife discussing money plans with your husband, a new college graduate considering your first career, or a retiree considering helping a family member, remember that your own financial security is paramount.

How do we build our own wealth? There are many ways to go about it; below, we will cut through the bewildering number of possibilities and help you get focused on the most effective strategies.

START YOUR OWN BUSINESS

Why Investing in Your Own Company Delivers the Biggest Return by Far

Starting a business is by far the best way to build your own wealth today. When you are trying to build wealth, you need to recognize that the world still offers obstructions as well as opportunities. If you are a highly educated woman, chances are good that you have pursued a corporate career. Working for a large company may make sense in the early years, so that you can develop great experience in a field. However, in the corporate world, women are still earning seventy-seven cents on the dollar compared to men. The glass ceiling is very much alive, and the ranks of women at the most senior levels are thin. Many women leave the corporate life to start their own business precisely because they realize that they will never earn as much as their male counterparts, particularly at the senior level. They then take their excellent skills and put them to work in a small business.

Between 1997 and 2011, when the number of businesses increased in the United States by 34 percent, the number of women-owned businesses increased by 50 percent—a rate one and a half times the national average.[3] When you own your own company, you have a chance to level the playing field in terms of your salary, bonus, and even preferred insurance rates. "The great equalizer for women in my mind is entrepreneurship," says Marsha Firestone, Ph.D., the founder of Women Presidents' Organization (WPO), a nonprofit membership organization for women who serve as presidents of multimillion-dollar companies.

Today, two out of every three new businesses are started by women.[4] "Many [women business owners] come from the corporate world, where they've hit the glass ceiling or the level of flexibility they seek is not available. They know they can do just as well—or better—on their own, and so they go into business for themselves," explains Ana Harvey of the U.S. SBA.

Although the prevailing view is that women are running mom-and-pop-style operations, Marsha Firestone says research shows that "the fastest-growing segment of women-led companies are those that have more than a million dollars in annual revenue."

The *World Wealth Report,* published each year by Merrill Lynch and Capgemini, reveals that the majority of all global wealth is created by family-owned businesses. Business-owner data also reveals the potential for greater earnings for business owners rather than employees. In the top 25 percent of earners, entrepreneurs make more money than those who work for employers. The average small-business-owning family earned $185,350 in 2007, compared to $64,207 earned by non-business-owning households.[5]

If owning your own business becomes your sole vocation, you'll be able to set your work schedule and get excellent tax breaks. If it's a secondary interest, you will gain more financial security in the new freelance economy. This is the era when your business vision can come true at any age, and there's a lot to consider when starting your own business. As Oprah Winfrey says on her website, "What I know for sure is that if you want success, you can't make success your goal . . . the key is not to worry about being successful; but to instead work toward being significant—and the success will naturally follow."

We realize there are many excellent resources available to help women start businesses. In this section, we want to dispel some of the myths surrounding this path to wealth building and help you focus on the most important things to know before you get started.

To Succeed in Your Own Business, Start with a Good Idea

We want to dispute the widely held belief that you must only start a business that reflects your deepest passion. Although that would be ideal, this daunting preconception can stop you from pursuing the best way to build your wealth. According to Marsha Firestone, the single most important characteristic of the women who have created businesses that earn more than $1 million per year is that they focus on some type of innovation. That means that the idea for your own business might be found in something simple—improving the way you do an everyday task, inventing a better version of an existing product, or coming up with a less expensive way to deliver a product to market, thereby drastically reducing costs. There are also many success stories of women who started a business based on a beloved hobby like working with pets or gardening.

Understand the Limitations of a Service Business

Many people decide to start a business based on providing a service. If the service is something that is provided by you, the growth of your business will be limited by the number of hours in your day. A good example of this is a massage therapist who works at a gym and decides to leave the gym to take only private clients. The growth of her business will be limited to the number of hours in a day in which she can give massages. Service businesses do not have property, manufacturing plants, or equipment, which means that they do not have assets that could be used as collateral for a business loan. Eventually, in order to expand a service business beyond what you can personally do, you will have to hire employees who do what you do, and these employees may or may not be able to provide the same level of excellence you provide in giving the service.

On the other hand, people who are excellent at providing a service can translate this excellence into a products-based business. For example, a Pilates instructor can consider writing a book on Pilates, creating DVDs to sell, and marketing a line of clothing to wear during Pilates classes.

Products do not require you to personally interact with each potential customer. You write a book once, and it can be read by millions, for example. You can standardize excellence much more easily in a product than in a service. Many products take equipment to produce, and these assets can be financed through business loans. There are tax incentives and subsidies available from the federal and state governments to businesses that hire employees. In the long run, a products-based business generally provides you with more personal flexibility than a service-based business. As your business becomes more successful, you can hire others to run it while you sit back and enjoy the benefits of ownership.

Start Your Business in Twenty-four Hours

If you're feeling overwhelmed by the task of starting your own business, don't be. Getting started now takes only a few strokes of the keyboard, thanks to technology. Jane Applegate, America's leading small-business expert and the author of *201 Great Ideas for Your Small Business,* declares to reluctant entrepreneurs: "Only in America can you wake up in the morning with a great idea and start a business by nightfall. Anyone can do it in a day. It really is the American dream." You used to need between ten thousand and twenty thousand dollars to set up a business. Now you can accomplish it with less than five thousand dollars, and do most of the work on your computer.

SMALL BUSINESS TIPS

These helpful tips come from author and small-business management expert Jane Applegate.

- Set up your preferred business structure—a corporation, partnership, or limited liability company (LLC)—and register it with your city, county, or state online through websites like Rocket Lawyer or LegalZoom.
- Open a business bank account online.
- Surf your way to a Web domain registration site (examples include Go Daddy and Network Solutions) and register a name for your website.
- Set up Web hosting, fill in a design template, and have a website on-line before bedtime.
- Hire outsourced talent to service your business from sites like ELance .com. They handle all the tax forms and arrange payments between you and your freelancers or employees.
- If you need marketing help, go to a website like growyourbusinessnetwork.com.
- Set up a cloud-based telephone system on RingCentral.com, or go to Google Voice and set up a "follow me" phone number.
- Take a step into social media for your new business by setting up a Facebook fan page, a Twitter account, and a LinkedIn page.
- Order your promotional materials on sites like 4over4.com, Zazzle.com, and 1800postcards.com.
- Finally, before you rest your head on your pillow, you can announce your new venture through PR Newswire or EnFlyer.com.

Do Your Research and Write a Business Plan

The most important investment you can make is taking the time to write a business plan. It is absolutely critical to figure out if there is a market for your business idea and to figure out how much money it will cost to get started. There are a number of great online resources and software programs you can purchase to help you write a business plan. You must get very clear on the costs of running your own business and understand how you will pay for these costs. The high failure rate of new businesses can be overcome by smart planning. If you are new to working with numbers, hire a good accountant to help you develop a business plan, and bounce your ideas off people with experience in the field you want to enter if you are not highly experienced. Take advantage of the wisdom of retired executives available through SCORE (www.score.org), which provides free small-business training and mentoring. The more research you do in advance, the more likely your business is to thrive.

Be Able to Cover Your Living Expenses Before Quitting Your Day Job

There are conflicting ideas on how much money you need to set aside when leaving a job to start your own business. Conservatively, you need to have two to three years of living expenses put aside—because that's how long it's going to take for a new business to start generating cash. It's always a good idea to keep your day job as long as possible. Use your spare time to write your business plan and source materials, and when you absolutely can't move forward unless you quit your job, then it's time take the plunge.

Fund Your New Business Sensibly

You can fund your new business from savings or by obtaining financing. Often, the cash used to start a business comes from an unexpected source. For example, some women have launched businesses by using a divorce settlement or a lump-sum payment received after they have been laid off. If you intend to fund your business from savings, you should fund it from personal savings, not your 401(k) plan. You can withdraw funds from your 401(k), but this is a very unwise thing to do. First, if you are younger than fifty-nine and a half, you must pay a withdrawal penalty and taxes, which means that you are receiving only forty cents of every dollar you have put away. Second, you are potentially devastating your retirement. Your business may or may not work, but you will certainly grow older and need those funds in the future, regardless of how the business does.

Although it may be tempting, also avoid using the excess value in your home as collateral for a home-equity loan to start your business. If the business does not take off, you may not be able to cover the second mortgage payments and may, tragically, lose your home as well as your new company. If you do not have enough personal savings to fund a new business, and many people don't, then you will need to look for financing.

- **Borrow against your 401(k):** To finance your start-up costs, you might consider borrowing against your 401(k), but this can happen only while you are still employed and working on your new business on the side; once you leave your corporate job, you must repay the loan, so this is a very short-term solution.

- **Check out SBA programs:** You can investigate loan-guarantee programs available from the Small Business Administration, which has many good options for women looking to start their own businesses. The SBA does not make loans but does provide loan guarantees to encourage banks to lend money to you. Again, you are more likely to get funds for a product-based business—one that has equipment, a plant, or property that can be used as collateral for a loan. It is much more difficult to get a loan for a service business, and almost impossible to get a bank loan for a service business without years of demonstrated cash flow from multiple clients.

- **Don't place high hopes on the banks unless you have other collateral:** It is extremely rare for banks to give noncollateralized loans to start up a business. The bank may give you a loan if you have other assets to pledge, such as a personal portfolio of securities. It may make sense to pledge a personal securities portfolio in order to get the funds to start your company; your securities can continue to grow while you launch your business. In this case, negotiate for long repayment terms, or an interest-only loan, to give yourself two or three years before you have to start repayment. Make sure the securities are conservatively invested so that you don't face a margin call if the markets go through a bad period. (A margin call means that the value of your collateral has fallen and the bank wants to sell the securities to pay back the loan.)

- **Take a personal loan from friends and family:** Many people turn to friends and family for personal loans to start a business. In this case, share your business plan, draw up a promissory note, and make sure family members have reasonable expectations of when you can repay the loan. Offer to pay interest and take out a life-insurance policy that would repay your family member should you die unexpectedly. These policies are usually very inexpensive if the benefit amounts are small.

- **Take a part-time job or a second job:** You may find it necessary in the beginning to take a part-time job or a second job to fund your living expenses while working on your business. This is not as bad as it seems—as long as you can cover your overhead, you can give your business the extra time it needs to become self-supporting.

- **Live on your partner's salary while starting the business:** If you are in a relationship, you may be able to join forces with your partner to support you and your family while you are starting your business. This can be an exciting family decision, and if the business takes off, your partner may be able to quit the nine-to-five routine and join you in working on the business. It is critical to share the business plan with your partner and to have regular financial meetings so he or she understands the progress you're making and setbacks you may be experiencing.

- **Max out your credit cards as a last resort:** Some famous businesses were started by maxing out credit cards; this is a much less likely scenario today due to tighter credit standards and smaller credit lines.

Beware the Dangers of Angel Investors and Venture Capital

If you have a terrific idea, you may be able to attract the attention of angel investors or venture capitalists. These are individuals who are looking to invest their capital in start-up businesses. Although this route may be appealing, angels can be distinctly devilish to new business owners.

First of all, angels and VCs expect you to give up a huge percentage of the equity in your business in exchange for their funds. Often, you end up owning less than 20 percent of your own company if you seek funding from these sources.

Also, angels and VCs want a quick, high return on their investment. They often want to see growth rates of 30 percent per year or more. This may be anathema to your idea—they may force you to sacrifice quality in order to obtain steep growth rates, as opposed to letting the business grow more organically.

In addition, these investors want an "exit strategy." They want to sell the company and realize a high return on their funds. You may want to create a business that could stay in your family for generations—therefore, you may have a very different time frame in mind. Make sure you agree with the strategy that the VCs or angels envision before you sign up.

Flexible Hours Do Not Exist

Women have been in search of flexible hours for decades in an effort to balance their personal lives and professional lives. However, do not start a business if you think it will mean having all kinds of glorious flextime. Running your own business only means that *you* now control your hours, not your boss. Let us be clear: If you want to succeed, you must not sacrifice work hours in favor of outside activities. Author and business expert Jane Applegate says, "There's certainly advantages to being self-employed, including lots of personal flexibility, but you'll definitely be working twice as many hours overall."

Choose a Legal Entity for Your Business

There are several different choices available when it comes to choosing a legal entity for your business. We strongly urge you to consult with a good business lawyer to discuss the pros and cons of each. In general, if you are going to be the sole owner of a small company, you might want to start as a single-member limited liability company, or LLC. This type of entity provides you with legal protection in case you are sued, but it taxes your income only once. By contrast, if you set up a corporation, the company pays taxes—usually quarterly—and then you pay taxes again on money the company distributes to you as a dividend. This often doesn't make sense for small companies. You may find that you wish to set up your LLC in a state other than the state in which you live. Many LLCs are registered in Delaware, for example, because Delaware has favorable LLC laws.

If you are starting a business with one or more partners, you should compare the advantages of an LLC to a partnership or an S corporation. A good business lawyer can help you make the choice. And it is critical that you have a very thorough legal agreement with your partner or partners before the business starts, so that you agree on how to split profits, make decisions, and most important, how to dissolve the partnership if things don't work out.

TAX BENEFITS AND BURDENS

When you are launching your business, it's absolutely imperative that you are aware of your tax benefits and burdens and keep on top of them. To understand the tax issues better, we consulted with Barbara Taibi, a director in the Personal Wealth Advisors Group of EisnerAmper LLP, a New York–based tax and consulting group. She has more than twenty years of public accounting experience and more than fifteen years of experience in income tax planning and tax return preparation. Barbara explains, "I see a lot of women and men in businesses that could have worked, but then they always say, 'I can't stand all of these tax rules and additional forms; I can't deal with this and I don't want to do it anymore.' Unfortunately, it is some of these additional forms that have the worst penalties for noncompliance. If they had assigned this responsibility to someone else, it might have been different."

With Barbara's expertise, we have laid out key tax and planning measures for you to pursue with the assistance of an accountant that will make you rich and keep you happy.

Take Advantage of Greater Business Expenses

When you are a salaried employee, there are very few expenses that you can deduct to lower your tax burden due to limitations on deductible amounts. One of the great benefits to owning your own business is the ability to offset a large number of your expenses against your business income, thereby lowering your taxable income. It is absolutely key to keep excellent expense records now that you are no longer a salaried employee.

Time Your Income

When you are a self-employed person, you have some flexibility on how much income to declare each year for tax purposes. Income, for tax purposes, is defined as business revenue (which is generally sales of goods or services) minus business expenses. By timing your cash receipts and the payment of expenses, you may be able to take advantage of the graduated tax rates and fall into a lower tax bracket. It is crucial that you work with a good accountant to take advantage of all the ways you can time income, expenses, and depreciation on plant and equipment.

Choose to Account for Your Business on a Cash or Accrual Basis

There are two ways to legally account for your income as a business owner: a cash basis or an accrual basis. A cash basis means that the income and expenses are declared when they are received or made; an accrual basis means that income is declared as the service is given. For example, a spa may sell a series of five facials at one time for a discounted price. On a cash basis, the income would be declared when the five facials are purchased. On an accrual basis, the income would be declared as each facial is given over the entire year. As a cash-basis business owner, you can manage your cash flow by managing how you make purchases and pay company expenses. For example, if you pay expenses on a corporate credit card, you can declare those expenses in the year that you purchased the items on your card, even if you pay back those card balances in the following year. This would allow you to lower your income for tax purposes while preserving your cash.

Take Advantage of the Home Office Tax Deduction

If you are starting your business in your home rather than renting an office, your home office can create a significant tax deduction. Your home office space must pass two important tests. It must be used exclusively for the office and no other activities, and it must be your principal place of business. Many people convert their garage for this purpose. A legitimate home office allows you to deduct the percentage of your housing expenses equal to the percentage of the home used as the office. For example, if you are using 30 percent of your total home space as an office, you can deduct 30 percent of the costs of your home as business expenses, including depreciation on the house, rental payments, electricity, mortgage interest, utilities, and even repairs. Make sure to keep scrupulous records, as the IRS loves to audit for home-office expenses. It is never a good idea to deduct a significant percentage of your home as a home-office expense—the IRS will insist that you document this and may visit to verify that you are not exaggerating the square footage used for the business. The exception here may be a small apartment, but then it is hard to declare that the space is being used "exclusively" for the business.

Use the Health Insurance Deduction

If you're self-employed, you can deduct 100 percent of the health insurance premiums you pay for yourself, for your spouse, and for your children. If you are a sole proprietor without employees, you may be able to get more reasonably priced health insurance through the Freelancers Union, which operates in most states.

Take Advantage of a SEP

When you're self-employed, you have some interesting opportunities to plan your retirement by creating a Simplified Employee Pension, also known as a SEP. Contributions to a SEP are tax deductible and your business pays no taxes on the earnings of the investments. You are not locked into making contributions every year; each year, you can decide whether, and how much, to contribute to the SEP. There are no filing requirements with the government for your SEP. There are a number of specialized rules that need to be followed, so it is best to discuss a SEP with your accountant or financial advisor.

Catch Up on Retirement Savings with a
Defined Benefit Plan

A qualified defined benefit pension is the traditional pension plan in which the employer bears the risk of providing the promised level of retirement benefits to participants. The defined benefit plan limit is based on the benefit to be received at retirement, not on the annual contribution. Each year the plan's actuary determines the required annual contribution based on several factors, such as age, salary level, and years of service, as well as interest rate assumptions. The maximum annual benefit for which a plan may fund is the lesser of 100 percent of the participant's compensation up to $195,000 (indexed for 2010). For participants closer to retirement, contributions to a defined benefit plan may exceed the 100 percent, or forty-nine-thousand-dollar, limit imposed by defined contribution plans. This may be advantageous if you are a business owner who is approaching retirement age, has never started a retirement plan, and wishes to put away as much money as quickly as possible. Keep in mind the administration of this plan is more expensive and complex than a 401(k) or a SEP, and that you should consult a pension benefits expert to see what is right for your company.[6]

Deduct the Interest Expense of Borrowing Money

You may be taking on debt to purchase equipment or grow the company. The interest expense is a business deduction to you, and that could be a fairly significant number. By contrast, the only interest expense you can deduct without a business is your home mortgage interest and investment interest on money borrowed to buy investment property (i.e., a margin loan).

Choose the Right State for Your Business

"Residency issues are a huge deal," says EisnerAmper accountant Barbara Taibi. "We're seeing a lot of business planning and a lot of retirement planning based on how the state treats business income or how the state treats you as the owner because eventually this is all flowing to you anyway."

When you set up a new business, it's critical to look at states that are friendly to small businesses and have fewer filing requirements. For example, Florida, Texas, and Nevada have no state income tax. If you're an Internet-based business and you don't need to live in a high tax bracket state, consider moving to a tax-friendly environment. Since state regulations are constantly changing, consult Internet resources like the Small Business Council's ranking of best and worst states for small businesses. Keep in mind that taxes are only one aspect to consider when launching your small business; a trained workforce and your own preferred lifestyle may cause you to trade off taxes for other factors.

Tax Burdens

Many entrepreneurs throw in the towel too early because they never figure out how to work the system. When you are successful in a corporation, you have applied yourself to navigating the company and engaging with departments to make your life easier and your work more effective. Use these skills and apply them to your own business. Whenever possible, your efforts should be focused on growing the business and not on paperwork. Here we're going to outline the headaches of the self-employed and the solutions that work for the experts.

Outsource the Administration of Payroll and Payroll Taxes

One of the burdens of owning your own business is payroll. Bottom line: Payroll tax is a nightmare, and there is no difference between having one part-time employee and five thousand full-time employees when it comes to dealing with the IRS. You have the same payroll reporting requirements, and they're very strict. They're voluminous both on the state level and federal level. One of your best investments is to hire a payroll company, such as ADP or Paychex, to handle payroll for you. Alternatively, consider using a service like Elance, which offers a virtual workforce and handles virtual employee paychecks through an escrow account for you. These options are inexpensive and eliminate the time-consuming payroll issues that distract you when you'd rather be growing your business.

Outsource Bookkeeping

Bookkeeping is extremely frustrating and overwhelming for the new business owner. For women who are fastidious about the bills, it is easy to get bogged down in accounting and have little time left to concentrate on growing the business. On the other side of the curve, many new business owners don't even attempt to keep track of the books until they come to the end of their first year and need to file their taxes. They are then left with the gargantuan task of re-creating the previous year.

Get a bookkeeper who has Quicken skills, and keep your books up to date. Alternatively, buy the Quicken software, set it up under the direction of your accountant, and commit to spending an hour each week inputting data on your business schedule.

Make Estimated Tax Payments

When you are an employee, tax is automatically withheld from your paycheck, leaving you with very little to worry about. As a self-employed individual, however, it is critical to file estimated tax payments every quarter. It is much easier to come up with quarterly payments than to be hit with a large amount of unexpected cost on April 15 each year. If you do run into trouble, however, the IRS will often be willing to accept a payment plan that allows you to pay off taxes over time. Keep in mind they may only do this if you make a good faith effort to pay estimated taxes going forward.

Keep a Separate Checking Account for the Business

It is critical to apply for a separate tax ID number for your business and to set up a separate checking account in the name of your business. You must keep all business expenses separate from personal expenses. Ideally, take a lump sum and transfer it to your personal checking each month for your personal use.

Understand the Tax Payments Due for a Partnership or S Corporation

Sometimes owners are unaware that if the business is a partnership or an S corporation, you pay tax on the income that's earned every year versus the cash distributed to you. This may present a challenge to find the cash to pay taxes if there has been no distribution. On the positive side, if you've built up accumulated income and paid taxes, those distributions are tax free when they finally come to you.

CHOOSE A FEMALE INVESTMENT ADVISER

Even if you don't elect to start your own business, you may be accumulating money through the investments in your 401(k) plan at work, a rollover IRA if you have changed jobs, or a personal portfolio of liquid assets that you have either earned, received in a divorce settlement, or inherited. You will need to decide how to invest these assets. Although some studies have shown that we women don't particularly like to talk about investing or spend time thinking about the subject, we, as a group, are starting to accumulate a good deal of financial wealth. In fact, according to data released by the IRS, nearly 1.2 million women in the United States have more than $1.5 million in assets, and these numbers are growing.[7] The good news is that we women are actually very good at investing money. You have every reason to feel confident that you can take charge of your own investments.

You may be surprised to learn that one strategy for increasing your odds of building real wealth is to choose a female investment adviser to work with you. Although men dominate the ranks of financial professionals, and for that reason you may think a man can better help you manage your assets, consider the research findings in this section before you make a decision. There are several important characteristics you need in a good financial adviser: great skill at investing, a good ability to carefully manage risk, and the discipline to avoid too much trading, which—because investors are taxed on a per-trade basis—tends to erode your fortune. Women investors have been exhibiting great strength in the above areas, which means you may have a better ally in a female investment adviser than you would in a male adviser. In addition, there is a less numbers-driven reason to consider a female investment adviser: Women tend to adopt a holistic view of their money, and a female adviser will understand that your money constitutes just one part of your very full life.

Female Hedge Fund Managers Earn Better Returns than Male Managers

In 2009, the National Council for Research on Women published a comprehensive report, *Women in Fund Management,* which takes a look at how female fund managers performed versus their male counterparts during the financial crisis of 2008, among other issues. We highly recommend that you read this report, which is available for free on the Internet. The report was spearheaded by Jacki Zehner, who was the first female trader to be made a partner at Goldman Sachs and who is now a top philanthropist and advocate for women in finance. The report highlights the fact that women hedge fund managers performed better during the financial crisis. "We focused on data from hedge fund managers because they are unconstrained in their trading," Jacki notes.

For the study, Hedge Fund Research, Inc. (HFRI), a company that tracks statistics about hedge funds, created a composite index of twenty-two female-owned hedge funds and compared their returns to those of the broader HFRI Fund Weighted Composite Index, which tracks more than two thousand individual hedge funds. The data is quite startling. The report looks at the fact that female managers outperformed male managers significantly during 2008. The women-manager index was down 5.41 percent that year, whereas the hedge fund composite index was down 19.03 percent during the same period.

This was not a fluke; during the period between January of 2000 and May of 2009, the female-managed funds had an annualized return of 9.06 percent, versus only 5.81 percent for the composite index. The female-managed funds had more consistent returns as well; the standard deviation was half that of the male-managed funds. The biggest one time loss in a month, called the maximum drawdown in hedge fund speak, was -10.86 percent for the female-managed funds but a whopping -21.42 percent for the composite index. This led the female-managed funds to generate a much higher Sharpe ratio, or return per amount of risk taken—1.06 versus 0.43 for the composite index. In plain terms, the female-led funds vastly outperformed the composite index by every measure of professional money management![8]

Men Are Driven by Testosterone to Trade

One of the foremost reasons women did better in the fund-management study is that women are more cautious than men about overtrading. Experiments by scientists in the U.K., published in 2007 by the University of Cambridge, show that when men trade and their trading produces positive results, they experience a surge of testosterone, which feels good and leads them to trade even more. This testosterone surge leads to competition with other male traders for dominance as well as excessive risk taking. Women are not affected in the same way by testosterone, so we don't tend to over-react and overtrade.[9]

A study conducted in 2001 by Brad M. Barber of the University of California–Davis and Terrance Odean of the University of California–Berkeley, titled *Boys Will Be Boys: Gender, Overconfidence, and Common Stock Investment,* analyzed the investment behavior of more than thirty-five thousand households. All else being equal, men traded stocks nearly 50 percent more often than women. This added trading drove up men's costs and lowered their returns. This tendency was observed again in a 2010 survey conducted by Vanguard Investments. Of the 2.7 million people with IRAs at the company, 10 percent more men than women abandoned their investments at the low point of the 2008–2009 financial crisis, which means they missed the rally that followed.[10]

Women Make Fewer Investment Mistakes

A 2005 report by Merrill Lynch surveyed five hundred men and five hundred women on their experience with investing. All investors had investable assets of at least seventy-five thousand dollars. According to the report, "while all investors make mistakes, women make fewer mistakes than men." Women are far less likely to hold an investment too long (35 percent of women versus 47 percent of men) or wait too long to sell a winning investment (28 percent of women versus 43 percent of men). Men were also more likely than women to allocate too much to one investment (32 percent of men versus 23 percent of women), buy a hot investment without doing any research (24 percent versus 13 percent), and trade securities too often (12 percent versus 5 percent). More troubling, the men were much more likely to repeat the same mistakes and not learn from their experiences.[11]

In addition, a 2005 study at the University of Cologne, which studied U.S. mutual funds run by female and male portfolio managers from 1994 to 2005, found that the female managers took fewer risks, had more consistent investment styles, and avoided overtrading when compared to the male managers. These are exactly the types of characteristics women want from their managers and advisers, and are the types of characteristics that allow portfolios to survive in times of financial turmoil.[12]

Women Excel at Complex Investment Decision Making

One of the salient facts about today's investment world is that investment products are getting more complicated. Performing intricate and unemotional analysis is something that women excel at, given what many studies have identified as our superior ability to handle detail and to revise our initial hypothesis. As noted in the fund-management report, "Women . . . tend to take into account more decision-making detail. They consider information that does not confirm their initial decision, where men tend to ignore this new information . . . therefore women's decisions tend to be better when complexity increases, whereas men's outcomes tend to be less positive as the complexity increases."[13]

We see this in the HFRI fund data, which show that men had much more volatile performance and much higher one-time monthly losses, to a maximum of 21 percent per month. Women's maximum loss was 10 percent per month, less than half. This means if women saw that a trade was going against them, they were willing to admit their mistakes and sell the holding rather than hang on, adhering to their initial reason for buying and incurring bigger losses, as the men did.

Women Look at Investing Differently

We have found that women adopt a holistic view when it comes to money. We women look at money in terms of how we are going to use it for ourselves and our families, and a female investment adviser tends to understand this motivation. A woman will think twice about making a risky investment, since she is considering the ultimate use of her funds—whether for retirement or as a legacy for her children. She is much less likely to make a decision without considering all the ramifications. Jacki Zehner, who worked closely with some of the top men on Wall Street, has chosen to work with a female investment adviser for her own funds. She says, "There are huge reasons why I choose to use a female investment manager, including all of the issues around risk taking. In general, women have a different sort of attitude around money, in that money is a means to an end rather than an end in itself. Women tend to think of money and say, 'My goal is not to have a lot of money; my goal is to have a great life.'"

When you consider all the evidence above, you have to conclude that women certainly possess better investment skills than many people realize. Of course, sex is not the only criterion you should examine when choosing an adviser, and there are vast differences in the quality of female advisers just as there are in the quality of male advisers. But perhaps now you are convinced that being female gives *you* an advantage as you approach investing, and it might be an advantage in the adviser you select as well.

BUY A VACATION HOME

In the United States, most people buy their primary residences first and invest in a vacation home later. In this new economy, however, it is time to take a second look at this conventional approach. There are some amazing opportunities out there: a vacation home can pay for itself, provide secondary income, and become an oasis for your future retirement.

Cora Bett Thomas is the founder and CEO of Cora Bett Thomas Realty and a member of the Who's Who in Luxury Real Estate. Her business covers an area that runs all the way from the South Carolina Low Country to the Florida border. Thomas brokered the sale of the 2,300-acre luxury waterfront community Hampton Island in 2003: it was one of the largest East Coast land deals on record. With a thirty-plus-year history in the business, Bett agrees that renting your primary residence while buying a vacation home works to enhance your quality of life as well as your personal wealth.

She also notes that buying a vacation home is a growing trend among women.

I have been in the real estate business since 1975. Each and every year, I've noted women taking charge of the investments for their families as well as investing wisely with long-term goals in mind. The woman who travels is often more versed in the advantage of second-home investments and will act on her knowledge and thus reap great rewards later in time. Her choices are made with two main factors in mind: those factors are the potential for appreciation plus an opportunity to experience firsthand the community and make a better decision as to the appropriateness of the community for her family retirement later on. Is it the right fit? That is wise thinking and planning. Climate, lifestyle, community involvement, and of course, resale value (appreciation) are all considerations. After all, you make your money when you purchase.

Thomas adds,

Women should listen closely to their intuition when shopping for a vacation home—or any property, for that matter. Women have an advantage; it's often called a gut instinct. It speaks to them the moment they step inside a property. Additionally, women are in touch with their feelings and emotions, therefore better understanding that intuitive message being sent to them. I find the most evidence of that kicking in when it comes to the reaction to *location*—the key to real estate!

Listen to your intuition, review the facts, and take it all into account.

Why Your Great Escape Is a Wonderful Nest Egg

Imagine owning a dream beach house off the coast of Santa Barbara or in the Hamptons, a ski home in Vail or a lake house in Vermont. It is managed by a professional management company (not you) while the property shelters your income and earns a few extra thousand dollars a year. While you're paying down the mortgage, the property is appreciating (adding value to your portfolio). Long after the mortgage is paid, it continues to pay you by continuing to appreciate. Think of the pleasure you'll experience visiting this beautiful location each year with friends and family.

For example, a woman of our acquaintance bought a small, furnished one-bedroom condo on the beach in Dauphin, Alabama, for $183,000 in 2004. She put 20 percent down and worked with a local bank to arrange the mortgage. The mortgage payment was $909 per month. The insurance was

$900 per year and the condo-association fee was $176 per month, which also included hurricane insurance. During the peak season between May and August, our friend was able to rent out the property for $2,000 per week. In the off-season, she was able to rent it out at a lower price. She used a management company to arrange all the bookings, feature the house on its website, and maintain the property. For its services, the management company charged a fee of 20 percent of the monthly rent. Our friend's real estate play, which fed both her financial and emotional needs, carried a fairly low risk because of her careful planning.

Paying rent on your main residence may also save you thousands of dollars in the long term, particularly if you are likely to experience multiple relocations. According to the 2010 Census, the average American moves 11.7 times in his or her lifetime. If you are continually selling and buying your main residence as you relocate over and over again, you put yourself at risk of losing money, especially in an unstable economy. Renting your primary residence can sometimes save you money, particularly if you are likely to experience multiple primary-residence relocations. "When you're moving from one place to another, you may take a twenty percent hit on selling your own home, and you may have to pay a lot more for the next place you're going to, even if it's offered at a distressed price," explains Thomas. Purchase a property that you keep in your investment portfolio for long-term appreciation. If you are subject to moving frequently, this plan allows you to invest in your retirement home and have it paid in full when the time arrives.

Mortgages

You have two ways to finance the purchase of your vacation home. The most common way is to use a mortgage lender and borrow against the value of the property. You will most likely find that a lender in the area will give you the best loan because they are in the best position to get you a fair appraisal on the value of the house. It's essential to go after a fixed-rate mortgage while interest rates are at historic lows, even if an adjustable-rate mortgage initially looks enticing. You want to stay in charge of your payments and not suddenly find yourself at the mercy of the local bank.

Alternatively, if you have a large portfolio of personal securities, you could take a secured loan against that portfolio rather than a loan against the house. However, you may not be able to enjoy as large a tax deduction if you take this route. The total interest that you can deduct for up to two mortgages is $1.1 million: the interest you can deduct on a secured personal loan is limited to the total interest you earn on that portfolio, which is usually less than $1.1 million.

Factors to Consider

Among the most important factors to consider when buying your vacation home are the location, the condition of the property, and the price you can charge for the property as a rental. "At the end of the day, what's on the ocean is going to rent for more money than what's on the next block," explains Thomas. "Your goal should be to buy the best property you can in the best neighborhood you can afford."

It's also critical to research the best property managers in the location, understand their fee structure, and make sure they will manage the property properly and maintain it well. When you're busy in another location, your management company is the only one that's taking care of the home, and you don't want your vacancy rate to suddenly increase because of a disgruntled renter's bad review online.

When buying a property, make sure you do additional research on top of what the broker shares with you. Look at what people have said on the Internet about the property, or ask local residents. A number of things can be deceiving to a buyer who doesn't check independently. For example, a broker may position a property as being "within walking distance" of a beach when it's actually a six-block walk to the beach—farther than is comfortable for some people.

When you are shopping for a vacation home, you can put yourself in a particularly strong financial position if the property can serve as a year-round rental as well as a seasonal vacation residence. If the vacation-rental market crashes, it's still a desirable place to rent full-time. An example would be a rental property that is both near the ocean and near a college town, which would have a steady supply of student renters. You will get a higher rental income and you will have a better chance of selling the property, whatever the economic environment is.

Other factors to consider include

- **Insurance costs:** Vacation rentals are one of the places insurance companies are redlining. Shop for your insurance carefully and choose a company that will stand by you in an emergency. Review the insurance protection against hurricanes and flooding.

- **Green is not necessarily better:** Although green living is a growing trend in primary residences, it may not make you any "greener" (i.e., richer) when it comes to your rental property. Cora Bett has found that people go for convenience rather than environmental responsibility when they're choosing a vacation spot, especially if they have children.

- **Beware of foreclosures:** If you buy a foreclosed property, know that you may not be able to resell it. Avoid foreclosed properties in heavily foreclosed areas. Buy your foreclosure in a neighborhood where, no matter what, the property will resell because the neighborhood is strong.

- **Beware of new subdivisions:** According to Cora Bett, people who buy in brand-new subdivisions usually want to sell in five years. One of the reasons for this is that, as a landlord, you may be competing for tenants against another new local development with even better amenities.

- **Put together a great team:** Enlist the help of trusted professionals, including an insurance broker, a financial adviser, a CPA, and a tax attorney. You may also want to create strong relationships with a cleaning crew, a gardener, a handyman service, and a local council member.

- **Become a property magnate:** If you own a successful rental property that has greatly increased in value, you may have an opportunity to keep your money working for you by buying additional vacation-rental properties and not paying taxes on the purchase. With an IRS 1031 exchange, you may acquire, for example, two properties of lesser value in exchange for your current property without paying capital gains tax. You may want to consider using the equity in your current vacation rental to refinance the property and buy something in a comparable area to expand your real estate empire.

INVEST LIKE A BILLIONAIRE

There are millions of articles on the Web encouraging investors to buy the same stocks as Bill Gates, Warren Buffet, or Carlos Slim, the world's wealthiest billionaires. This advice seems at best confusing and at worst irrelevant, since most people don't have the same diversification strategy that these mega-investors have. However, there is one thing that many of the world's billionaires, including Oprah, do have: a private company that is staffed by people who do nothing but select and watch after their boss's investments. This company is called a family office.

We believe that you can learn to think like a billionaire's family office, and that this is the best approach to take with your money. A family office offers the Rolls Royce of wealth-management services—integrated advice on investment management, tax planning, estate planning, philanthropy, and financial education for future generations. According to the 2010 Multifamily Office Study, conducted by the Family Wealth Alliance,[14] the top seventy-two multifamily offices currently manage a staggering $357.3 billion in the United States; the average amount of assets under management for each client is $49.6 million. Carol has been running a family office on behalf of a number of clients for the last ten years; prior to that she worked for the Rockefeller family office. Carol is hired by billionaires to create family offices for them, so she is an expert in this area.

Develop an Investment Philosophy

One of the principal jobs of a family office is to help families develop an investment philosophy. The vast majority of families working with the firms surveyed by the Family Wealth Alliance use the family office to create an asset allocation, to select and monitor investment managers, and to select alternative investments, such as hedge funds or private-equity investments.

We all know that the financial markets fluctuate every day, often to an alarming degree. Turn on any financial news program, and you can hear how much the Dow is up or down for the day, hear about the latest interest-rate move, or about the trading patterns of the day's hot stock. There is tons of information out there but very little useful guidance—and almost no sense of long-term strategy. Family offices receive the same conflicting information, but are savvy in the ways of Wall Street and the brokerage community. They know that a broker selling you products is a salesperson and cannot deliver completely objective advice. Investors working with brokers are expected to look out for their own interests, according to the standards set by the SEC. Registered Investment Advisers are held to a higher standard, but that does not necessarily completely protect your money. That is why family offices develop an investment philosophy and write an investment policy statement for their clients before they begin investing.

One assumption that underlies all family-office investment philosophies is long-term thinking. Family offices consider investments in light of generations, not weeks or months or even a year. Of course, the family office makes sure that a family's short-term cash needs are met and that there is always sufficient money available to meet expenses. But long-term thinking is critical to investment success, and can be practiced by everyone. For example, it is much better to start saving for a child's college education when she is born rather than when she becomes a teenager; the power of compound interest means that you can start with a smaller initial investment than you would otherwise. Thinking for the long term can also mean having the patience to wait for the right time to sell an investment. For example, waiting to sell a valuable piece of art until its style is popular again, even it if means waiting a couple of years, might be a better decision than selling it at a fire sale price today.

Like a family office, you need to develop an investment philosophy and policy before you approach the markets. Some elements of your investment philosophy are going to be universal—good practices that all investors should follow, regardless of their personal preferences—and some are going to be unique to your own situation. We'll explore the universal elements first.

Adopt the Universal Keys to Good Investing

The first key to investing is to realize that the only reason to make an investment is to achieve a return on it. The fact that you like the broker, like to attend events sponsored by a particular bank, or that your friends are making the same investment are not good reasons to invest your money. The only reason to invest is that you think you will receive all your money back, *plus* an appropriate return. So the first universal principle of your investment philosophy should be, "I am going to invest my money only where I think I can make a return; that is, I have conviction when I invest."

The second key to investing relates to the question, Why do you believe that this particular investment will give you a return? This is one of the principles followed by Warren Buffet. He is famous for investing only in companies and businesses that he understands. Certainly, in the post-Madoff world, this is an important tenet. Not understanding how an investment proposes to give you a return is a big mistake. So the second key is, "I invest only where I have an understanding of how it will make money for me."

This leads us to the third universal key: It is critical to have the information necessary to monitor investments so that you can determine whether your original conviction and understanding prove to be correct. Unless you get detailed monthly information, you can't tell how the investment is doing. You should choose only investments that give very detailed disclosure of how they are performing and how fees are being charged. So the third universal key is, "I invest only where there is transparency on an investment's performance and fees."

We now have the first three universal keys of our investment philosophy: conviction, understanding, and transparency—or CUT. With these, we can "cut" through a great deal of hype and focus in on only the most suitable investments. Any investments that don't pass muster, that don't meet the criteria of these first three keys, won't make the "cut"!

Customize Your Philosophy to Reflect Your Preferences

After you adopt the universal principles of good investing, you need to take your own fundamental inclinations and preferences into account. If you like bargains and hate to overpay, you are probably going to be happier following the value-investing path. If you love looking for the next great success, then growth investing will be more appealing to you. The good news is that growth investments sometimes outperform value investments, and value investments sometimes outperform growth investments, so your natural inclination will be most successful at least some of the time. Understanding whether you are a growth or a value investor by preference is critical to investment happiness. It is impossible to get a value investor excited about high-priced, high-growth investments, just as it is impossible to get a growth investor excited about a company that to her looks half dead but to a value investor reveals hidden potential. The key is to adopt the principle, "I invest primarily in my favorite style."

How much risk are you really comfortable taking? How did you feel when your portfolio swooned during the crisis? Understand that this could happen again in your lifetime, and invest accordingly. Be honest with yourself about how well you handle market volatility. The principle here is, "I accept only an appropriate level of risk." Your financial adviser should spend a great deal of time with you to make sure that he or she understands your risk tolerance, and it is crucial that you are honest about this subject. Don't let an adviser talk you into taking more risk than you are comfortable assuming.

How much time do you have to devote to understanding the markets and participating in them? For example, we know a woman named Julie who no longer trades stocks, because she doesn't have enough time to watch the market closely every day. It is part of her investment philosophy that if she can't devote the amount of attention required for trading individual stocks, then she would rather invest in well-managed funds. Here the tenet is, "I invest in a way that makes sense given the amount of time I have to devote to it."

How strongly do you feel about funding guns, tobacco, or alcohol? For some investors this is a big problem, and they will be happier if they avoid making money on these types of investments. How strongly do you feel about funding community banks, alternative energy, or organic farming? There are investments that fall in the "socially responsible" or "sustainable" categories that will help you fund the things that are important to you. If you want to make these kinds of investments, you should seek out experts who are familiar with the growing number of options in these areas— many traditional advisers simply don't know where to find the best socially responsible or sustainable funds. The tenet here is, "I invest in a way that comfortably reflects my values."

In summary, your investment philosophy should reflect three universal investment best practices—conviction, understanding, and transparency—which will help you "cut" through the noise in the market. You should then consider your style, risk tolerance, time commitments, and values as you decide where to focus your energy. Armed with this personalized investment philosophy, you can now map out a strategy. You can even write up a simple document to share with your financial adviser that reflects your investment principles. This will be the beginning of your investment policy statement.

Develop an Asset Allocation for Each Portfolio

The first step in turning your investment philosophy into a smoothly functioning portfolio is to develop an asset allocation for each pool of money. Your financial adviser will help you with this task. An asset allocation is the mix of cash, stocks, bonds, and other investments that you choose to have in your portfolio. The appropriate mix will depend on the amount of time you have available for investing, your risk tolerance, and the purpose to which you want to put each pool of money. You may have one particular asset allocation for your long-term retirement plan and quite a different asset allocation for investments that will eventually be used to buy a home. Before you start picking funds or individual investments, make sure that you and your adviser have crafted the correct asset allocation first. You might like to see what the world's wealthiest individuals are doing in terms of asset allocation by consulting the World Wealth Report, published each year by Merrill Lynch Global Wealth Management and Capgemini, and available for download on the Internet. The 2010 report stated that wealthy individuals around the world kept 17 percent of their assets in cash and 41 percent in fixed-income securities—a much more conservative asset allocation than is normally promoted by many financial advisers.[15] Don't be afraid to insist upon the level of cash and fixed-income securities that will make you feel comfortable.

Insist on Quality Guidelines for Selecting Investments

It is not enough to create an asset allocation, however; you should also create quality guidelines for your financial adviser and make sure they are adhered to. In all cases, you want to have the highest-quality investments, managed by the most experienced team possible. If you are considering funds or portfolios, you want to see the longest track record possible, with good performance during difficult markets. Although all financial investments come with the disclaimer that "past performance is no guarantee of future results," the truth is that a fund with good past performance is a safer bet than a fund with no past performance to evaluate. Each type of investment has its own particular set of criteria—for example, investors judge corporate bonds differently from high-yield bonds, small-capitalization stocks differently from large-capitalization stocks. If this is new territory, ask your adviser to help you develop a set of criteria to judge the quality of your investments.

Use Online Tools to Assess Mutual Fund Quality

When selecting investments, it is helpful to use ratings agencies to help you assess the quality of any mutual funds you are considering. Most online brokerage websites will give you mutual fund ratings from a company called Morningstar. If you are investing in mutual funds, you can set minimum standards by insisting on funds that are highly rated by Morningstar. There is very little reason to invest in a mutual fund with fewer than three stars. Another good rule of thumb is to look for investment management teams with at least ten years of experience working together. You can also assess the track record of a fund by comparing its performance to that of its corresponding investment index. Your adviser can provide this information for you. You can also look up mutual fund performance information on free websites like Yahoo! Finance, which offers a great deal of detail on mutual funds. You can also set up an online tracker for your funds so you can see their performance every day.

It is also important to look at the size of the fund. Beware of mutual funds or ETFs (exchange-traded funds) below $200 million in size—they are just too small to operate efficiently. Don't let your adviser put you into a brand-new fund with no track record—many brokers get paid higher commissions for selling new funds. This helps them, not you!

Separately Managed Accounts

If you have a large amount of cash to invest, your financial adviser may suggest that he or she set up separately managed accounts for your money rather than mutual funds. Separately managed accounts, which are created for you and have a personal portfolio manager, offer the advantage of allowing the portfolio manager to more carefully manage the realized gains and losses in your portfolio by deciding when to buy and sell securities. It is very important to investigate the track record of any adviser who is proposing a separately managed account. If the account is going to hold different types of assets—for example, stocks and bonds in the same account—ask the manager to create subaccounts for each asset class. The manager should also give you performance information for each asset class separately, as well as for the account as a whole. There should be a ratings number for the performance of bonds as compared to the appropriate bond index, and a number for the stocks compared to the appropriate stock index. Otherwise, it is very difficult to judge whether the account is performing well for you.

Pay Attention to Cash and Liquidity

There are two key tenets to consider when constructing your portfolios: the amount of liquidity, or cash, in the portfolio, and the degree of liquidity of the securities in your portfolio. The need for liquidity—or, more simply stated, the need to have cash—was painfully brought home during the crash of 2008 and 2009. Investors who had enough cash to feel comfortable were not so likely to panic and sell at the bottom. The degree of liquidity of your securities refers to how long it takes to sell an investment and receive your return in cash. On one end of the spectrum, most mutual funds and ETFs have daily liquidity. On the other end, private-equity-fund investments cannot usually be sold for ten to fifteen years, making them highly illiquid. Although there may be a secondary market for illiquid investments—that is, someone willing to buy them from you—you typically receive only 10 to 30 percent of the amount you invested back, so they are a very poor choice and a last resort when you absolutely must get some cash.

Make Sure to Diversify

It is critical that you specify to your adviser that you don't want to take too much risk by concentrating investments in just a few stocks or bonds. Most mutual funds hold more than thirty stocks, the minimum considered necessary to diversify a fund appropriately. Make sure that if you have a separately managed account, the manager is limited to the size of the positions he can take, which means that there should be a limit on the percentage of the total portfolio invested in any one stock or bond. A good rule of thumb is that there should be no more than 5 percent of the total value of the portfolio invested in any one fund, and within a fund or portfolio, there should be no more than 2 to 3 percent invested in any one stock or bond. This rule does not apply to smaller accounts, with a value of, say, five thousand dollars or less—in cases like this, you may have to invest in just one or two funds until your assets grow.

If You Are Considered a Sophisticated Investor

Depending on your income and net worth, you may be classified by the SEC and your brokerage firm as a *sophisticated investor.* A sophisticated investor must have either a net worth of $2.5 million or have earned more than $250,000 in the past two years to qualify. Once you are classified this way, you can be shown investments that have a higher risk, or less detailed financial disclosure, than investments shown to non-sophisticated investors. The assumption is that you can afford to lose 100 percent of the investment, that you have a high degree of knowledge of markets, and you can make decisions about complex investment products. All these assumptions may be false, however, even if you have the required net worth and income. Do not invest in products for which you are not given enough information to thoroughly understand the risks you are taking. Don't rely on the fact that the investment carries the name brand of a top firm—insist on understanding where your money is going.

Hedge Funds and Alternative Investments

If you are a woman with a large portfolio, the chances are good that you will be offered the opportunity to invest in hedge funds, private placements, or other so-called alternative investments. These investments are usually not regulated by the SEC or any other governmental body, so they are inherently riskier. Hedge funds, for example, often have lockup periods—it can take months to get your money back. In the wake of the latest financial crisis, many hedge funds have imposed *gates,* which means that if all the investors want to get out of a fund at once, a "gate" is slammed shut and an orderly liquidation takes place, sometimes over a couple of years.

The prevailing wisdom used to be that you were compensated for the lack of liquidity and additional risk in hedge funds by much higher returns. However, the performance of many hedge funds was dismal during the crisis, and they did no better protecting investor wealth than traditional investments, which have significantly lower fees. If you plan to invest in any alternative or hedge fund investments, you must have a clear understanding that you are most likely paying much higher fees and getting less transparency, less regulatory oversight, and less ability to redeem your cash. The returns you earn should compensate for all these negative characteristics—if they don't, then stick to traditional investments. According to the 2010 World Wealth Report, wealthy investors with more than $1 million in investable assets put, on average, only 6 percent of their total worth in alternatives[16]—so don't be pressured to overinvest in illiquid alternative investments.

Ask for a Blended Benchmark

Your financial adviser should be able to help you accurately measure the performance of your assets against an appropriate benchmark. Remember, you are paying the manager a fee to manage your assets, so the fund should make more money using an active money manager than you would make using a passive index account.

In order to assess how your manager is doing, each type of investment should be measured against an appropriate benchmark. Your large-capitalization U.S. stock investments should be measured against the S&P 500 index, for example. To make matters more confusing, there are actually several versions of the S&P index, including those with dividends and those without dividends, among other variations. Work with your adviser to make sure you are using the right benchmark. It is also possible for many advisers to create a "blended benchmark" that reflects that same percentage allocation as your portfolio. For example, if your portfolio has 60 percent U.S. large-capitalization equities and 40 percent municipal bonds, you can have a blended benchmark of two indices in the same ratio and use that to judge the performance of your account. This is easier to do if you have separately managed accounts than if you have mutual funds. If you are investing in mutual funds, each will be measured against an index; your job will be to measure the performance of your total portfolio correctly. Ask your adviser for options.

Your Investment Policy Statement

Once you have set your investment philosophy, asset allocation, and quality standards, you can put all these elements together into an investment policy statement that you can give to your financial adviser. Most family offices and most institutions, like pension funds, provide their own policy statements to their investment advisers. There is no standard form for these statements, but there are certain elements common to all of them. Creating a written document that contains all these elements will make your intentions clear and will ensure that there are no misunderstandings between you and the people who manage your money.

To give you an idea of what an investment policy statement might look like, let's create a hypothetical example for a woman we'll call Susan Smith, a forty-five-year-old professional who works as a corporate marketing executive and lives in California. After taking care of her liquidity needs and fully funding her retirement accounts, Susan wants to grow her wealth, so she has decided to create an investment portfolio that she plans to leave untouched until retirement. She has seventy-five thousand dollars to invest today and, based on her budget, can contribute a good chunk of her bonus each year, so she plans to add another twenty thousand dollars annually. Susan cares deeply about environmental causes and travels frequently, so she is interested both in socially responsible investments and in international stocks, particularly those from Asian countries. She realizes that she does not have a very high risk tolerance, however, so she wants a fairly stable and conservative portfolio. Her investment policy statement might look something like the one on page 43.

INVESTMENT POLICY STATEMENT FOR SUSAN SMITH

This document describes the investment policy for my personal investment portfolio.

Initial investment amount: $75,000.

Tax status: This is a taxable account.

State tax: I am a California resident.

Structure: This portfolio is part of my revocable living trust. [See page 45.]

Purpose: The purpose of this portfolio is to create wealth that I can live on in retirement.

Percentage of my liquid assets: This portfolio is 50 percent of my liquid assets.

Percentage of my total assets: The portfolio is 30 percent of my total assets.

Ultimate distribution: I plan to pass on any money I don't use to my sister's children and my alma mater.

Time horizon: I expect to invest this portfolio for the next fifteen years, or until retirement, whichever is later.

Liquidity requirements: I do not require any current income from this portfolio. I will use this money in retirement. I am keeping cash in other portfolios.

Liquidation of investments: I want only investments that can be sold every day. I don't want locked-up investments.

Diversification: No one fund should be more than 5 percent of the portfolio.

Risk tolerance: I am a low-risk investor. I would like to limit the possibility of investment losses. However, I want some equities and commodities so the portfolio will grow.

Style preference: Although I know my investments should comprise a variety of styles, I am a growth investor and I prefer to invest 60 percent of my U.S. equities allocation in growth companies and 40 percent in value-oriented companies.

Values: I do not want this portfolio invested in the traditional "sin" stocks. Do not invest in alcohol, tobacco, gaming, or military contractors.

Interests: I am interested in socially responsible investments, international investing—especially Asian equities—and clean technology. I like commodities, including gold.

Avoid: I don't want real estate funds, as I own two buildings and have enough real estate in my net worth. I don't want hedge funds.

Asset allocation:

Cash	10%
Municipal Bonds	50%
U.S. Large Cap Growth Equities	8%
U.S. Value Equities	6%
U.S. Small Cap Equities	1%
International Equities	10%
Socially Responsible Equities	5%
Commodities	10%

Rebalancing: I would like to rebalance the account at least once a year to maintain the asset allocation, unless we discuss otherwise.

Investment vehicles: Use mutual funds and ETFs for the investments.

Quality standards: No mutual fund should have fewer than three stars from Morningstar unless I give specific written permission to the adviser for an exception. I want funds to have a ten-year track record with the same team of investment professionals. I do not want to invest in any fund or ETF that has less than $500 million in assets, unless I give specific written permission to the adviser for an exception.

Position size: No one fund should comprise more than 5 percent of the portfolio.

Duplication: Please analyze funds to the best of your ability to make sure that there is not a great deal of duplication in the underlying securities.

Performance reporting: I want to see each fund or ETF compared to the appropriate benchmark. I also want a blended benchmark that I can use to monitor the results of the total portfolio.

Information access: I want online access to my portfolio, as well as statements in PDF format emailed to me each month.

Communication with adviser: I expect to speak to my adviser at least once a month. During a crisis, I want to be able to reach my adviser every day if necessary. I will be the one communicating with my adviser.

These instructions shall remain in effect until I submit written modification of them.

Structures to Hold Investments

In addition to choosing investments, family offices make sure that the right legal structures are used to hold assets, given the family's tax and estate planning situation. Sometimes an LLC is the right answer; other times, a family limited partnership makes better sense. Even if you are single, it is still critical to hold your assets in the right form, which may be a Revocable Living Trust, which we explain next. The key point is this: don't assume that having investment accounts in your own name is the best way to hold your assets. The choice of vehicle and which state to hold the vehicle are critical. Some states, such as Alaska, Delaware, and South Dakota, have progressive trust laws. You do not need to be a resident of these states to have a trust that is domiciled in the state. Consult a good trust and estate planning attorney and consider your options.

THE ADVANTAGES OF A REVOCABLE LIVING TRUST

A revocable living trust can hold all your assets during your lifetime and distribute them to your heirs after you die without the assets having to go through the probate process. It is called "living" because you create it during your lifetime, and "revocable" because you can change it at any time. Once the trust is created, moving money into it is as simple as opening an account in the name of the trust and transferring the funds into the account.

The trust must be drafted by a good estate-planning attorney, who will help you include all the right provisions, such as the following:

- You are the trustee of your trust, and you can change the terms any time.
- All your accounts and assets are in the trust's name (e.g., the Susan Smith Revocable Living Trust).
- A revocable trust names a successor trustee should you no longer be able to act on your own behalf. This means that if you are in a car accident and go into a coma, there is already a designated person in place who can legally take over and manage your affairs.

When you die, assets in the revocable trust do not go through probate court. This means that your estate is kept a private matter—in contrast to assets in probate, which are a matter of public record. Any assets held in your own name are subject to probate and public scrutiny.

You still need a will with a revocable living trust. If you so choose, you can have a special "pour over" will drawn up, which names the trust as the beneficiary of any assets held in your own name that you have not specifically put into the trust. These assets are then distributed according to the wishes of the trust. This is especially useful if you should suddenly die without having time to put assets in the trust. You also still need a will to designate a guardian for your children, which cannot be done with a revocable living trust.

Here are some other advantages of a revocable living trust:

- Your beneficiaries will receive distributions much faster from the trust than from your estate, which can take years to be settled in court.
- If you own a business, the revocable living trust's designated trustee can carry on quickly after your death under the instructions in the trust.
- You can name more than one person to act as trustees after your death: for example, you can have one trustee make decisions on behalf of your business and another manage trust distributions to your beneficiaries.

Get on Top of Your Budget

You may be surprised to learn that many very wealthy people work with monthly budgets to manage their spending. The Family Wealth Alliance's 2010 Multifamily Office Study showed that 97 percent of family offices offer financial-planning services and that 77 percent of their clients take advantage of them.[17] Clients of family offices usually have meetings with a personal accountant, who goes over all their past and projected spending needs to make sure that their investments are correctly positioned to meet those needs. Many more wealthy individuals started working with a budget after the latest market crash, when they discovered to their dismay that they did not have sufficient liquid assets to meet their ongoing lifestyle requirements—because, for example, too many assets were tied up in illiquid partnerships, hedge funds, and private-equity investments. Individuals who have inherited money also know that if they want the money to last, they need to live on their investment income rather than draining the principal. Otherwise, even a sizable inheritance can disappear rapidly through overspending.

If you plan to think like a family office, you should have a budget for your spending. A 2007 survey by MSN Money revealed that only 40 percent of Americans use a household budget.[18] Contrast this with the whopping 77 percent of wealthy families who use their family office's financial-planning services, and you, like them, may come to recognize the value of this powerful tool.

A simple way to keep track of all the money you spend is to use a debit card for all purchases rather than cash. You will always have to spend some cash, but by reducing this amount, you can monitor the majority of your expenses. In addition, financial-planning software like QuickBooks can help you understand exactly how much you are spending. You can open a personal "company" on QuickBooks and use the excellent features of the program to categorize every expense. If you have online access to your bank account, you can download your monthly debit card expenses to QuickBooks and then add in your monthly credit card expenses (also by accessing your credit card accounts online) to get a full picture of your personal spending. Each expense should be categorized—restaurant meals, personal grooming, clothing, medical, household expenses, and so on. If you decide to create a dating budget, as we suggest in the next chapter, you can create a dating category and capture all dating expenses easily.

If the task seems too overwhelming, you should consider hiring a part-time bookkeeper to create a personal QuickBooks company on your behalf; you may be able to have that person come to your home only one day a month and get the entire job done. We also recommend that while you are entering expenses into QuickBooks, you or your bookkeeper scan all business and personal receipts and put them into electronic folders, organized by vendor, that mimic the categories you are using in QuickBooks. You can keep the paper receipts as well, but it will be much easier to find copies of receipts once they are scanned. Once all receipts are scanned and all expenses entered into QuickBooks, enter in your monthly income. You can then see whether or not you are living within your means. You will also understand the extent to which you are using your credit cards—remember that you are spending this money even if it doesn't feel like you are. Knowledge is power—you can decide what you need to adjust only once you see what you are really doing. Then, you have choices.

Take a look at your expenses by category for each month—ideally, take a look at two or three months at a time. Now you can see where the cash is going, and decide if your long-term goals are being met by these spending habits. If you want to save for a vacation-home down payment, for example, you may need to cut back in some other area, or you might want to start a small part-time business to increase your income. No matter what you would like to achieve, the first step is understanding where you are today so that you can have choices about how to move forward toward manifesting your vision and making your dreams come true.

Thinking like a family office involves thinking strategically, staying calm, and planning rather than reacting. Once you adopt these habits, your chances of increasing your wealth by investing in the financial markets will rise dramatically, and the first pearl of wisdom will be yours.

CHAPTER 2

ROMANCE AND MARRIAGE

THE SECOND PEARL OF FINANCIAL WISDOM:
A Woman Should Require Good Finance in Her Romance

OUR FASCINATION WITH ROMANCE, which is one of the most marvelous aspects of our lives, often sends even the most sensible woman into a state of blind denial. A grain of sand can enter our shell: when dating, we do not see the money we're spending. We do not judge if this money is being spent effectively. We do not make our money work for us in a way that delivers the relationships we fantasize about. Once we get into a committed relationship, we do not discuss our financial style, situation, and plans with our partner. We do not ask for full financial disclosure before we marry. Sometimes, we are left in the dark even after we are married, if we choose to defer all financial decisions to our husbands. We may bankrupt ourselves by overspending on dating before ever having a real relationship or find ourselves bankrupt at the abrupt end of what we had hoped would be a lifetime marriage. Hence the second pearl: *A Woman Should Require Good Finance in Her Romance.*

In this chapter, we want to share with you ways in which your relationship with money has a great effect on your partnerships. It is a fact that 60 percent of couples who divorce in the United States split over money issues. It is time that we honor ourselves by practicing good financial habits ourselves and seeking partners who do so as well. While this can't prevent every breakup, financial sanity in dating, committed relationships, and marriage increases the odds for long term stability and romantic harmony.

Women in the United States no longer need a dowry to find a husband. In fact, 22 percent of women outearned their male partners in 2007.[1] When approaching the dating game and the search for a husband, many women still wistfully long for the Cinderella story to happen to them. This often leads them to enter into unions armed only with information about their emotional or sexual compatibility and with very little substantial financial information about the partner they are devoting a great deal of time and resources to dating in the hope of getting married. If we are willing to discuss money with our partner, we are much more likely to create a satisfying and long-lasting union.

THE GRAIN OF SAND IN THE OYSTER SHELL

Do you know a woman who . . .

- Spends extravagantly on clothes to entice each date?
- Is worried about her partner's gambling habits but won't confront him?
- Is paying for her boyfriend's lifestyle and feels discouraged?
- Is getting married but doesn't want to upset her fiancé with a prenup?
- Wants to start a business with her husband but feels she needs direction?

It is our hope that, by adopting the strategies we discuss in this chapter, you will be able to handle the financial aspects of your search for love, and your resulting partnerships, in a way that honors your character and your relationship, protects yourself, and enhances your romance. Once you marry, we want you to preserve your love and yourself by practicing smart financial strategies with your spouse.

BUDGET FOR LOVE

Today there are nearly 50 million single women in the United States,[2] and many are seeking to become part of a couple. Unfortunately, it appears that much of the spending women are doing to prepare for dates is unplanned for and ends up on credit cards. Now that the average household owes nearly fifteen thousand dollars in credit card debt,[3] there couldn't be a better time to budget for love.

Women often find themselves in debt when they invest more than they can afford in preparation for dates. In a small Match.com poll of approximately five hundred singles, 65 percent of women said they "spend more than $50 on preparing for [a] date"; the survey also found that women generally spend more than men.[4]

In a cosmopolitan city like New York, a woman might spend a minimum of fifteen dollars on a manicure, thirty on a pedicure, forty on a blowout of her hair, sixty on a bikini wax, thirty on a new top for her jeans—that's a total of $175 before she even leaves the house for her first date, whether she is paying for the date itself or not. If she is shopping for three dating experiences or more in a month, her romantic pursuits can tally into thousands of dollars over the course of a year.

As new money norms develop around dating between men and women in the twenty-first century, women may be spending more now than ever before. In a study of more than five thousand American singles between the ages of twenty-one and sixty-five plus, 41 percent of women say they "would offer to pick up the check on a first date."[5]

Dating should not cause a woman financial stress, but it often does. If she is using credit cards to pay for her dating expenses, her financial deficit may ultimately have a negative impact on her relationship prospects. Match.com found that 57 percent of singles they polled said that "debt has an impact on how [they] view potential partners," and it would cause them to reevaluate their relationships. A whopping 74 percent of singles said "more than $5,000 of credit card debt is a turnoff."

Whether you are in a relationship or single and looking for a relationship, you should be allocating money in your regular monthly budget for dating. When you calculate the amount you are spending on dating, you should include money spent on romantic trips and events as well as on wardrobe and beauty products and services.

A dating budget allows you to do just that. To get started on a budget, identify your financial requirements—and the style you want to project in romance—by answering the following questions. Some items may already be in your regular budget; others need to be accounted for on an ongoing basis.

- Do you usually pay for dates, or do you split the checks?
- Do you need to hire a babysitter?
- Do you shop for something new to wear every time you have a date?
- Do you buy lingerie before a new date?
- Do you require travel expenses?
- Do you clean your car before dates?
- Do you hire a pet-sitter for dates?
- Do you get a manicure and pedicure before a date?
- Do you get your hair cut or colored before a date?
- Do you get facials, massages, or bikini waxes before dates?
- Do you need to purchase birth control?
- Do you plan to use online dating sites that charge a fee?
- Do you expect to attend an event where you will meet potential dates?
- Do you plan to take up a hobby in order to meet potential dates?
- Do you employ a personal trainer, or maintain a gym membership, to keep in shape for dating?

SAMPLE MONTHLY DATING BUDGET

Manicure and pedicure	$50
Waxing	$75
Hair	$40
Lingerie	$50
Shoes	$60

Clothing	$100
Travel	$100
Dating websites	$25–$40
Events	$50

You may find that you spend a great deal more on dating than you thought you did. In fact, you may be spending more than you can reasonably afford. Now is the time to adjust your dating budget—before you make a permanent commitment—so that you make the most of the funds you have available. For example, our friend Marlena rarely buys new clothes for dates; instead, she started a dating-outfit exchange with a group of women, who swap dating outfits and accessories with one another whenever the need arises. Marlena uses the money she saves to invest in a professional blow-dry (forty dollars) and a professional makeup application, which she gets at the cosmetics counter at her local department store when she spends twenty dollars on one of the products used in the application.

CONSIDER A PROFESSIONAL MATCHMAKER

There is one very important item that some highly successful and wealthy women are adding to their dating budget: the services of a professional matchmaker.

Successful executive women who can allocate $10,000 to $150,000 or more in the search for the right partner have an opportunity to make a unique investment. If you're reading this book, it's unlikely that you ever left your career or your housing payment up to chance, yet so many women leave the question of finding their life partner to whimsy, luck, or the hand of the gods. When a woman is highly successful, she is apt to be preyed upon by con artists and gold diggers, as we will discuss later in this chapter, so it is crucial that she thoroughly screen potential serious mates, and a matchmaking service is one way to go about this process.

It's key to have a strategy once you become serious about finding a life partner, especially when finances and security are at stake. If you're an ex-

ecutive woman of means looking for the ultimate partner and tired of sift-
ing through men you meet at cocktail parties, holiday resorts, and luxury
hotels, there is another avenue. We do not advise pinning all your hopes
on a matchmaker, but we believe that an elite matchmaker provides a much-
needed service for a discerning, accomplished single woman who can afford
the expense.

CEO Amber Kelleher-Andrews and her mother, Jill Kelleher, of Kelleher International are among the top matchmaking experts in the world.
Amber says that 85 percent of their clients enter into relationships and half
of them get married within a short period of time. A decade ago, her San
Francisco–based firm already had four hundred marriages on the books.
They have forty matchmakers working for their clients at any one time, as
well as scouts and recruiters in cities across the United States.

Amber, who has seen an increase in the number of women approaching
her company in recent years, says, "It's the practical side of how a woman
thinks. She has her biological clock ticking and seeks security. Men can
date for fifty-plus years before having a child. Women like that the men we
suggest for them are screened, not married, and have the income level to
support such a search. We don't work with gold diggers, but rather with successful women who appreciate a man at the same level of success or higher."
Her company also rejects a large number of candidates for its database.
Out of seven hundred to nine hundred applications per month, Kelleher-
Andrews may pick only thirty. "Kelleher International will take you only
if you're accomplished, passionate, physically fit, free of addictions to tobacco, alcohol, and drugs, clinically sane, marriage-minded, realistic about
yourself and your prospective partner, and in possession of a good attitude."[6]

The company searches both inside and outside the people in its propri-
etary database and, when necessary, creates a personal marketing campaign
just for an individual client. For example, one of Kelleher International's
clients was a woman in Florida who has a large yacht and spends most of
her free time on the water and on the boat. Although they could have introduced her to dozens of professional, handsome businessmen in her area
and nationwide, a specialized search was created. "For her," says Kelleher-
Andrews, "a man who doesn't live this same lifestyle would not be an ultimate fit. So we ran a series of ad campaigns in *Boating International* and

Showboats magazines—two high-end publications in Florida—to attract men who have boats."

Kelleher-Andrews has often reflected on the importance of good finance in her own romance. She says, "I feel the freedom to be more romantic with my husband when we have our house in order and our finances are not the main topic of discussion. Money is definitely a mood killer. It's also important to note that children make this very real. You can be poor and have a great time together as a couple for years, but once the kids arrive, the romance goes out the window unless you have money under control. Age is a factor, too."

Many successful women are not ready or able to spend ten thousand dollars or more on a matchmaker, but there are opportunities to benefit from their work if you qualify. Matchmakers often seek out attractive, successful single women as matches for their male counterparts. If you are approached, it's important to check if the company that approached you is reputable.

A single woman may also want to call a few prominent matchmakers to say that she is available. She will be profiled by the matchmaker, and the matchmaker will decide if she would make a good fit for her database. If a woman agrees to be entered into a database, she should speak frankly with the matchmaker about her expectations. There is a chance for rejection in taking this course of action, but nothing a successful job seeker hasn't experienced in her career. Enlisting the services of a professional matchmaker simply increases your chances of finding the right partner.

SPOT THE POOR FINANCIAL MATCH EARLY

While we all hope that love will conquer all challenges in our relationships, there are some issues we may encounter in a potential partner that almost guarantee a lifetime of heartbreak and financial ruin. No matter how sexy the man, how dangerously exciting the player, if you want to plot a course to wealth, you will have to make hard choices if certain issues are present. Even though you may have fallen in love, you will need to leave a man who exhibits the warning signs of a major personality disorder. He may be a con artist, gold digger, or display the signs of a serious addiction to gambling or pornography. Men with certain telltale behavior patterns will most certainly put your financial security at risk and will make it impossible to build your wealth personally.

Bettyann Glasser, a psychotherapist and life coach who has worked with hundreds of men and women with addiction and personality disorders, gives clear direction on this matter. Use your business skills to make sure you see your romantic situation clearly. You would not put up with negative behavior from a colleague, boss, or employee: your romantic relationships need to be handled with an equally clear head. In both cases, you must take appropriate action to protect yourself and your interests.

Beware the Con Artist

The con artist is alive and well today, and he will target a busy professional woman looking for love. The National Institute of Mental Health estimates that approximately 1 percent of the U.S. population (more than 3 million people) has an antisocial personality disorder, which is one of the hallmarks of a con artist.[7] An antisocial individual shows

> a pervasive pattern of disregard for, and violation of, the rights of others . . . [This disorder] begins in childhood or early adolescence and continues into adulthood. People with antisocial personality disorder may disregard social norms and laws, repeatedly lie, place others at risk for their own benefit, and demonstrate a profound lack of remorse. [Antisocial personality disorder] is sometimes referred to as sociopathic personality disorder, or sociopathy.[8]

If you are a woman with a great job who is happily building her wealth, you may become a target of a con artist simply because you are successful. The most typical sign of a con artist—a man with a hidden agenda, a sociopath who will put your financial security at risk—is that his words do not match his actions. He may be extremely sexy or charming, but the picture doesn't add up. "The key [to identifying con artists] is to look for men who don't do what they say they're going to do," says Glasser. If a woman wants to protect her financial stability, this behavior signals that it's time to walk away.

BEWARE A POTENTIAL CON ARTIST IF YOU CAN ANSWER YES TO ANY OF THE FOLLOWING QUESTIONS

- Does he ask to borrow money and then fail to pay it back within the agreed-upon time frame, or according to the agreements made between you?
- Does he seem to have no close friends, no close family, and no clear history?
- Does he fail to show up for events, meetings, or dates that were clearly arranged in advance?
- Does he watch pay-per-view sports or pornography at your home without asking and without offering to pay the bill?
- Does he offer to pick up the tab at restaurants but forgets his wallet and asks you to pay?
- Does he ask you to pay for the gas in his car because he doesn't want the charge to appear on his business credit card?
- Do you find yourself paying for holidays, events, or other purchases that he had previously agreed to pay for?
- Does he ask you to invest your life savings in financial ventures for which he shows you no documentation?
- Does he say he is starting a company and ask you to invest in it? Does he ask you not to consult your attorney about the investment?
- Does he claim to be a money manager and, as such, does he ask to manage your wealth?
- Does he claim to be wealthy, and dress as such, but fail to invite you to his home?
- Does he ask you to introduce him to your well-to-do friends? Does he ask them for money, or ask them to invest with him?

Busy, successful women are particularly vulnerable to con artists because they often don't have time to monitor the behavior of their boyfriends or significant others. Although the situations in the questions above may seem like mere annoyances and disappointments when a relationship is new, they can become extremely serious in marriage or when a couple is living together.

We know a woman who suffered disastrous consequences from being married to a sociopathic con artist. Sarah and Frank were married ten years and owned a small marketing business. Sarah became the face of the business, running development and sales for the company, while Frank managed their business and personal finances. Each year, Frank would ask Sarah to sign their tax return, and she believed he always paid their business and personal taxes each year. In fact, when the marriage disintegrated, Sarah was horrified to discover that Frank had never actually paid any taxes. He had only pretended to do so. They owed three quarters of a million dollars to the U.S. government, *and* they were getting divorced. How had Sarah missed her husband's criminal behavior? Upon later reflection, she admitted that her partying habits, her desire to concentrate only on what interested her in the business, and her willingness to ignore Frank's inconsistencies around money issues—after all, she loved him, didn't she?—meant that she hadn't been paying attention for years.

Many women, like Sarah, fall victim to the "surprise con," in which it seems impossible to detect suspicious behavior. But even in these situations, there are often early warning signs that reveal how a man will behave around money in the long run. Some of them may seem perfectly normal at first glance. For example, a man may be making business deals on the side with her friends' husbands, taking money out of their joint account, and getting clients through her connections. These may all be legitimate pursuits agreed upon by the couple. However, when a little whisper in a woman's ear says, "Hey, something's fishy here," that's a survival signal that should be heeded.

The bottom line is this: loving a man is no excuse for becoming blind to financial red flags. If a woman is paying attention, she can stay in the truth, process the facts, and deal with financial infidelity and liars effectively. If a woman has finally decided to confront a man's behavior, conversations should be straightforward and to the point, says Glasser. She recommends setting boundaries and using clear language like the following: "I cannot lend you money right now. I cannot do the things you have asked me to do. After you get your financial house in order, maybe we can start again."

Beware the Gold Digger

Women now control more than half the wealth in the United States,[9] so it's not surprising that men have joined the legions of women who marry or enter relationships for money. "These men used to be called gigolos," explains Glasser. But the women they prey on don't have to be extremely wealthy; they just have to be wealthy relative to the men. "I saw one man at my practice who never told me the first names of the women he dated," Glasser continues. "He would say, 'She's my Hamptons house. This one is my house in the Poconos. This one's going to give me my next job.'"

A gold digger may be hard to spot at first, because he may not directly state his desire to be financially kept. Rather, he often has many reasons why his career has not taken off and why you should support him in the short term. Or he may act like he is quite wealthy, but he in fact has made an art of being charming and getting invited to parties and weekends where others foot the bill and he never reciprocates. The gold digger may subtly train you into supporting him by rewarding your financial generosity with love, affection, and attention and by withdrawing when you question why he does not contribute financially. He may feel that his contribution of being very good-looking, much younger, an entertaining companion, or even a good listener is equivalent to your financial contribution. You may or may not agree with his assessment.

Although we now live in an era when couples can choose to have any financial arrangement that works for both of them, no matter how unorthodox, women need to make sure that their partners are not in the relationship *only* for the money. Otherwise, as wealthy men have known all along, your lover will most likely vanish if the money runs out or when you get tired of footing all the bills. When a woman is supporting a man, it is critical that she protect herself with a prenuptial agreement if they marry; otherwise, she will most likely end up paying alimony if the union fails. This also applies to cohabiting couples, who should sign a cohabitation agreement to avoid claims for continuing support should the relationship end.

BEWARE THE POTENTIAL GOLD DIGGER IF YOU CAN ANSWER YES TO ANY OF THE FOLLOWING QUESTIONS

- Does he have a vague artistic ambition—say, to be a painter or a musician—and blame his inability to earn money on outside circumstances when he really isn't working to make a career happen?
- Does he avoid saying he just plain doesn't like to work, but all behaviors telegraph this message loud and clear?
- Does he pretend to be rich and dress very nicely, but in fact never pays for anything and gets rather offended if you ask him to contribute?
- Does he make it clear that he expects you to pay for all dates?
- Is he very vain about his looks and does he think that the pleasure of his handsome company should be paid for?
- Does he think that his Olympian prowess in the bedroom is ample contribution to the relationship and therefore he should not be expected to pay for dates or trips?
- Is he more attentive to your every need when you buy him clothing, take him on trips, or pay off his debts?
- Does he pout and withdraw attention when you are not putting out the money?
- Do you feel like he will leave you if you don't pay for everything?

The Addict

One of the most disappointing realizations a woman can have is that the man she loves is an addict. Addiction comes in many forms, from alcoholism to drug addiction to pornography addiction to compulsive gambling. All these addictions wreak emotional havoc on those close to the addict, and spell certain relationship disaster. The financial consequences alone are astounding.

According to drug-rehabs.com, a heroin user spends $10,032 per year on his habit, and more than $200,000 in a twenty-year period. A cocaine habit costs nearly $9,000 per year, or as much as $180,000 over twenty years. These figures are conservative, and vary according to how much an addict buys, but they paint a good general picture.[10]

The legal substances that addicts abuse also make a hefty dent in a couple's financial savings. A heavy drinker who drinks a six-pack of domestic beer a day is spending $3,000 each year at a minimum, and likely much more on additional beverages if he is an alcoholic. And although pornography addiction seems like it might be more emotionally challenging for women to deal with, there are even worse financial consequences for a couple. "When viewing pornography rises to the level of addiction, 40 percent of . . . addicts lose their spouses, 58 percent suffer considerable financial losses, and about a third lose their jobs," according to Dr. Patrick Fagan of the Family Research Council.[11] Pornography addicts often pay for their addiction by running up huge credit card bills that can eventually become the responsibility of their spouses.

BEWARE THE POTENTIAL ADDICT IF YOU CAN ANSWER YES TO ANY OF THE FOLLOWING QUESTIONS

- Does he drink alcohol until he is clearly drunk every night—an entire bottle of wine or several hard-liquor drinks?
- Does he need to smoke pot almost every day to remain calm?
- Is he extremely moody, and do you suspect he is taking drugs such as cocaine?
- Does he disappear every night for hours on the Internet, and can you tell he has been looking at porn when you check the browser history on the computer?
- Does he constantly bet heavily on sports? Is he distracted when he has placed large bets and is he very moody because he has risked a great deal of money?
- Does he trade stocks constantly in amounts he cannot afford? Is he always on edge about the stock market?
- Does he constantly visit doctors to get prescriptions for pain medications or antianxiety medications? Has he asked you to get prescriptions for him or does he buy pills through online pharmacies?

* * *

In this chapter, we want to put special emphasis on the male compulsive gambler. The attractive and charismatic nature of such a person covers up a host of issues that may not be evident early on in a relationship. It is often very difficult for a woman in this situation to distinguish between reality and fantasy, and to acknowledge the level of danger she is in when she embarks upon a relationship with a compulsive gambler.

First of all, gambling is legal, socially acceptable, and even sexy. Participation is increasing at a rapid pace as the Internet welcomes new gamblers who would never have indulged in a trip to Las Vegas or Atlantic City in the past.[12] Often compulsive gamblers mask their addiction by suggesting that "it's a harmless game of cards" or "it's just a few trades" on E*TRADE. Gambling is now a $40 billion industry in the United States and growing.[13] If betting on "the big game" appears to be occupying too much of your partner's attention, expect financial devastation in the future. "The average debt incurred by a male pathological gambler in the U.S. is between $55,000 and $90,000," according to Gregory L. Jantz, author of *Turning the Tables on Gambling*. He continues, "The average rate of divorce for problem gamblers is nearly double that of nongamblers."[14]

The compulsive gambler is one of the most dangerous men a woman can meet because his very nature can seem so attractive to relationship seekers. "I can tell you that compulsive gamblers, particularly male, action-seeking compulsive gamblers, have a lot of flash, a lot of charm, a lot of charisma," explains Renee Siegel, a licensed independent substance abuse counselor, nationally certified gambling counselor, and executive director of the ABC Wellness Centre in Scottsdale, Arizona. It's hard to spot red flags. Common signs of the compulsive gambler are that he carries a lot of cash, appears incredibly generous, and is charming and charismatic. Over time, the danger signs become more obvious. Bill collectors call his home often. He disappears for long periods of time, doesn't answer his cell phone, and is not at work when he's scheduled to be at work. He is often depressed or exhibits erratic emotional behavior. (Among addicts of all kinds, compulsive gamblers have the highest suicide rate.[15]) He may often produce something Siegel calls shut-up money: even though he doesn't have enough money to pay the mortgage, he will drop a thousand dollars on the table and say, "Go buy something."

A gambling addict will often make the woman in a relationship feel like she knows less about money than he does, and will use that ploy to distract her from the issue at hand. According to Siegel, the gambling addict has "bizarre cognitive distortions that make him believe that he's capable of solving all sorts of financial problems. Women sometimes feel really guilty, because their partners often do, actually, have an intellectually greater knowledge about money than they do." Siegel has found that male gamblers are much brighter than "the average bear—usually an IQ of 135 or higher."

Gambling addicts will also try to shift responsibility for what they have done. A compulsive gambler will attack his partner, accusing her of being an extravagant spender, blaming her with accusations like, "If you were a better wife . . ." When the gambler is confronted about his problems, he usually promises never to do it again and emphasizes that he has the situation under control.

In addition, these men usually lie about the amount of debt they are in. Siegel, who was married to a compulsive gambler for many years, says, "It's like the alcoholic who says he's drinking a pint when he's drinking a fifth. You might think the gambler has twenty thousand dollars in debt, as I did—that's what I knew about—and in fact, it's three quarters of a million."

Even under this constant financial duress, female spouses very often stay with their husbands. The best thing a woman can do is to get her husband into Gamblers Anonymous, to a trained therapist, or into a specialized treatment program. Renee advises women who choose to pursue a relationship with a recovering compulsive gambler to make sure that the man meets all the following criteria if she wants to stay in the relationship; each of these actions is key to a healthy financial and romantic partnership with a man recovering from a gambling addiction:

- He attends Gamblers Anonymous or psychotherapy sessions or both.
- He has a sponsor in Gamblers Anonymous.
- He has done a pressure-relief program in Gamblers Anonymous.
- He accepts responsibility for his past actions.
- He has repaid all his debts.
- He maintains his own financial accounts, separate from yours.

* * *

If a woman's partner is a compulsive gambler, a pornography addict, an alcoholic, or a drug addict who is not in recovery, her financial future is extremely grim. She can look forward to debt, hospital bills, psychiatrist bills, parenting costs, and expensive divorce or legal fees. If the signs of addiction are clear in the first three months of a relationship, the financially responsible move is to leave. A woman shouldn't doubt what she is experiencing. As Bettyann Glasser explains, "When a woman says, 'Oh, but I love him,' she is making excuses for her choice to stay. Isn't it hard to live that way?"

MAKE THE BEST FINANCIAL MATCH

One of the best ways to ensure a happy partnership and a secure marriage is to make a great financial match. By this we don't necessarily mean marrying a wealthy man—rather, we mean finding a partner whose financial style works well with your financial style. Often, women are swept away romantically and fail to take a hard look at financial compatibility before marrying or moving in together. Here, we will discuss strategies to evaluate your financial compatibility long before you get to the engagement phase of your relationship. Getting to know each other financially will only strengthen your love. Since 60 percent of divorces are caused by financial problems,[16] it is critical that you work out money issues before you marry.

Know the Kind of Financial Partner You Want

If you are looking to get involved in a serious relationship, we advise you to first think about what you want your partner to bring to the table financially even before you begin dating. It is important to have a vision of your preferred marriage and family setup. Do you envision both of you working, or do you want to stay home to raise children? Do you want to be the main breadwinner while your husband raises the kids? Do you want to be PONC—Pets Only, No Children—and use your income to travel the world? It is important to find a partner who shares the same basic life goals in order to be happy. It will not work to try to convince an artist or a stay-at-home-dad type of man to become the sole breadwinner, nor will you be happy if you want to be at home and your husband expects you to bring home half the household income. Being honest with yourself on these crucial lifestyle choices is the first step. Early in the dating process, you need to discover the goals and dreams of your date, to see if they can match. If they can't, it is better to determine this early and move on, before you become too attached and then try to rationalize away these key differences.

Assuming that you and your date are looking for the same type of long-term relationship, the next step is to evaluate his basic financial habits in the early stages of dating. Here, we'll focus on five top traits to evaluate: personal financial management skills, financial integrity, financial realism, financial style, and financial negotiating skills. As you evaluate your potential mate, look at your own habits in these areas. You cannot expect to be attractive to a man with good financial habits if yours do not add up as well.

Personal Financial Management Skills

Long before you met your man, he developed personal financial management skills, and you will quickly see them in action. On the most basic level, is he a responsible individual? Does he support himself financially, or is he still living off his parents? Does he have a job, or is he in school, working toward a degree? Is he able to handle the expenses of a place to live? Can he handle the expenses of a car or his monthly commutation ticket or both? Does his life seem chaotic? Is he always in some kind of financial jam? If so, he may have very poor financial management skills, or this may be a red flag that you are dealing with an addict or a con artist, as we discussed earlier in this chapter. On the other hand, if he is able to manage his own life financially, chances are good that he will be a good financial partner and you will be able to manage finances well together. To get a little more information, you can ask him whether or not he does a budget every month, and compare how you both go about tracking expenses. This will also give you a great deal of information without prying too deeply at the beginning.

Financial Integrity

The next thing to try to evaluate is financial integrity. You want to partner with a man who meets his financial obligations honestly. You can find out some things about this by asking questions. How does he feel about paying taxes—has he filed every year, or does he boast about not bothering to pay or cheating the government? If the latter, this is a huge red flag. Does he pay his credit card and other bills, or is he constantly being declined when he tries to make purchases (or, worse yet, does he ask you to whip out your card)? Does he boast about scamming his company by filing false or padded expense reports? Many of these behaviors can be the signs of a dangerous sociopath. If he doesn't display financial integrity with others, he won't display it with you. On the other hand, if he seems to be extremely honest and conscientious, you will be in good hands and will be able to build a life together. It goes without saying that you must also have financial integrity, or an honest man will not be attracted to you once he learns the truth about your lack of values.

Financial Realism

It is critical that you observe a healthy attitude of financial realism in your man. His spending should not outstrip his means, and he should not carry a heavy load of debt. If a man insists on a lavish lifestyle that he cannot afford, he may be extremely insecure and out of touch with financial reality. His desire to impress will only lead to ruin, and if you marry him, you will be responsible for the many debts he continues to accumulate. It may not be easy to evaluate whether a man is living beyond his means in the early stages of a relationship—it may only be possible to discover this at a later stage of commitment, when more financial disclosure is customary. However, if you know he has a relatively modest job and he exhibits a fancy lifestyle, beware. It is good to have big dreams, but if a man only dreams and pines for a millionaire lifestyle without working for it, you may be saddled with a disgruntled husband who will never be happy with what you can both realistically achieve.

Financial Style

Another thing to evaluate is whether you like your partner's financial style. Do you think of him as cheap, or do you find him generous? These impressions can be very subjective, and what one woman may think of as incredible cheapness may strike another as admirably thrifty. If you love to clip coupons and shop at consignment stores, you need to find a man who also places a high value on frugality. If you love to stay at five-star hotels and tip generously, you need to find a man who agrees with your approach to spending. Many power struggles can be avoided by paying attention to how the two of you handle money, and whether you have similar spending habits. You will be able to learn more about a man's saving and investing habits as the relationship progresses, but his spending style will indicate a great deal about his approach to money early on. This trait may not be a deal breaker, the way financial integrity or financial realism is, but differences in financial style can cause a great deal of friction in a long-term partnership or marriage.

Financial Negotiating Skills

As soon as you start dating, you and your man will be entering into financial negotiations. Who will pick up the check on the first date? How about after you have been dating for a month or two? How about after six months? As your relationship progresses, there will be more and more opportunities to discuss who is paying for what. Some women expect men to pay for everything; others feel more comfortable and more independent when they share half the costs. Some women far outearn the men they date and want to pay for lavish vacations their men could never afford. All these situations require communication and negotiation. Ideally, you will both be able to discuss finances in a civil manner and come up with a system that works for both of you. Red flags to watch out for include the passive man who pays but acts resentful, manipulating you into paying without having an honest discussion about it. You should also avoid the bully who feels he owns you because he has paid. You need to keep an eye out for the gold digger, who never contributes anything. Even assuming your financial styles match, financial negotiating is a crucial skill you will need to make a long-term relationship work.

Moving Toward Commitment:
Full Financial Disclosure

Once you decide to become a committed couple, you need to begin working toward full financial disclosure. If you have decided to invest more time and effort into developing a relationship with someone, it is time to begin to dig deeper into all areas, including finances. Although there is no right time table for getting information, we are assuming that by the time you are ready to talk about living together or getting married, you should also be disclosing more specific personal financial information. There are five areas in particular you need to discuss: income, financial obligations, credit ratings, financial goals, and the handling of joint finances. We know this is not easy stuff—it is so much more fun to look at apartments together rather than at credit ratings—but it is essential that you know what kind of person you are moving in with before you do so. It is even more crucial before you tie the knot—you may become legally responsible for your husband's obligations, so you need to know exactly what his financial picture is like before you decide to take it on. You need to decide how much both of you want to commingle your finances before you merge households.

What should you do if your man refuses to participate in financial disclosure before making a serious commitment? We know men who croon that all will be revealed "after the wedding." We seriously advise against marrying or moving in with someone who will not disclose financial information to you. His stonewalling is a very big red flag. He may be a chauvinist who thinks women are either incapable of understanding family finances or have no right to the information; ask yourself if you want to live with this type of person. Read *Innocent Spouse,* a memoir by Carol Ross Joynt, who was saddled by huge debts she had no idea existed after her husband's untimely demise. If he refuses to disclose financial information, your man may be a con artist who does not want you to see the evidence of his financial misdemeanors, or he may have given you a false name and actually cannot produce a credit report under that name. He may be a control freak who will make your life miserable and who will never treat you like a full partner—you may not want to live under the "rule" of a petty Attila the Hun. He may be extremely wealthy but living beyond his means and not want you to really know about his multiple lawsuits, alimony payments, and other financial obligations. Knowledge is power, and without knowledge you should not commit to moving forward into a situation where you share living arrangements and financial obligations. Continue to date if you like, but don't commit financially to a man who won't share information with you.

Take a Look at Joint Income

In order to decide how to split expenses when you decide to live together or get married, it is essential to understand how much money each person makes. For couples who work at salaried jobs, this is not difficult to verify—just show each other a pay stub. For business owners, the question is much more fluid—many business expenses, such as travel or home-office rent, reduce taxable income but improve after-tax cash flow. You need to sit down with each other and share realistic numbers based on the last couple of years. For wealthy men and women, income may include proceeds from investment portfolios, family trusts, and dividend checks in addition to, or in lieu of, a salary. However, a wealthy person may have no control over trust disbursements, for example, so he or she may have less financial flexibility than an entrepreneur.

Once numbers are disclosed, you may be surprised to find out that you are among the 22 percent of all American women who outearn their husbands; the number is 25 percent if your husband does not have a college degree.[17] If you are under the age of thirty, are single and childless, and live in a major city, you probably earn quite a bit more than the men in your town—17 percent more if you are in New York City, 12 percent more in Los Angeles, and 15 percent more in San Diego, for example.[18] Now that you understand who has the greater earning power, it is time to look at financial obligations, so there is a true picture of net cash available.

Examine Financial Obligations

If either of you has ongoing financial obligations, these will reduce the amount of cash available to fund joint expenses. Financial obligations in the early years usually include school debt, car payments, and credit card bills. In later years, obligations include the support of your children, any child support or alimony payments if you are divorced, and mortgage payments on properties you own. If you have experienced financial difficulties, you may also be responsible for past-due medical bills, tax installment payments, or payouts under bankruptcy or other creditor agreements. A simple list of your financial obligations should be shared with your mate, so that both of you understand where all the cash is going.

It can be helpful to break financial obligations into mandatory and discretionary categories. You may spend a great deal on antique cars or boats, for example—this is really a discretionary obligation, compared to court-mandated child support. Asking your significant other to share a list of his financial obligations will be a good test—can he produce this list? Can you? If both of you are capable of producing the list, it shows that both of you are aware of and handling your obligations. If he cannot produce a list and is totally disorganized, you need to decide if you want to assume this chore for both of you as a couple or not.

Share Credit Reports

One of the most reliable ways to gauge your potential mate before you move in together is to share credit reports. Credit reports are assembled by ratings agencies, so your man cannot manipulate or hide data—the credit report will tell the unvarnished truth, which can often be an enlightening story. First, take a look at his overall credit score. Then look at the details—you will be able to see if he has late payments, bankruptcies, or other summary judgments against him. You definitely need to know all the facts before you make a commitment to sign a lease or buy a house together. If your man has a good credit score and pays his bills on time, you can feel more confident in joining your households.

You will also need to come clean and present your own credit report to your partner, so make sure it is accurate. Although you cannot hire "credit doctors" to erase problems, you can improve your score by making all your payments on time—not even one day late—and by never borrowing more than 30 percent of the credit available to you. Helpful online credit monitoring reports can guide you to ways to improve your own scores. Companies like myfico.com will monitor your credit report and send you an email alert if your credit score changes.

Discuss Financial Goals

Now that you have a good handle on income levels, financial obligations, and credit scores, it is time to switch gears and talk about the future—what are your man's goals? If he has had financial problems in the past (which you can see plainly from his credit report), how is he working his way out of these problems? Is he expecting you to handle more expenses than you normally would while he digs himself out of a hole? How do you feel about doing that? Again, this is the time to be brutally honest with yourself. If your man does not have a good track record in handling money, you have no evidence that this will change in the future.

If your man is financially responsible, it is still a good idea to discuss financial goals with him. Now that you are a couple, what are his goals? Does he plan to start a company, make partner in a law firm, or work for your business? How much money does he envision going into joint plans versus his personal goals and investments? If he wants to compete in triathlons around the world, for example, he may need to keep a good deal of his cash flow to meet this goal. It is better that you know this in advance, rather than assuming that you are sharing the same vision of the future. Your own goals are also important, and you need to express them. If you plan to take on debt to go to business school for an MBA, he needs to know that. If you want to start a family and stop working within two years, this should be openly discussed rather than making it a covert agenda. If you want to sell your business within five years and retire offshore, you need to make sure he is agreeable to that plan.

Discuss How to Handle Joint Finances

Armed with the knowledge gleaned from full disclosure, you can now discuss how to handle financial arrangements after you join households. At this point, you can relax because you have a clear picture of what you are committing to—there are no financial secrets waiting to disrupt you after you have moved in together.

Of course, we hope you discover that your man is an excellent financial manager. Life is not always perfect, though, and if you have fallen in love with a man who has poor financial management skills but is willing to reform, you may decide to take the risk and move ahead. In this case, you can protect yourself by making sure you do not expose yourself to his potential pitfalls. Make sure you do not open any joint accounts, either checking or credit, for at least two years. If you plan to marry, seriously consider a prenuptial agreement (see page 72). Better yet, consider getting engaged and living together, or sharing joint finances for at least a year, before you marry. Do not enter into a lease agreement that you could not afford to carry on your income alone. Do not put his name on a mortgage or on a property deed, especially if you are providing all the funding. If you lend him money, or agree to pay off his bills, make sure all your agreements about repayment are documented in writing. This way, if he disappoints you and remains a financial disaster, you can extricate yourself with minimal damage to your finances.

If your man is a good financial manager, on the other hand, it will be easy to create financial arrangements that suit you both. A good way to start is to have one joint checking account with two debit cards for joint expenses, while the rest of your finances are maintained separately. Both of you can contribute proportionally to the joint account. For example, if you make $100,000 per year and your man makes $50,000 per year, you may agree that you will pay two thirds of the joint expenses while he pays one third. If one of you has a private company, as described above, it may take a bit more analysis to figure out a fair way to split expenses. After a year or so, you may also want to have a joint savings account to which you can both make contributions—this is ideal for major joint expenses that require advance planning, such as a house or an expensive vacation. As trust grows over time, you can share more.

CHOOSE TO HAVE A PRENUPTIAL AGREEMENT

We feel that signing a prenuptial agreement is one of the best ways to increase the odds of having a happy marriage. According to one law firm, a prenuptial agreement is "a written contract created by two people before they are married. A prenup typically lists all the property each person owns (as well as any debts) and specifies what each person's property rights will be after the marriage." If you are able to negotiate the terms of this emotionally charged document with your fiancé before your marriage, chances are good that you will never need to use it. If your marriage fails, however, you will be relieved that you have already agreed to the major terms of your separation and will not waste money on divorce lawyers who do nothing but attempt to destroy your ex-spouse financially.

Prenuptial agreements demand that we revolutionize our thinking about our money and ourselves. Divorce is a $28 billion industry today.[19]

We believe you don't need to contribute any more money than necessary to that pot. The reality is that 65 percent of the time, women initiate a divorce. Current research shows that more than 20 percent of first marriages end in divorce within five years and 40 percent of first marriages end in divorce within thirteen years. Although 75 percent of those divorced eventually remarry, 65 percent of those second marriages also end in divorce. More sobering, studies show that in the United States, women's income drops between 24 and 26 percent after a divorce, whereas men's income drops only between 6 and 15 percent.[20] Given the statistics, chances are good that you will be very glad you insisted on signing a prenup before you walked down the aisle.

Since ancient history, women have been protecting their assets with marriage contracts. According to Janet Johnson, professor of Egyptology at the University of Chicago, the oldest known marriage contracts were recorded in ancient Egypt, where women had full legal rights as far back as approximately 2686 BCE).[21] The traditional Jewish marriage contract, the *ketubah*, which is designed, in part, to protect a woman in the event of divorce or her husband's death, is also thousands of years old.

So we advise you to follow the traditions of your wise female ancestors and take the opportunity to love freely but plan sensibly. Although there can be some intense moments during prenup discussions, it's good practice for a woman and a man to explore their greatest financial and emotional fears before they get married, just as they will have to do throughout their married life. The prenup is an absolute declaration of the love and respect you feel for your partner. After all, with a prenup, you have an opportunity to satisfy your partner's need for financial security.

We know a couple for whom a prenup has only enhanced their marriage. Laura, a media executive, and Jake, an investment banker, decided that signing a prenup was a wise decision before they got married. Jake earns $15 million per year, and believed that he had the most to lose in the event of a divorce. However, Laura, who has a portfolio worth more than $1 million, actually believed that she had the most to lose. She wanted to keep her portfolio in her own name after she got married, as she had inherited this money from her father. When Laura hired a well-known divorce attorney—one with a reputation for being extremely aggressive—to negotiate her side of the prenup with her fiancé, he was really hurt. Jake didn't expect Laura to take decisive action, as he was the one with more assets. But as Laura explained, she was protecting both of them and their future children. Ultimately, this rather emotional prenup situation led to a much stronger marriage. As Laura says, "We trust each other completely, we have a plan for dark days, and we're taking care of each other now and in the future."

Who Should Have a Prenuptial Agreement?

Prenups are used widely by the very wealthy, but anyone with assets or the potential for future assets should consider such an agreement. Prices for a good prenup can range from two thousand to more than twenty thousand dollars, depending on the complexity of the assets held by each person prior to marriage.

To determine whether you could benefit from a prenup, ask yourself the following basic questions about your assets and liabilities:

- Do you outearn your partner?
- Do you own, or own part of, a business?
- Do you have a degree or license that represents the potential for major earnings in the future?
- Do you own a home?
- Do you have a stock portfolio?
- Do you have a savings account?
- Do you expect an inheritance?
- Do you have a collection of valuables, such as jewelry or antiques?
- Do you have college loans?
- Does your partner have college loans?
- Are you supporting family members, including children or elderly parents?

When a relationship ends without a prenup, a woman may be forced to give up her home or homes, her savings, her salary, and her future inheritance from her parents, even if these assets have nothing to do with her spouse and were accumulated years before he came on the scene. In addition, these disputes are usually settled in public—in an angry battle between lawyers, or at the whim of a judge. Without a prenup, a woman is suddenly power-less over her financial future. On the flip side, financially punishing a male partner because he had certain expectations about the end of his marriage is a deeply undesirable situation. Imagine if he is also the father of your children.

Prenuptial Agreements, Step by Step

Vikki Ziegler, a family law attorney, TV analyst, and author of the book *The Pre-Marital Planner,* outlined some key steps to take when considering a prenup. She divides the process into three stages.

The First Stage: Information Gathering

Evaluate your current financial circumstances and determine if you have any property, bank accounts, retirement accounts, or possible inheri-tances that you want to protect in the event of a divorce. If you do, take a financial inventory of all your assets to determine what you want to remain segregated. The list should include all your assets, debts, income, and ex-penses, as well as your credit report.

The Second Stage: Starting the Prenup Conversation

After you have completed your inventory, it is time to broach the dif-ficult subject with your partner. Be sensitive to his emotional attachment to money. Timing is everything—choose a time and date when you both are at ease and not occupied mentally. You might broach the topic by say-ing that you love your partner and want to spend the rest of your life with him. Then you should speak matter-of-factly about how important it is to discuss financial matters. You could ask him what he thinks about the idea that, if you should ever get divorced, assets that you accumulated to-gether should be shared, but assets acquired before the marriage should remain separate. See what your partner's response to that position is. Don't talk over each other; make sure to listen. You may learn that your partner is not opposed to the concept or may have a different approach. Adding that a prenuptial agreement will make a divorce less acrimonious and expensive for both of you is a real plus in the conversation.

The Third Stage: Working with Lawyers

It is important to ensure that you have several months to fully disclose all your assets to your respective attorneys. The more organized you are, the better the prenup will be—trust us. It is also very important that you and your intended retain separate counsel. Topics that you will want to discuss with your attorneys include

1. the division of property acquired before the wedding date and the division of property acquired after the wedding date;
2. the division of responsibility for premarital and postmarital debts;
3. the ownership of marital residences, including who moves out in the event of divorce;
4. the division of financial responsibilities during the marriage;
5. the divorce laws in your state of residence—community property versus equitable distribution;
6. alimony obligations;
7. the distribution of property upon the death of either spouse;
8. life insurance coverage;
9. how to protect business interests before and after the marriage.

Vikki Ziegler also told us that

women are earning more in this day and age and are becoming more realistic about divorce rates. The number of women requesting prenuptial agreements seems to be increasing year to year at a rapid pace. In addition, some women are requesting stipulations in their prenups for sunset clauses, which automatically terminate the terms of the prenup on a certain date in the future. This is to protect the breadwinning woman from being held to a prenup after being married for an extended period of time.

By choosing to be a financially savvy bride, you can say your vows with confidence, knowing that you have protected your assets as you pledge your love.

MAXIMIZE YOUR VALUE AS A COUPLE

If you have followed our advice in making the best financial match, you have wisely chosen a mate who is a good fit for you. If you share values, are financially responsible, and are willing to open up to each other and discuss finances in a straightforward manner, now is the time to embark on an exciting adventure of living together and maximizing your joint income.

Rather than offer you advice on what to do, we'd like to share with you the thoughts of two couples who have excelled at meshing their professional lives and creating long-lived, thriving marriages. Both our power couples are highly admired and famous in their fields. Each couple has come up with a unique way to work together and to thrive in their partnership. We'll see common threads and different choices by learning from these fascinating couples.

We'll first speak with Barbara Taylor Bradford, the novelist, about her marriage and partnership with movie producer Robert Bradford. Barbara is one of the world's best-selling novelists. According to the official Barbara Taylor Bradford website, she has published twenty-seven books, all bestsellers, and has sold more than 85 million copies worldwide in forty languages and in ninety countries. Barbara Taylor Bradford met her husband, Robert, in London. "We were introduced by friends and it was an instantaneous attraction. About a year and a half later we got married and I came to live in New York," explains Barbara.

Robert Bradford was a successful movie producer in Beverly Hills and New York before he met Barbara. In the 1950s, he served as a vice president for Samuel Bronston Productions in Madrid. Among his film credits from this era are *John Paul Jones, El Cid, Fifty-five Days in Peking,* and *The Fall of the Roman Empire.* In the 1960s, Bob was an executive producer for Hal Roach Studios in Los Angeles. He later became the executive vice president and CEO for Franco London Films S.A. in Paris. While at this major independent French film company, he oversaw major productions, including John Frankenheimer's *Impossible Object.*

When they married, Barbara was an established journalist in London's Fleet Street, but she had become a reporter on the *Yorkshire Evening Post* when she was sixteen. Four years later she went to London to work on a women's magazine, and later moved to the *London Evening News*. Once she and Bob were married and she was living in New York, she wrote eight books on interior design, which were published by Meredith Press, Simon & Schuster, and Doubleday. She also had an interior design column that was syndicated to nearly two hundred newspapers in the United States.

In the early seventies, the Bradfords were living in Paris, where Bob was running Franco-London Films.

> I was able to write my column in Paris, and send it back to the syndication service in New York, but I also returned to New York every couple of months, where we still had an apartment, to do research and interviews and collect material for the column. However, I had always wanted to be a novelist; I had sold my first short story to a children's magazine when I was ten years old. It was around 1976 that I had the idea for *A Woman of Substance*. At that time, I wrote an outline for the novel, showed it to a friend who was an agent, and he arranged for me to meet an editor at Doubleday. Eventually, the book was bought on this twelve-page outline and 150 pages of manuscript. It came out in 1979.

A Woman of Substance became an instant bestseller, eventually selling 28 million copies worldwide. Barbara has written twenty-five novels since then. In 2011, she delivered her twenty-seventh, titled *Letter from a Stranger*.

"I am lucky to have married a movie producer," Barbara says. Robert Bradford has made ten of his wife's books into miniseries or movies of the week. Barbara twice took on the challenge of writing the screenplay for these movies.

In an interview with us, Barbara makes a very important point for couples who are considering maximizing dual incomes by working together. Barbara and Bob both had excellent careers in their chosen creative fields and a strong marriage for more than a decade before working together.

> If you want to work with someone to whom you are married, you have to have a solid marriage. You have to love the person, trust and respect them. Otherwise, if you don't, you will have chaos in the office, upsets, and anger, and will take all that home. It's not merely a colleague, it's your

husband or wife. Perhaps it won't work for a lot of people, because there could be a lack of trust or respect. Also, you really have to be on the same wavelength with your husband (or wife). I had been married to Bob for sixteen years when *A Woman of Substance* was published in 1979. It was only when he got involved in the making of *A Woman of Substance* several years later that we started working together.

The couple is never in the same location together during their workday, even during collaborations. "This is the best for us. I am working in my office at home and Bob goes to his office on Park Avenue. I need to be alone when I'm writing. And Bob certainly does not need me to be involved with the nitty-gritty of movie producing," she says.

Barbara and Bob share a mutual reverence for each other's expertise, creativity, and independent spirit.

I read a script of one of my books and give him my opinion, and sometimes a few suggestions. He likes to discuss casting with me, but that's always a tough one. Not because we disagree, but the right actor for the part might not be available. I would never want to be a casting director! But I am a sounding board for Bob. However, for the most part, you must let the filmmaker make the film. Bob has other people who are essential sounding boards: the director, the line producer, and the cameraman. I am very much involved because it is my book, but it's not about going to the office every day and being under each other's feet. We work in separate places, except when he is filming and he invites me to go to the set if I want.

Barbara emphasizes that it's important to understand the person you are married to if you are going into business together. "I am very strong, independent, and quite opinionated, but Bob understands me because we've been married for years. As for my work, I don't show anyone a new book until it is a finished product. Bob would never encroach on my writing and I don't do that to him, either. It's two different crafts. A film is watched; a book is read."

True mastery and success in business collaboration enters the picture when couples can benefit from each other's area of expertise. Robert Bradford

used a lot of new ideas when he became involved in the marketing of Barbara's books.

> Bob believed that a book could be marketed like a movie. For instance, he
> was the first to take a full-page advertisement on the back page of *The
> New York Times* for a book. Also, he has always hired outside public rela-
> tions people to promote my books. This is because he realizes that a pub-
> lisher can only do so much because they have many authors to cover. Bob
> supervises my entire career," Barbara adds. "He has also created a global
> franchise that has succeeded extremely well. He is not heavy-handed with
> publishers and he puts his own money where his mouth is. Bob is the one
> handling the financial side of our business, but we do have discussions.
> And of course, we have financial advisers.

We feel it's valuable to understand that Robert Bradford and Barbara
Taylor Bradford did not enter their marriage with the intention of becoming a business success story. Their marriage started with true love. "The
business part was almost by accident," explains Barbara. "When we got married I was a journalist, and he was making motion pictures. Bob didn't know
I was going to write novels. Nor did he know he would make those novels
into television movies."

If you dream of running a successful small business with your husband, you will enjoy meeting Bob and Melinda Blanchard. In one of their
books, *Live What You Love,* the Blanchards recount their adventurous life
as serial entrepreneurs—they've started nine businesses over thirty-six years,
written five books, been married, and had a son. From packaging a line of
gourmet foods to running a top restaurant on the Caribbean island of
Anguilla, they have chosen to experience the ups and downs of entrepreneurial life as partners. The title of their book says it all—*Live What You
Love,* and they do.

The Blanchards have experienced both small-business failures and successes. They have a talent for picking up and being willing to start again
from scratch. Their businesses have been diverse, and they are never afraid to
tackle a new challenge. The couple's nine businesses range from Board
and Basket, a tabletop store they launched in 1976 right out of college, to
ARTECH—Alpine Racing Technology, which they own 25 percent of today

and expect to do $2 million in business in 2011. In 1983, they created a multimillion-dollar line of specialty sauces called Blanchard & Blanchard & Son that was launched after they lost almost everything in a store called Kids Connection. After they sold that company, they moved to Anguilla, where they now run Blanchards Restaurant and write books inspiring others to follow their dreams.

The huge success of the sauce company followed on the heels of a failure. The couple had borrowed a lot of money to expand their store chain in Vermont called Kids Connection at an interest rate of prime plus 2 percent, at a time when the prime rate was 19.5 percent. The high interest rates put them out of business. They ended up having a huge going-out-of-business sale and earned barely enough money to pay off the bank. They had to break store leases and were afraid they would lose their house. They literally buried their last four thousand dollars in the backyard in a small box for safekeeping. Undaunted, they decided to try again. Bob went back to work as a carpenter to make the mortgage payments while Melinda headed into the kitchen to create a line of specialty sauces. The fact that they had never run a food products company did not deter them. Bob remembers Melinda emerging from the kitchen saying, "I have twenty-four products developed. I want to take them to market. Let's build a trade show booth and go to the Fancy Food Show in California."

They were behind on their mortgage and it was a really rough time. They had spent most of their last four thousand dollars on bottles and glass and ingredients for the salad dressings and mustards. Bob built a trade show booth made from fixtures from the failed store. The Blanchards wrote thirty-five thousand dollars'-worth of orders at the show. They hired sales reps in fourteen states, and wrote orders for Bloomingdales, Neiman Marcus, and Macy's nationwide; they came back to Vermont with no way to produce the products. "We had a blender in the kitchen," says Melinda, laughing. "So we went back to the bank with the orders and said, 'We need money!' and they gave it to us! We hit the specialty food market just as it was taking off, and it grew from our kitchen into a twenty-thousand-square-foot bottling plant in three years. It just exploded."

The couple has loved sharing all their adventures together. Melinda says, "It sounds sort of corny but once we were married and had our child, we just couldn't imagine going in separate directions each day. We couldn't figure out why we would want to do that. For us, we got married so we could spend all our time together. If we had both established separate careers, we would have had disconnected lives that would have had to be blended tougher."

Bob and Melinda believe that having the same ultimate goals made a big difference. Over the years, they've made an effort to declutter their lives of excess. This has made some financial decisions easier and their vision for their lives and priorities more clear. Melinda says they're not spendthrifts and they don't spend a lot on extras. Unlike so many couples, they seem to be able to agree on "needs" as opposed to "wants" when necessary. Bob might say that they need a walk-in cooler because the one they've got is worn out and rusted. If Melinda replies that they can't afford a new one, Bob will usually agree and just fix the old one.

Melinda believes that "communication" is the single most important word that comes to mind when discussing how to achieve business success in a marriage. "I think that you just can't keep anything to yourself, because it festers and it turns into a problem. We really share all of our feelings, all of our thoughts, and all of our ideas, good and bad. If we're worried about our staff not performing correctly or the food not arriving on time, there are times that we may not always agree on a solution but we talk and work it out."

Over the years, one of the Blanchards' biggest decisions has been about how to spend money or when to take a risk regarding their investments. "For us, wine is a big investment. Sometimes we bring in a huge order directly from France and it can be a fifty-thousand-dollar decision. And I tend to do it a little more easily than Bob," says Melinda. "I think it used to be the reverse, but again, we do make these decisions together." Roles have reversed over the years, says the couple. Bob was the more laid-back of the two early on, and Melinda says, coming from New York, she was less patient. Now their attitudes have flip-flopped a bit.

The Blanchards suggest that you remain flexible with your business idea, and if your business plan hits obstacles, be willing to change course. When the Blanchards first came to Anguilla, they thought they would start another sauce company, but realized that the cost structure would make that impossible. Determined to find a way to live in Anguilla, they changed course and opened a restaurant. Over the years, they've also written five books and now spend some of their time inspiring and coaching budding entrepreneurs.

Through all the business changes, the Blanchards have never questioned their partnership. "If there's something major to be decided, then we do it together. I think part of what makes it work is that we don't compete with each other at all," says Melinda.

> I cannot think of a single situation where either one of us has felt even a twinge of competition. I think we simply both have the same goals of getting the job done in whatever business it is we're doing at the time. We're very quality-minded. We don't need meetings. Working together is just our life. We've gone through stages over the years where we've wondered together, "Are we business partners or are we a married couple? Where are the priorities and where does one leave off and the next begin?" We've come to realize that we're obviously both. Learning how to weave your personal life together when you work with your spouse and learning how to weave it together with the business takes a little time. We've had things we had to overcome and things we've had to figure out together, but we've never had the discussion, "Should we do this anymore?" That's never been an issue.

Investing as a Team Sport

Now that you are maximizing your incomes, chances are good that you are generating more cash than you are spending. If that's the case, then it is time to start investing as a couple. By following the advice we have set forth as part of our first pearl of wisdom—invest like a billionaire—you should be ready to create an asset allocation and an investment policy for each pool of money that you are considering for investment. When investing becomes a team sport, there are several ways to maintain harmony in your marriage while investing in a way that is comfortable for both of you.

According to financial adviser Holly Dustin of Ledyard Financial Advisors, the single biggest mistake couples make is delegating the task of investing to only one person. Says Dustin, "I think it's important for both parties to take an interest and be responsible and know what is happening so one of you can't say at a later time, 'Oh, I thought *this* was the plan.' I think you've got to be engaged and help make the plan so you aren't surprised."

Simply opting out of financial discussions is not fair to the spouse who is left to make all the financial decisions. It is easy to be a Monday-morning quarterback and to blame your partner if things don't work out. You both need to make decisions together, or to agree to keep your investments separate and look after only your own money.

If you're a woman, opting out can be a very dangerous choice—as we previously discussed, it's not uncommon for men to take advantage of women in financial situations. You may feel that your husband is genetically better equipped to invest than you are, but as we learned in chapter 1, recent studies show that women are actually much better investors than men because they do not experience testosterone surges when trading. Even if your husband is a professional money manager, you may have a valuable perspective to bring to the table. There are millions of ways to make money, and it is important that you are both comfortable with the investment choices you make as a couple.

If the two of you have similar financial styles, chances are good that you will have similar investing styles. If this is the case, it may be very easy for the two of you to agree on an asset allocation for each portfolio and to approve or select money managers or investments. On the other hand, if one of you is very conservative and the other is a risk taker, it may make sense to keep investment funds separate. Holly Dustin explains, "If the man is very aggressive and wants 100 percent of his portfolio to be in stock, and the woman is very conservative and would like a much more balanced portfolio, you have a couple of options. You could meet somewhere in the middle and establish a compromise position or, in a scenario that I find works better, you could keep your money in separate investment accounts and have a little fun comparing whose portfolio performs better."

As the heads of your family office, you and your husband should meet regularly and discuss how your investments are doing. We advise you to meet once a month, or if that seems too overwhelming, at least once every quarter. Ideally, we suggest you meet with your financial adviser as a team. Use your adviser to provide reports that compare the returns of your various investments to the appropriate benchmarks. Review your statements and performance reports together before meeting with your adviser, and develop a list of questions if you are not comfortable with the performance your funds are achieving. Ideally, you should attend all meetings with the adviser together—this ensures that there is no misunderstanding about instructions, new investments, or sales of existing holdings. Again, make joint decisions that you are comfortable with, or simply manage your own money.

Even if you decide to manage your money separately, you should meet and discuss your separate investment accounts with each other. Chances are good that you both plan to rely on income from the investments for retirement, and you need to keep each other abreast of what is happening. You may be able to help each other and learn from each other's experiences. Communication is the key.

Together, you can develop strategies for handling the markets. For example, you can create mutually agreed-upon stop losses for each type of investment (e.g., if an investment goes down by x percent, you agree to sell, no matter what). You can also agree on how often to rebalance your asset allocation and how to invest new funds. By creating policies as a team, you will only enhance your marriage as you grow your wealth.

CHAPTER 3

MOTHERHOOD

THE THIRD PEARL OF FINANCIAL WISDOM:
A Woman Must Nurture Her Prosperity in Motherhood

THE DECISION TO BECOME A MOTHER is life changing: women who decide to devote themselves to the next generation embark on a wonderful journey, one that has major financial implications. The quality of your experience as a mother will very much be affected by the financial decisions you make—when to have children, whether to work or stay home, and what happens if you are facing remarriage and the creation of a blended family. Your children's attitudes and ability to handle money will be shaped by what you teach them about finances. Your child may become a superstar and need your financial guidance at an early age. You may choose to become a dog parent without kids. This is why our third pearl of wisdom—a woman must nurture her prosperity in motherhood—is so important. It is imperative for all members of the family that women combine motherhood and finance in a way that enhances the quality of life.

In focusing on our families, we often forget ourselves. We feel torn because we feel we have to choose between motherhood and making money. When we try to combine both, we can feel exhausted. If we are caught up in the day-to-day dramas of children, it is hard to step back and remember that there are big picture issues to consider.

THE GRAIN OF SAND IN THE OYSTER SHELL

Do you know a woman who . . .

- Wants to have children but has not met a husband and is in her thirties?
- Needs additional income and wants to work from home?
- Wants to teach her children good money habits but doesn't have a plan?
- Wants to encourage her child's dream of modeling?
- Has remarried a man with three children and is raising a blended family?
- Is adopting her first dog and needs to understand the financial commitment?

We hope you will be open to the new opportunities that are presented here. We are much more likely to enjoy the experience of motherhood and to continue to prosper when we have a strategy in place. The solutions we offer are innovative and exciting, allowing you more freedom and the ability to keep building your wealth.

PLAN FOR CHILDREN EARLY ON

If you decide to have a baby in America, you will quickly discover that the laws in this country are not very supportive of the economic needs of motherhood, starting from the day we give birth. More than half (55 percent) of women who had a child in 2010 were in the labor force, yet the United States is one of the only countries in the developed world that does not require companies to provide paid maternity leave.[1] According to *The Wall Street Journal,* in 2008, only 16 percent of employers offered full-time maternity pay, down from 27 percent in 1998.[2] Maternity and paternity leave has become scarcer due to the economic recession, part of the trend to cut employee costs. This lack of support for maternity leave means that working women are delaying childbirth, often out of economic necessity, while they pay off college loans and start to get on their feet financially. Unfortunately, delaying childbirth may mean facing fertility issues later on—which can drive the cost of motherhood right back up again.

In America, the choices women make about when to have children have major economic consequences. The cost of raising just one child from birth to age seventeen is $200,000.[3] Choosing to have a baby later in life can be even more financially challenging, as in vitro fertilization (IVF) and other medical treatments often add anywhere from $5,000 to $100,000 or more to the cost of parenthood. Here is an example of a few of the costs associated with fertility treatments—and they're conservative estimates:[4]

IVF Procedure: $7,000 (not including medications)
Hormonal and sonographic monitoring
Ultrasonographic egg retrieval
Sperm preparation
Embryo culture
Embryo transfer

Donor Oocyte Cycle: $25,000
Donor compensation ($8,000)
Donor screening costs
Donor medication recipient synchronization
IVF procedure
Recipient transfer
Pregnancy test

Frozen Embryo Cycle: $3,500
Blood tests
Sonograms
Embryo thawing and preparation
Embryo transfer
Pregnancy test

Frozen Embryo Cycle Ancillary Procedures
ICSI (intracytoplastic sperm injection) $1,000
Hatching $1,000

Blastocyst culture	$1,000
Embryo cryopreservation	$1,000 (includes first year of embryo storage)
Testicular sperm extraction	$3,500
Donor sperm	$400 per specimen
Embryo storage	$600 per year after the first year

Already, in 2011, more than 7 million women between the ages of fifteen and forty-four use infertility services, according to the Centers for Disease Control and Prevention.[5] More and more women are incurring the costs of fertility treatments as they choose to delay motherhood. In particular, college-educated women are putting off having children until later, presumably to establish their careers. It's a trend the 2010 census calls the "delayer boom." This delay means that there are many more childless women in their forties than there were in earlier decades. Ten percent of all women between the ages of forty and forty-four were childless in 1976. In 2010, the figure was nearly double, at 19 percent.[6]

We don't want to tell women when to start a family, but we want to reiterate that, for women, the fertility clock is a reality. Between the ages of twenty and twenty-four, a woman's likelihood of infertility is 3 percent. That figure rises to 32 percent between the ages of forty and forty-four. Between the ages of twenty and twenty-four, a woman's likelihood of getting pregnant as a result of having unprotected sex is 100 percent; that likelihood drops to just 36 percent between the ages of forty and forty-four.[7] And even IVF does not always deliver the desired results. In cumulative delivery data collected by Dr. James Grifo at the New York University Fertility Center from 2003 to 2008, at the age of thirty, women who have had IVF have a 62 percent delivery rate. When a woman has IVF at the age of forty, the delivery rate falls to 28 percent; at age forty-two, it falls to 14 percent. Those results are from a single attempt at IVF where stimulation and egg retrieval are done. Repeated attempts result in higher cumulative pregnancy rates; that is, the numbers reported are per one attempt.[8]

The fact is, a woman's fertility drops dramatically as she heads into her forties, and the risk of having a child with Down syndrome or birth defects increases exponentially. By the age of forty-five, a woman has a one in thirty chance of conceiving a child with birth defects.[9] So we believe that when a woman reaches her twenties, it's important for her to become familiar with some of the basic costs associated with delaying child-birth. She should also familiarize herself with the various options that may give her extra time to plan motherhood on the schedule that works best for her.

Just as the birth control pill was the solution to unwanted pregnancy in the 1960s, egg freezing may be the solution for women who now want to postpone pregnancy. Freezing a woman's eggs until she can find the ap-propriate partner or is ready to have more children gives her an opportu-nity to stop time for a while, and ensures that she can carry viable eggs to fruition. Egg freezing is not a guaranteed path to motherhood, but more than a thousand babies have been born from frozen eggs worldwide. Women don't have to forgo parenting because of early menopause or other health issues. Women don't need to marry badly to secure a chance at mother-hood. They can plan their children in a financially savvy way with their partners.

This controversial procedure is much more expensive than birth control, and is not covered by insurance. It costs approximately fifteen thousand dollars—sometimes more—and additional fees are incurred for maintaining the frozen eggs at an appropriate facility. Some women need to go through two egg-freezing cycles just to produce enough usable eggs, but it's a viable option, and much less expensive and less risky than facing IVF down the road.

"I've wanted kids since I was twenty-one years old, yet I've also been obsessed with the advancement of my career," explains a woman we know named Elizabeth. "Somehow the right guy didn't come along. When I turned thirty-seven, I had already started mourning the children I wasn't able to have. I was crying at the sight of baby strollers in the park and I knew I had to do something. Then a friend who works in finance told me she used last year's bonus to freeze her eggs. And I knew this was it, it had to be done. Twenty thousand dollars later, I have twelve eggs in the bank. My clock is still ticking, but the volume is lower and I may have bought myself some time."

A woman who freezes her eggs undergoes the same treatment program as a woman undergoing in vitro fertilization. An orientation session educates women how to inject daily hormones at home; then the next step involves a hormonal "trigger shot." Nurses are available to discuss questions and explain side effects. Although many women inject themselves with the medication, nurses can be hired to administer shots at home. The treatment cycle continues with ultrasounds and in-clinic monitoring, and concludes with the egg-retrieval process itself. While a woman is under sedation in an operating room, her eggs are located with transvaginal ultrasounds and are retrieved by inserting a needle in the ovaries through the wall of the vagina. The actual procedure lasts about thirty minutes. After a few hours in the recovery room, some women are able to return to work and others may need a few days off.[10]

Women have been financing egg freezing by borrowing from their 401(k)s, taking loans from family members, and even accepting gifts from boyfriends—all in an effort to lock in a chance at motherhood. Although it is optimal for a woman to freeze her eggs while she is still in her twenties, some experts believe that the experience can be traumatic at that age, and that women in their thirties are better adjusted to the idea.[11]

The biologist Dr. Raffaella Fabbri and the clinician Dr. Eleonora Porcu invented egg-freezing technology at the department of obstetrics and gynecology at the University of Bologna. One of the purposes of their work was to find a way to get around the Roman Catholic Church's ban on freezing embryos, and to use egg freezing as a way to at least partially eliminate the moral stigma of embryo freezing. They also wanted to give women the opportunity to have babies after they had undergone cancer treatment.

"As you know," says Dr. Porcu,

men can create sperm easily before having chemotherapy, but until recently women had no opportunity of preserving their fertility. The first patient with cancer in the world to give birth from her frozen eggs was a patient of mine who had ovarian cancer and who had undergone an oophorectomy. She lost her ovaries, but before the operation we froze her eggs. After four years, she had her eggs inseminated and fertilized, and after the transfer she became pregnant and she had two very nice daughters, very nice little girls. This was the best satisfaction in my career.

The scientists' intentions were not to create the procedure so a woman could wait to reach the boardroom before she got pregnant with her first child, but they do take into account the new lifestyle demands of women in the modern age. Many women are using egg freezing to stake a claim at motherhood as their fertility chances shrivel into their thirties.[12]

Dr. Fabbri believes that egg freezing is an excellent idea if a woman has a good career and has not found a partner by the time she has reached her thirties, but that she should not seek to postpone motherhood much further than that. "I think egg freezing is a good solution for women who have some reason to postpone their fertility, but that doesn't mean it's a good idea to have a child at sixty or more. I think that's immoral and unethical, and it's especially bad for the babies. Babies need to live with young people and to have a young mother and a healthy mother, not a young grandmother."

Dr. Porcu, who is a director at the Infertility and IVF Center at the University of Bologna, is concerned that the science she helped create sometimes sends the wrong message to women about the fragile nature of their fertility. She is an advocate for what she calls prestigious motherhood and fertility awareness.

She says, "Be aware that your fertility is really fragile, and that when you are forty you will probably have a very low chance of becoming pregnant. Try to become pregnant as soon as you can. Besides, you *can* have it all—a house, a job, a child: we women are better than men at organizing things."

Porcu waited to have her first child for nearly a decade after she was married for fear she would be ostracized by her colleagues and placed on the "mommy track." She didn't even reveal that she was pregnant until her seventh month. Today, she is deeply concerned that the delayer boom is only lining the pockets of leaders in the reproductive marketplace, who offer false promises to infertile couples.

Egg freezing is becoming increasingly popular because it avoids producing a large number of embryos that will be preserved in medical limbo for years. The alternative, says Porcu, is to freeze eggs, which can be destroyed without any moral compunction. Dr. Porcu has worked with leading doctors, such as Nicole Noyes at the NYU Medical Center in New York, to spread awareness globally about this less controversial option.

"One important thing to remember," says Dr. Porcu, "is that eggs belong to women, whereas embryos belong to both men and women. If a married couple gets divorced, there are problems, very unpleasant problems, that cannot be settled in court regarding the fate of their embryos."

Clearly, we should all be lobbying our employers to support parenthood and maternity leave in this country. But meanwhile, it's time to put some money aside if motherhood is part of your long-term plan. These costs, if necessary, may be shared with a partner, but for now, be aware that part of your savings may have to go toward your commitment to motherhood.

BANK ON DIGITAL MOTHERHOOD

Today, technology and social media offer mothers the gift of a home-based career based on their new expertise: motherhood. As a group, digital moms, better known as the Twitter Mom Brigade in the tech circles, are raking in millions in product endorsements, sponsorships, and income from social events. In this section, we'll explore this fascinating way to earn a good living and be home with your children at the same time—every mom's fantasy. We'll explain the difference between a successful blogging career and a hobby. We'll talk about building your blog into a platform that corporations will want to connect to. We'll describe how you remain employed by your company while you raise your family by taking over the social media marketing for the firm. As with any other profession, being a top Twitter Mom takes a good strategy. Camilla is a top online media expert, creating blogs, videos, and other content for major publications, and will show us how it's done.

Mommy Bloggers Are a Big Business

According to emarketer.com, there are almost 4 million moms who blog.[13]

Moms who blog have become important marketing partners and powerful allies, spreading the word about products and services to 32 million moms who go online in the U.S. In total there are 3.9 million women with children under 18 who write blogs, covering a wide variety of subjects including parenting, couponing, travel, automobiles, and technology. While they share one thing in common—having children—they are a diverse group, which is a benefit and a challenge for marketers.[14]

Many mommy bloggers are making a good living, especially when they move from writing to product endorsements and other related deals. Robin Raskin, founder of Living in Digital Times, has created a series of conferences and exhibits that bring the mommy bloggers and the tech industry together. Says Robin,

> We started a series of conferences and exhibits around products that are appropriate for moms for a number of reasons—whether because they're stylish, or extremely mobile, or efficiently designed, such as a camera you can hold in one hand while you're holding your baby in your other. I'd say top bloggers are making $60,000 to $80,000, while others struggle. Some women bloggers are successful because they have a particular expertise: fashion, cooking, and technology come to mind. This is not quite up to where the corporate jobs would be, but their quality of life becomes a lot easier. And when they are ready to reenter the corporate world, if that's what they want to do, they have the skill set to do so.

However, making a living as a mommy blogger is not a given, and many women are spending time writing but not figuring out how to connect with an audience and monetize their blogs. According to a Technorati survey, 48 percent of mommy bloggers receive fewer than 1,000 unique visitors per month, and only 2 percent receive more than 100,000 visitors per month. Corporate bloggers receive the most unique visitors per month: 312,783, on average.[15]

Develop Your Platform

If you plan to make money blogging, tweeting, and expressing yourself in the digital world, your blog content (including text, video images, and audio), on whatever device it appears, has to function as your platform. In order to build a consistent platform, you need to develop your voice and have a clear vision of what your blog is about. Then and only then can your platform attract advertisers, sponsors, partners, product placement, content aggregators, event planners, media, and attention.

Developing your platform—whether you are writing about your children or something else that renews your spirit or emphasizes your career expertise—involves answering the questions below. The answers will allow you to write a short business plan for your blog.

To Define Your Strategy
- What are your goals for the blog?
- Are you using the blog to tell stories, share advice, and impart information?
- Do you plan to document events?
- Do you want to promote products, a cause, or something else?
- How many viewers would you like the blog to have?
- Do you want to write alone or take on cowriters and guest bloggers?

To Find Your Topic, Ask Yourself:
- How are you unique in this world?
- What excites you, and what are you ready to talk about for the next two years?
- What are you passionate about?
- What topics do you want to learn more about?
- Are you an expert in a field that others want to read about?
- Is there a topic—such as baby clothes, gluten-free cooking, style for moms, autism, working from home, "green" cleaning, raising bilingual children, marrying into the military, or kids' art—that you could write about every day?

To Define Your Style, Ask Yourself:
- What is your style and how would you express that in conversation over the Web?
- What tone do you want to use: your natural voice or a journalistic style?

- How open are you willing to be about your personal life or subject?
- What types of media do you want on your blog—words, pictures, music, etc.?

To Find Your Competitive Positioning, Ask Yourself:
- How many other blogs are out there on your topic?
- What is the size of the audience for these other blogs?
- How does your blog differ from others on your topic?

To Find Your Audience, Ask Yourself:
- Do you have a built-in audience—such as an alumni network, professional association, or members of the local chamber of commerce—that would follow your blog immediately?

To Find Your Corporate Partners, Ask Yourself:
- What companies might be interested in partnering with you, either because they're going after the same audience as you are or because they reflect your opinions and values?

A WARNING ON WRITING ABOUT YOUR CHILDREN

How will your children feel about reading what you wrote in the years to come? Writing about every move Tommy is making now may sound like fun, but it's also important to reflect on how much of your child's personal life you want to broadcast publicly. Are you exposing your children to dangerous predators and pedophiles? Do you want photographs of your children to fall into the wrong hands? Remember that you cannot control who is looking at your blog unless you set access limits! Be safe and protect your children!

Commit to Blog Production

Now that you have defined your blog, it is time to make a commitment to producing it. First, you need to decide where you are going to post and build your blog. Three top choices to consider are WordPress, Blogspot, and Tumblr. Be sure to review the fine print, as it is constantly changing. Make sure you own the copyright to anything you write on your blog. You need to understand that any personal photos you post on the Web are actually in the public domain and no longer copyrighted, unless you take steps to protect them through adding watermarks or disabling the ability to print through JavaScript tools. This technology is always changing, so make sure you are up on the latest if you plan to use original images in your blog.

Writing blog posts every day may sound easy, but producing, writing, editing, and posting a blog is at least two to four hours' work per day for a committed blogger who wants to see a return. Responding to and moderating reader comments if you allow them on your blog, sending out at least ten tweets a day, and emailing the companies and individuals mentioned in your blog can take another two hours per day for a seasoned social media expert. Know the amount of time you have available, and use it wisely. It's best to plan your time in advance—to make a schedule and stick to it. Answering the following questions will help you know what to expect.

- When will you be blogging—morning, afternoon, or evening?
- How much time do you currently spend tweeting, posting to Facebook, and engaging in social media?
- How many images do you plan to load for each blog?
- Will you be adding video regularly to the blog?
- How many words a day do you plan to produce? Three hundred or more?
- Are you sending emails and tweeting companies or bloggers to let them know you have covered them in your blog?

Make sure all your accounts are linked to save time as you broadcast each installment of your messages. For example, it's possible to set up your Twitter account so that your tweets are automatically posted on Facebook and LinkedIn, as well as on your blog. Remember: it's called *social* media. You are not a lone wolf mom, so go at it with the goal of being social on all available platforms.

Finally, establish early on with your family that this is your home-based business. If you are to succeed, everyone in the home needs to respect the time you've committed to the blog. If you're blogging for yourself, remember that this is an entrepreneurial endeavor that may lead to new income, more education, and better connectivity—but it's still a start-up. Give it the investment of time it needs to get on its feet.

Keep on Top of Blogging Trends

What makes a blog appealing changes often, so it is crucial to use online resources to educate yourself on the latest findings. The preferred length of videos, the right amount of words, and the right combination of words and other media can create a strong following. Make a point of consulting Mashable.com, TechCrunch.com, and Scobleizer.com for everything from apps to optimizing distribution and readership.

Develop a Following Online and Offline

Now that you have an appealing blog, it is time to develop a following. Your audience development must include online and offline actions. As an independent blogger trying to gain positioning, you may be served by joining a blog aggregator. BlogHer is the Internet's largest community for female bloggers. The site reaches 25 million women per month.[16] The BlogHer network works on a revenue-sharing basis. If your blog gets 1 million impressions or more per month, your cut is 60 percent of the revenue. If you get fewer than 1 million impressions, the revenue share drops to 50 percent.[17] One million impressions per month is no easy task. Many women will not make money, but there are opportunities. To take advantage of them requires strategic planning.

Offline, it's a good idea to seek out like-minded tech-savvy moms. As Robin says, "If you walk into Starbucks at ten o'clock in the morning on any given day, you'll find a group of moms with baby carriages planning their next business." Follow them, promote them on your site, see what events they're planning, and even reach out to them to stage group events. Following other moms on Twitter and on blogs, and commenting on their activities, blogs, and tweets are some of the quickest ways to gain followers on Twitter and subscribers for your blog yourself.

Attract Advertisers and Brands to Your Blog

When you have a defined subject for your blog, it's easier for advertisers to align themselves with your content and for large companies to approach you with free products to test and write about. To keep your readers' trust, you will disclose these relationships. For example, if your blog is called Sports Mommy and you write about testing women's athletic gear and jogging strollers, major companies know to target you with sneakers, running shorts, cameras, water bottles, yoga mats, and other products. It's easy for them to determine that you're a member of their target demographic.

"Nowadays, brands and bloggers are able to connect through networks like Mom Central and Business 2 Blogger, which play matchmaker between brands and blogs," explains Ryan Pulliam. "If you are starting out in the blogosphere, we highly recommend joining these networks and other communities, such as BlogHer, which are helpful resources to streamline and fast-track the overall process."

Monetize Your Blog

Once you have a following on your blog, you can start staging sponsored events, negotiating deals with content aggregators, and even adding an e-commerce element to your site for brands that fall in line with the vision of your blog. Blogging alone will rarely make you any significant income. "It's not about you and your writing," explains Robin Raskin. "It's about your audiences and who they are—who they are is really your most valuable asset."

A recent Nielsen study showed that more than half of U.S. women blog readers have purchased a product based on a blog recommendation.[18] That's why companies like Clorox and Procter & Gamble are engaging with mommy bloggers in new ways. "We're past the Web banner stage now," says Robin Raskin. "We're up to the stage where Procter & Gamble has a little minisite on my site about cleaning clothes. Clorox the other day announced they were doing a site with one of the mommy bloggers about keeping clean and organized, and that they were going to be the money behind it. As the big companies realize that social media is the best way to stay close to their customers, they are finding moms to work with them. That's the way to get to the big numbers." Kraft launched an online talk show hosted by prominent mommy blogger Soleil Moon Frye, who used to be the star of the hit TV show *Punky Brewster*.

Consider a Corporate Social Media Role

Another way for moms to pursue a blogging career is to take on the role of social media expert for their companies and work from home. Ryan Pulliam suggests that women who want to leave the workplace in pursuit of motherhood should consider becoming a social media or community manager (or both) instead.

> If you feel you are qualified and confident in your ability to fulfill this role, then it may be advantageous for both and you and your company. If your company does not currently have a social media point person in place, it may be an opportunity for you to be proactive in carving out a role that fits your personal, parenting, and professional style. Corporate blogs are a great way to promote business, drive traffic, reach wider audiences, and connect with influencers. You may want to consider learning more about this role so you can begin to work in-house—literally—and still maintain a valuable position within a company. Why would a company hire an outside social media consultant or expert when they already have you on staff?

If you are about to approach your corporation about being the social media point person or executive for the company, know your selling points. Don't think that being older puts you out of the running for the role. Ryan, who currently consults for big-name brands and celebrities to help "socialize" and stay current on all their digital needs says that while,

> people right out of college may be more technology-savvy, they cannot necessarily be trusted to handle the corporate message of the company and interact efficiently and intelligently with executives and multiple departments. Furthermore, they don't have the experience to knowledgably answer questions about the business or handle political situations adeptly.

This is a role that interacts and engages with customers in a new way, and that requires a different way of thinking, executing, and adjusting to ever-changing technologies and trends. Women who are in an executive or management-level position can easily learn how to use social media if their technical skills are not up to par. Do not make this the focal point for selling yourself. Focus instead on your more advanced inherent skill sets—such as higher-level experience, responsibilities, earned credibility, and accountability—which are all important attributes in social media leadership.

Don't be intimidated by social media experts. Remember, you're handling the message of the company and that's where you're an expert. With such a rapid advancement and adaptation of social media and mobile technology, companies have had to keep up with an explosive growth rate in a short amount of time. This has created a gap between having the qualified or required skill set and having the level of experience needed to take on the responsibilities and decision making that accompany a department head role, especially in a corporate setting. For example, you may have been a real estate lawyer or a commercial chef for ten to twenty years, whereas Twitter launched in 2006 and corporations are still figuring out how to use it effectively and safely.

You don't need to be an expert, but you do need to know the basics. Go to BlogHer.com and Mashable.com, which have how-to guides. If you still feel in the dark, hire a social media consultant or a student to sit down with you for a few hours a week until you have a basic understanding of the technology. Become proficient in the main platforms like Twitter, Facebook, and Tumblr. Learn how to add links, load video and photos, and use your company's blog.

Grow with Your Blog

Finally, a blog is an evolving business: it may develop into an e-commerce site, or even an app. Stay current on mobile technology by creating a simple low-cost mobile Web version of your website. This is a great way to connect with your users and stay on top. You're a mom—we know you're good at adapting! Who knows? You may start a new company through your blog, or position an existing family business in the digital universe. It's up to you.

RAISE YOUR KIDS TO BE WEALTHY

Just as you learn to value yourself financially and build your own wealth, you can raise your children to be wealthy as well. We know that of course you first want your kids to be healthy and happy. Wealthy probably comes far down the list of what you wish for your children. But wouldn't you want your children to be highly educated, to travel the world, to be able to explore beloved hobbies, and to contribute to society? We are sure you want your children to be able to maximize their potential, to enjoy their lives, and to leave the planet in slightly better shape than they found it. But all these things imply that your children will earn enough or have enough money to live life in something other than survival mode. We are sure you don't want your children to live in an unsafe neighborhood because they can't afford to live in a good area, worry about paying bills, and never be able to lift themselves above a minimum-wage lifestyle.

We want to share with you five things you can do to inspire your kids to live out their highest potential as human beings and maximize their chances of becoming wealthy adults. It is well known that many of us have spent years trying to undo negative messages we received in childhood. Today, we are much more aware of the psychological cost of discouraging children. Mothers have a golden opportunity to avoid planting negativity into their children and sow thoughts that will program them for success, happiness, and wealth. This is the lifelong gift you can give to your children, regardless of the financial wealth you have—or don't have—to pass on to them.

Set a Great Example

This common piece of advice is the best and easiest thing that you can do to encourage your children toward financial greatness. Do your children see you and your partner embracing work that you love, eager to face the challenges that work sends your way? Or do they see you drained, discouraged, and resentful? Your attitude toward work is one of the primary drivers of your children's attitude toward work. If you don't love your current work, are you in school, training for a better life, starting a business on the side, or planning to job hunt? If so, then your kids will learn that it is okay to make changes and to seek to improve your working life. If you don't love your work, then don't expect them to show much enthusiasm for getting an education, which, in their minds, will only lead to a life of misery.

As you embrace *The Seven Pearls of Financial Wisdom,* you will naturally show your children how to be involved, responsible, and enthusiastic stewards of wealth. Your willingness to learn about money, live within a budget, and carefully take responsibility for your finances will speak louder than any lecture you can give. No matter what your means, choosing to live responsibly, avoid massive debt and financial chaos, and building for your future will show your children how to live well. Society and television will teach them how to *consume;* it is up to you to teach them the value and joys of *contributing.*

Joline Godfrey, in her excellent book *Raising Financially Fit Kids,* urges parents to make financial values explicit to children. Godfrey is the CEO of Independent Means, Inc., a company that provides innovative learning experiences for high net worth families. Independent Means' custom programs help families raise financially thoughtful family members and responsible beneficiaries. "We help families design what I sometimes refer to as a drip, drip, drip process," Joline said in an interview with us.

> Financial education is a process, not an event. A weekend program is a great idea, but not enough. Kids need to see behavior modeled. They need to hear financial values spoken out loud, repeatedly, drip, drip, drip: "Saving is essential;" "Sharing is good;" "Managing your allowance well is expected," et cetra. And they need regular opportunities to practice financial skills. Families that "drip" values, messages, and practice on their kids in a regular, thoughtful way—whether it's once a week, once a month, or once a quarter—are doing better than nothing, which is what most families do. Just do *something* in a constant way, and kids will have much greater potential to mature as financially thoughtful, secure adults.

Joline also emphasized the importance of modeling the work ethic and fiscal responsibility you want your children to develop. "Families say, 'I want my children to have a good work ethic,' and I remind them that to have a work ethic, you have to work or at least see people work. It doesn't mean kids have to watch you head off to a conventional workplace every day—that's so twentieth century—but showing kids what it means to be engaged in purposeful activity is critical."

If you tell your children that they should save money and live within their means, yet you are constantly in credit card debt and at risk of losing your house because of late mortgage payments, then your words will be hollow and have no real impact upon them. On the other hand, if you set an example of financial discipline and positive feelings about the possibilities that money brings into your life, then you will set a standard that your children are much more likely to embrace.

Furthermore, it's important to give your children many opportunities to practice making business decisions and investing money before they reach adulthood. Today, Dune Thorne is a managing director at Silver Bridge Advisors, where she works as a financial adviser for sophisticated and complex families with multiple family branches and generations. Dune is also dean of the Silver Bridge Institute, an educational initiative that runs forums, seminars, workshops, and customized educational sessions for their affluent families. Dune's interest in this work started when she turned eighteen and became responsible for a family trust that her grandfather had set up for her.

The adviser I was assigned to put me in a mutual fund that was an all-equity growth fund with a high allocation to technology stocks. At this age I didn't know any better and figured that I wanted to grow my assets so these smart advisers must know what is best for me. They never asked me what my goals were, which was primarily to use the money to pay for graduate school. The greatest learning experience was when the fund went down by seventy-five percent and I still needed to pay my business-school tuition each semester. Big picture, it was the right time of life when it happened. I was not married, I had no children, and business-school tuition was an expense that I felt strongly about paying, even if it took all my financial resources. This experience was so valuable because it made me realize how quickly wealth can be created and how quickly it can be lost, and how important it is to understand the timing of the cash flows.

Dune's research at Harvard and life's work in this field continue to reveal the financial education gap that exists for wealthy families around money matters. "When you grow up in a family of means, it can often be assumed that you automatically learn how to manage it, but this is not the case. Families need to set aside the time to not only teach their children but also share their money values and goals so that their children understand how the choices they make with their human capital and financial resources can impact the world and their legacy," says Dune.

Teach the Importance of "The Big Three"

From the beginning, it is important to emphasize that you can do three things with money: save it, spend it, or give it away. The goal is to train young people from the beginning that some portion of all money is given back and some portion is saved. You can do this by using shoe boxes or other containers and dividing their allowance and any monetary gifts they receive into three parts. You can explain that this is how everyone in the family handles money—if, of course, that is indeed true of your family.

A great example of this philosophy is the allowance contract that John D. Rockefeller Jr. drew up with his son John III in 1920, when his son turned fourteen. The contract, reprinted in *Smithsonian* magazine in June 2004, specified that 20 percent of John III's allowance would go to savings and 20 percent would be reserved for "benevolence," or charities. John III was to write down every dollar that he spent and provide his father with a receipt. If he didn't perform this task, then his allowance would be reduced. Conversely, if he did a good job with his money, then his allowance would be raised. It is clear that his father was treating John III as an adult, providing him with an incentive to do well and letting him know that there would consequences if he didn't comply with the agreement. Both parties signed the contract, thereby making John III responsible for understanding the terms of at least this part of his inheritance. There were rules to prevent cheating. John Jr.

also motivated his son to save by providing "match funding" for any extra amounts that John III contributed to his savings. Today's parents could do worse than to draw up a simple contract with their children along the same lines. Keep in mind that John Jr. was the richest man in America at that time; this did not mean, however, that his son got a fortune for an allowance.

MEMORANDUM BETWEEN PAPA AND JOHN REGARDING AN ALLOWANCE

May 1920

1. Beginning with May 1st, John's allowance is to be at the rate of one dollar and fifty cents ($1.50) per week.

2. At the end of each week during which John has kept his accounts accurately and to Papa's satisfaction, the allowance for the succeeding week will be increased ten cents (10¢) over the week just ended, up to but not beyond a total per week of two dollars ($2.00).

3. At the end of each week during which John has not kept his accounts accurately and to Papa's satisfaction, the allowance for the succeeding week shall be reduced ten cents (10¢) from the week just ended.

4. During any week when there have been no receipts or expenditures to record, the allowance shall continue at the same rate as in the preceding week.

5. During any week when the account has been correctly kept but the writing and figuring are not satisfactory, the allowance shall continue at the same rate as in the preceding week.

6. Papa shall be the sole judge as to whether an increase or a decrease is to be made.

7. It is understood that at least twenty percent (20%) of the allowance shall be used for benevolences.

8. It is understood that at least twenty percent (20%) of the allowance shall be saved.

9. It is understood that every purchase or expenditure made is to be put down definitely and clearly.

10. It is understood that John will make no purchases, charging the same to Mama or Papa, without the special consent of Mama, Papa, or Miss Scales [a family governess].

11. It is understood that when John desires to make any purchases which the allowance does not cover, he will first gain the consent of either Mama, Papa, or Miss Scales, who will give him sufficient money with which to pay for the specific purchases, the change from which, together with a memorandum showing what items have been bought and at what cost and what amount is returned, is to be given to the person advancing the money before night of the day on which the purchases are made.

12. It is understood that no governess, companion, or other person in the household is to be asked by John to pay for any items for him, other than carfare.

13. To any savings from the date in this account which John may from time to time deposit in his bank account, in excess of the twenty per cent (20%) referred to in Item No. 8, Papa will add an equal sum for deposit.

14. The allowance above set forth and the agreement under which it shall be arrived at are to continue in force until changed by mutual consent.

The above agreement approved and entered into by

John D. Rockefeller, Jr.
John D. Rockefeller 3rd

Giving your child this level of financial discipline is one of the best gifts you could possibly give him or her. Habits instilled when children are very young will last a lifetime. Your child will have the pleasure of seeing his or her savings grow and the joy of helping others while always knowing exactly what he or she is spending. Practicing the discipline of writing down everything that you spend will take away the mystery of seemingly "disappearing money." Programs and apps like www.mint.com make this a much less tedious task than it was in the 1920s; kids can easily record their spending online, track their savings accounts online, and open online charitable funds for giving.

Encourage a Sense of Possibility and Promote Individual Strengths

Interviews with successful individuals often contain stories of parents encouraging their children to go after dreams and take risks. Beyoncé Knowles is an example of a woman who credits her mother for a great deal of her success. Her mother, Tina Knowles, told CBS News that the family got behind Beyoncé because they could see her natural talent. "She just came alive and just had all the confidence, so I was like, 'Wow, who is that?' We encouraged her to do that because it brought out her personality."[19]

As a mother, you have the opportunity to provide the same type of encouragement to your children. Be the parent who says yes to their dreams and encourages them to explore various interests. Do not shut your children down by shaming their dreams or telling them that they are selfish, stupid, lazy, or will never amount to anything.

Parental support is critical for childhood development, according to experts. A recent study by researchers at the University of Nebraska studied hundreds of high school students and found a link between hope and expectations on the one hand and future educational achievement on the other.[20] They found that students who have high aspirations and put thought into their futures during their high school years tend to attain higher levels of education.

Scientific research is debunking the myth that children are blank slates. It appears that we are born with a strong set of innate talents and preferences. Dr. Nancy L. Segal runs the Twin Studies Center at California State University. She has spent the last seventeen years studying identical, fraternal, and virtual twins extensively. (Virtual twins are children brought into the same household at approximately the same age and raised as twins.) She has found that identical twins are the most alike in their thinking, fraternal twins somewhat less so, and virtual twins strikingly different. When it comes to intelligence, for example, only 25 percent of the differences between twins—virtual, fraternal, or identical—can be accounted for by their environment, whereas 75 percent can be accounted for by genetics.[21] The implication of this is that parents should be spending their time helping children identify their natural strengths and talents and helping them nurture those talents. If a child is great at math and science, for example, he or she should be allowed to focus on those talents early rather than being made to take honors courses in English, an area in which the child has little interest or aptitude.[22]

Joline Godfrey in *Raising Financially Fit Kids* suggests that you sit your teenager down and help him or her really understand what it costs to live the lifestyle he or she desires at the salary customary for an entry-level position in your child's chosen field. This great exercise will help overcome the fantasy images that kids get from reality TV shows and give them a real idea of what to expect once they are on their own. What will it cost to try to be an actor in L.A.? A writer in New York City? A veterinarian in Seattle? "There was a sixteen-year-old boy in one of our programs who was not excited about this whole business of financial education," says Joline.

> Unlike his younger brothers, he was quite resistant. Finally, he wanted his first car and his parents said to us, "Is there some way we can use the car as the tool for getting his attention?" We created a program that illustrates the expense of maintaining a car. As he realized his "free car" would cost about $6,500 a year to maintain, a light went on. He wants to maintain his car and take his girlfriend on a date and suddenly he is more interested in earning and saving money. His entrepreneurial spirit has been awakened. And this summer he's attending Camp Start Up. So you never quite know what's going to spark a child's imagination, but including them in their "real world" will help.

By helping your child understand the educational costs, the cost of living, the wages, and the taxes, you can help your teen get excited about real possibilities for the future and make choices that will support the achievement of his or her goal. The same holds true for a child who wishes to pursue an expensive hobby, sport, or vacation; make sure you explain what the costs are and how much this pursuit will impact the family budget. It does not help children if you struggle to provide them with ski trips and vacations when you cannot afford to save for their college education.

Push for Four-Year College Education

One of the biggest gifts you can give your children is the means—or, if not the means, the motivation—to attain a four-year college degree. Even if you cannot afford to fully finance a college education, making it clear to your children that you expect them to go to college is vital. Early on, you must be open with children about your ability to pay. If you cannot afford to finance college, it is even more important that you encourage your children to keep up their grades and excel in sports or other activities that can lead to a scholarship opportunity.

A four-year college degree confers three advantages: higher wages, higher lifetime earnings, and more job opportunities. Although some writers have recently suggested that the relative value of earning a college degree has declined, the data were presented in a misleading manner. Parents were given the impression that a four-year college education is no longer a good investment. However, according to a recent study released by the Georgetown University Center on Education and the Workforce, the earnings of college-educated individuals still far exceed the earnings of those who have not obtained a four-year degree. On average, high school graduates earn 68 percent more than high school dropouts; those who hold associate's degrees earn 26 percent more than high school graduates; those who hold bachelor's degrees earn 45 percent more than those who hold associate's degrees, and those who hold master's degrees earn 37 percent more than those with bachelor's degrees. Holders of college degrees earn twice as much as high school graduates. Although real wages for those who earned college degrees declined between 2000 and 2008, giving rise to lots of sensational press coverage, the rate at which college-educated individuals outearn those with only high school diplomas remained constant.

According to the study, college graduates earn anywhere from $600,000 to $900,000 more than high school graduates during their lifetimes. Given that the average college education costs $50,000 over four years, this is an extremely good investment. It is also important to note that it is much more difficult to graduate from college when you've taken time off after high school; according to the study, 70 percent of four-year-degree students under the age of twenty-three graduate versus only 16 percent of students over the age of thirty.

Looking forward, the study estimates that by 2018, 63 percent of new and replacement jobs will require at least some college, while 72 percent will require at least a bachelor's degree. Not pushing your son or daughter to graduate from college may mean dooming him or her to a lifetime of low wages and dead-end service jobs.[23]

Connect Your Children with Reality

If you are raising your children in an affluent environment, it is critical to instill in them a sense of financial reality. "I had a parent use the old Cosby line, 'Honey, you're not wealthy. You're poor. Your dad and I are wealthy,'" says Joline Godfrey. "Even when children have significant trust funds, they typically don't have access to them as children." Children from wealthy families still must learn about financial limits and self-discipline. They still need to master the ten basic money skills (see page 112). If you raise your children to have no idea what their lifestyle costs, how the family earns its money, or the value of your philanthropic contributions, then you cannot expect that child to be a responsible inheritor and to handle the fortune that you would like to leave to him or her. When a child in a wealthy family hears, "We can't afford it," he or she knows that is not true; nonetheless, it is the job of wealthy parents to say, "We are not going to spend our money in this way" and to teach good financial values to their kids. It is important to think twice about whether or not your son or daughter needs a new BMW or a hundred-thousand-dollar sweet sixteen party, even if all his or her friends are being indulged in this way.

Buying your child every possible thing he or she could ever desire and never saying no will create a very unhappy adult who has no sense of limits and is extremely angry to be kicked out of the fantasy world you raised him or her in. These children may refuse to attend school, party constantly with friends, and refuse to grow up. They will become unhappy, insecure adults with many of the problems we see acted out in the tabloids. Remember, their behavior is being funded by you if you continue financial support when children do not attend school or do not seek viable employment. It is sad to see children who "had it all" burn out with drug addiction, crazy behavior, or suicide. It is the job of wealthy parents to make sure that their children do not become overwhelmed by the family circumstances.

Even if a child will not have to work, due to income from an inheritance or trust fund, he or she will still need to be involved in the management of the investments that create the income and to understand how to work with the financial professionals who are managing the fortune. It is up to you to teach responsibility and balance and to show your children that money is not buying their happiness. It can't be said often enough: The most important things in life—including love—are priceless.

No matter how large the family fortune, the money will not be there to support future generations if the current generation spends it all. It is quite possible to blow $100 million on bad investments, a lavish lifestyle, and one or more expensive divorces in a matter of just a few years. Unless children learn from the parents how to live responsibly as wealthy individuals, their children and grandchildren may well be working-class again.

TOP TEN SKILLS TO DEVELOP IN AFFLUENT KIDS

This action plan will help guide you to family prosperity:

1. Learn to distinguish between wants and needs, and to delay gratification.
2. Understand the family history of creating wealth and practice the skills and values that made the family fortune.
3. Learn to live within a budget and to manage spending, savings, and philanthropy.
4. Understand how to read financial statements and interact with the financial professionals who manage the family fortune.
5. Graduate from college and, if possible, get an MBA in order to be able to participate in the financial decisions affecting the family fortune in an intelligent way.
6. Develop a meaningful career or find activities that bring a sense of purpose to life.
7. Learn how to interact with people from all walks of life.
8. Learn to handle requests for money from others in a gracious manner.
9. Develop a meaningful connection to the world at large.
10. Learn to accept and manage life as a very wealthy individual.

GROOM YOUR CHILDREN FOR SUPERSTARDOM

If your children are photogenic or athletic, you may be wondering just how far their looks and talents can take them. Your children may be advancing at the local level in sports, or they may be approached about modeling, or they may be begging you to help them become a superstar in the world of acting, music, or chess. This can be an exciting time for the family as your child receives more attention and fame.

Your child may become famous and wealthy or may use the skills learned in the spotlight to forge a successful career later as an adult. However, parents are challenged to help a child navigate the path of celebrity. This road can ruin the lives of their siblings, wreck the family finances, and rob them of their innocence. The road to superstardom is also expensive. With your guidance and protection, you can help your child and your family to travel this road in an intelligent and financially responsible way.

Understand the Impact on Your Marriage and Family

When you commit to raising a superstar child in sports, modeling, or entertainment, the investment of time you must make is enormous. If you are a mother with a career, it will be challenging, to say the least, to find time to take children to auditions and on trips for performances and competitions. Another responsible adult must be added to the mix, and this will require paying a caregiver to accompany the child. If you have other children, then you can expect to pay even more for additional caregiving support at home.

Be prepared for your other children to feel the impact of having a "star" in the home. If your financial resources are being invested disproportionately in one child, your other children may experience jealousy or feel your lack of attention. The bottom line is that child superstardom is a family commitment both financially and emotionally, and it should be addressed in family meetings.

It's very important to have regular strategic conversations with your partner or husband about the direction of your child's career and the family unit. When a sports star is injured, for example, the entire family is affected. Chemmy Alcott, Britain's number one alpine ski racer, has referred to being concerned about the selfishness of her passion. In her last major accident, which occurred in 2010, when she was twenty-eight, she recognized that her dangerous career impacts the entire family, as her brothers and their families cared for her until she recovered.

When a child in the modeling or entertainment field commits to a major motion picture or photo shoot, he or she needs to be uprooted from school for months at a time. It's not uncommon for such a child to live overseas with a parent on location. When Sasha Eden, a former child model who now runs an award-winning theater company called WET (Women's Expressive Theater), was slated to play a role in a film in Italy, her parents made the difficult decision that their marriage, Sasha's schooling, and the family unit were more important than a movie role for Sasha at that point in their lives.

There are amazing opportunities for children and young adults in many fields, but it's key to understand the choices you are making ahead of time.

Make Sure Your Children Love What They Are Doing

First and foremost, make sure that your child is really doing what he or she wants to do—rather than what *you* want him or her to do. Otherwise, your child won't stand a chance.

Chemmy Alcott began skiing at the age of eighteen months and competed in her first race at the age of three. She went on to represent Great Britain in three Olympics as a downhill skier. To facilitate her training, she spent every summer between the time she was eleven and the time she was nineteen in New Zealand because of the lack of snow in Great Britain. She also suffered a broken neck when she was twelve, the first of many injuries. In December of 2010, a fall at eighty miles per hour caused her to shatter her right leg, which put her out of World Cup competition; she immediately started rehab and plans to ski again in the Winter Olympics of 2014, despite the presence of nine screws and a metal plate in her leg from the injury. Her personal drive and passion have been key elements of her success in a very difficult sport. Regarding parental influence, Chemmy says:

> I think there is a really fine line between being a pushy parent who wants your child to be good in a sport and being an enthusiastic parent who just lets your child learn to love it. Ski racing is a tough sport, and if you don't have the greatest will to do it, then you won't become world-class in it. A lot of parents think, "Oh, I'd love my kids to be skiers," and the

kids are skiing for their parents and not for themselves. There's such a thin line between perfection and tragedy. . . . It's about making a passion, a hobby, and a love first and foremost, and making a career second.

Child Stardom in the World of Sports

Although you may wish to support your child's passion for a particular sport, it pays to be realistic about his or her talent. Listen to coaches and observe how your child performs in competitions before you take on major additional expenses that should perhaps be going toward funding other goals. On the other hand, if your child really does have a major, unique talent, athletic scholarships can support a dedicated young person through college as he or she rises in the sport.

Whatever your financial circumstances, we recommend keeping your child athlete focused on academics even as he or she excels in sports. A severe injury, such as Chemmy's fall, can quickly derail a promising career, and if a child has not kept up his or her grades, it will be very difficult to find an alternative career. In an article titled "Parents Raising Superstars," Tonya Shockley, mother of D. J. Shockley, formerly a quarterback with the Atlanta Falcons, stresses the importance of making academics your child's priority. She writes: "Our philosophy was school comes first, not sports. No grades, no play. We believed if you excelled in school, there would still be times for friends and fun. The goal was always to do your best and aim high."

If it really looks like your child has the talent to make it on the world stage, has the personal desire for a professional athletic career, and keeps up with schoolwork, then you should make sure you hire the best advisers possible to manage his or her career. Once offers for endorsements start coming in (and this is now starting at very young ages), a great sports and entertainment lawyer can help you negotiate the best possible arrangements. Terms keep changing, and generally the money that top athletes can earn only keeps getting bigger. For example, the number one choice in the 2010 NBA draft, John Wall, started with a $4 million salary from the Washington Wizards, and then announced that he had signed a $25 million endorsement deal with Reebok for his own signature basketball shoes before he had played even one professional game.

In the fashion industry, Teresa Pollman, a top model scout and talent developer, agrees that you need professional management. She is president of IMD Image and Modeling Development, based in Medford, Oregon. A former model herself, Teresa signs promising child models and actors and grooms them for success. She strongly advises parents to turn the management of their children's careers over to professionals for several reasons. First, children tend to take direction better from another adult. Second, professionals have the contacts to get maximum visibility for their children. Third, professionals know how to negotiate and are able to stay on top of the latest innovations in contracts and pay packages. She says, "It's like a parent sitting on the sidelines watching their child play soccer and constantly telling the coach what to do . . . you can't manage your child without having a personal conflict. No matter what, you're always going to think your child is the best. Which is completely natural. Sometimes children don't listen to constructive criticism from parents, because they don't trust that their parents know what they're talking about."

Teresa warns that as a parent, you can ruin your child's career by having an overly aggressive style. "I would say that fifty percent of the time the reason a child doesn't make it is because of the parents, who are so overbearing, they crush their kid's career. A good parent sits back, lets her child do what he needs to do, and supports him by giving him a hug and then allowing him to perform on his own. That's what we need from the parents: be really supportive, trusting, and responsible. That means bring your children to castings and jobs on time."

Succeed in Child Modeling

If your very young children are especially photogenic, you may be thinking about child modeling or acting. "I do what we call street scouting, which is the same thing as going into a mall. I like to go to outdoor areas that just have stores," says Teresa Pollman. "There is a place in Santa Monica that I love walking around, and there are beautiful people in every direction. I found this beautiful twenty-year-old plus-size model, which means she was a size ten to fourteen. She is absolutely gorgeous. She works almost every day in L.A. for us now. She was just in there shopping and I walked up and talked to her for a little while. You can literally be discovered anywhere."

Teresa recommends when you are approached by someone to get a business card and then do your research on that company. Find out what they're all about and how long they've been in business. Discover how long the person who is scouting has worked at the company. She also recommends calling the Better Business Bureau.

We spoke with Kristen Smith, a teen model discovered by Teresa. "I always get nervous before doing a photo shoot or fashion show. Mainly before a fashion show, but I think that's what makes it fun," she says. "You're nervous because you're excited, then there is the adrenaline rush, but the energy onstage is just, it's amazing. I just love going onstage and doing fashion shows."

Kristen went to the annual IMTA (International Modeling and Talent Association) competition in 2010. She won overall model of the year and got the most callbacks of any young woman there, according to Teresa. She won two thousand dollars at IMTA and she's on hold for *Seventeen* magazine and Abercrombie and Fitch. "I was discovered when I was twelve," says Kristen. "I was playing basketball and Teresa came to my game with a friend, and she saw me so she talked with my mom. We came in and met with Teresa and then IMTA came up and so we went to that. It's all been a great experience."

As part of the process, Kristen is taking modeling classes, which she says is teaching her "never to be disrespectful. Even if you don't agree with the client, always keep a smile on your face. Always be yourself, but never rude or loud. Never chew gum when you're meeting people and things like that."

Modeling has been an opportunity for Kristen to overcome some of her greatest fears. "The toughest thing is probably being so young and meeting people. I'm really shy and it's been hard for me. I'm not used to talking to people and being outgoing. So I have to put myself out there and get to know people, even if I don't want to. Going to IMTA really helped me."

At this time, Kristin is working mostly during the summer and just a few days during the school year. She says she is going to finish high school and then really go ahead with her modeling ambitions and is considering acting. Kristen's mother, Cindy Smith, accompanies her most of the time. "Anywhere that I travel, she'll come with me because of my age. I don't like going places alone," says Kristen. "I haven't traveled much. She's always coming with me and she's been a part of it, the whole way. My mother works, and that makes it kind of hard. Sometimes my sister will go with me because she's twenty-one. My goal would be to walk in Fashion Week. I was just asked to go to Miami for Fashion Week in a few weeks, so hopefully that all works and if I got to walk the show that would be one of my big dreams."

Teresa sees modeling as a great stepping-stone to so many other careers. Many young women will go into fields such as fashion merchandizing, photography, or become a makeup artist or stylist. "There are so many things you can do inside this industry. Look at people like Christy Turlington. She has her degree from NYU, is incredibly intelligent, and a successful businesswoman. Cindy Crawford has a great skin-care line. A lot of people go on to do these great things, and it's their modeling or their acting careers that gave them the confidence to accomplish their goals."

Approach Child Modeling and Acting with Caution

Although modeling and acting can be exciting for you and your child, the entire experience may have a deep psychological impact on a child, and you must be vigilant and monitor how your child is being affected. Marilyn Weiss, mother of Sasha Eden and Piper Weiss, was approached by a friend in an elevator in New York City about bringing Sasha to an audition for a toy commercial. Although her daughter didn't want to do it at the time, two years later, around the age of eight, she told her mother she wanted to do a commercial. Marilyn called a friend in advertising, interviewed two top talent agencies, and got her daughter an agent. She notes, "We always worked through experts, so that my children weren't victims and we didn't get drawn in by our enthusiasm for our child's talents alone."

From there, Sasha began to audition, and quickly began working. Marilyn's second daughter, Piper, who is five years younger, would accompany her mother to Sasha's auditions. People on the set would see Piper and request that she audition, too, and soon both girls were working. Although both girls initially liked child modeling and acting in commercials, there were difficult moments. Marilyn notes that children get tremendous attention when they are making it through rounds of casting calls, and can be very disappointed when they are rejected. This can be more difficult when siblings like Sasha and Piper go on casting calls and one is chosen while the other is rejected. Marilyn says, "It was so complicated when I brought my eleven-year-old to audition and the casting person took my six-year-old, who wasn't even there to audition. That creates tension between the sisters and the mother."

Success in childhood modeling and acting can seem extremely arbitrary—a child may be fantastic but just not right for a particular situation, and it can be disappointing to be rejected. You are truly at the mercy of however the people at the audition want to deliver the news. This can lead to extreme people-pleasing behavior in your child. Sasha says,

> Your child can become almost addicted to people-pleasing. That can be very unhealthy. You live for someone's applause. . . . You know if you get a job as a kid, you are worshipped on set. You're taken such good care of—assuming it's union—and your agent loves you and your mom is thrilled because you're finally making some money after fifty auditions. You get praised . . . and then when this doesn't happen, you think, I'm no good. I need to please. So it's just something to be careful of, especially under the age of two. You see this with a lot of child actors, especially the really young ones, who are so precocious—it's connected to the need to please.

Child acting can cause other problems. Piper recalls developing separation anxiety, because as a very small child she was required to go into audition rooms while her mother waited outside. She says, "When I was in second or third grade, I started to develop extreme separation anxiety because when I went into the audition room . . . I was convinced that when I came out, my mother wouldn't be there. This may have been caused by some of the scenes I read in the auditions. I am really glad my mom identified the problems and stopped my auditioning instead of pushing me toward it more."

Parents also need to look at the content of roles their children are auditioning for, to assess if they want their children exposed to adult subjects. Piper recalls being cast in a made-for-TV movie about a little girl who is molested. Her mother pulled her out when she saw the subject matter of the script, which she was not given to review in advance.

As in the world of sports, parents whose children want to act and model must assess the costs responsibly. Don't get sucked in by the many scams that abound, which prey on children and parents alike. Beware of being approached in the mall by a "talent scout" and being asked to fork over thousands of dollars for head shots. A reputable agent charges no money to look at simple photos of your child. Teresa Pollman notes, however, that you will need to make a considerable financial investment in photographs once you are under the wing of an agent. "Can you model with no pictures? No. It's like asking whether you can go on a job interview with no résumé. However, you don't want to be charged eight hundred dollars for photos that look horrible and don't include the services of someone to style your child's hair, makeup, and clothing. You must do research on the photographer to make sure he is reputable before you spend money."

Also assess whether you can reasonably travel to a distant audition site. Most auditions are held in New York or Los Angeles, and if you don't live in these cities, you will be spending thousands of dollars traveling to casting calls. You must determine how this will affect your child's education and school schedule.

Sasha was frustrated because her mother put the brakes on her acting career once she hit seventh grade, since she could not continue to attend her private school and also audition during the day. Marilyn wanted her daughter to have normal teenage years and to attend a top school, but Sasha wanted to attend a school for professional child actors and continue acting. Marilyn won the battle. Sasha says, "I was devastated when my mom said, 'I don't think I want you to be doing this professionally anymore.' It was really very painful. You have to be prepared for that as a parent. . . . In retrospect I get it and I appreciate her for doing that. I had the most amazing education [at Chapin, a private girls' school in New York City] and I'm much healthier now than I would have been if I had continued acting at that age. But it's hard for your relationship [with your mother]."

In addition, keep in mind that many acting and modeling jobs barely cover the cost of getting to the shoot. As Sasha says, "You have to be honest with yourself about the kind of hours you could potentially spend on a sound stage, in a studio without any light, just so your child can appear for one second in a commercial."

Teresa Pollman notes that a young person who wants a modeling career needs to be prepared to invest three years of time before it is possible to determine whether or not success is going to happen. You also have to be prepared to invest a minimum of three thousand dollars during each of those years to cover the costs of traveling to auditions, photos, and so forth, before your child begins to earn a living. That ten-thousand-dollar investment could earn nothing in return, or it could suddenly turn into a major ad campaign for which your child earns $250,000 plus residuals when the commercials air. "There is no other industry out there where you can make this kind of money at a young age," Pollman says.

Open a Coogan Account If You Live in California

If you live in the state of California, income earned by your child as an actor or athlete is subject to the Coogan Act, a law enacted in 1939 and named for the child actor Jackie Coogan, whose father and stepmother squandered his earnings. Whenever a child actor or athlete works under contract, employers are required to deposit 15 percent of his or her gross earnings directly into a blocked trust account, also called a Coogan account, set up in the minor's name. The earnings are the legal property of the child, but cannot be touched until he or she reaches the age of eighteen. Parents or legal guardians are required to establish a Coogan account no later than seven business days after a minor's employment contract is signed, and to furnish the minor's employer with a copy of a trustee's statement proving the existence of the account within ten business days of the start of employment.

Manage Your Child's Earnings Wisely

If your child does make it big in the entertainment industry, there will be earnings to manage and expenses to pay. In 2010, the top child earner in television was Angus T. Jones from the show *Two and a Half Men,* who earned $250,000 per episode. Miley Cyrus earned only fifteen thousand dollars per episode on *Hannah Montana,* but she made many times that on her concert tours. Other top TV child stars earned between seven thousand and twenty thousand dollars per episode. In a *New York Post* article, Hollywood talent agent Jackie Lewis, who represents many child stars, notes, "People think there is a pot of gold at the end of the rainbow for young TV stars, but let's think about the commissions given out once they get the pot of gold: 10 percent goes to the agent, 10 to 15 percent goes to the manager, 15 percent goes to the Coogan account, and then there's taxes. So even if a kid is making $25,000 a week, he or she may only see 30 or 40 percent of the money."

Sasha Eden suggests that if you plan to act as your child's manager, you should take a straight 10 percent or 15 percent commission, as a professional manager would, and then put all other earnings into accounts or trusts for the child's future benefit. The tabloids are full of stories of children suing their parents for mismanagement of their entertainment or athletic fortunes. If you don't have the skills and experience to successfully manage your child's career, it is wiser to pay a professional to make sure the funds are properly handled.

Keep in mind that although your child may be earning a great deal of money, these earnings may be short-lived and you will still need to save money for college down the road. Assume that you will need to invest your child's earnings until he or she turns eighteen—at that point your child will be a legal adult and college tuition must be paid. Meet with your financial planner and an attorney to determine if you can create trusts to protect your child's income until she turns, say, twenty-five or thirty.

Invite Your Children to Participate in the Management of Their Careers

Whenever possible, allow your children to understand the business side of their careers. As they grow older, they can become even more involved. Chemmy Alcott, for example, is very involved in the business and management side of her career. Like many actors and sports figures, she makes more money from endorsements than she does from her primary career, and she has always participated in the meetings regarding sponsorships and endorsements. She notes, "A lot of athletes don't want to know all the nitty-gritty, but I think I'm my own best salesperson. I don't understand how someone else can go into a meeting for me, representing me when I'm not there, and get a better deal for me than I can get for myself. In fact, it's gotten to the stage now where I just set up my own management firm."

Life After Child Stardom

It is quite rare for child stars to transition into stardom as adults, so make sure that you prepare your child for life after the limelight. In particular, give your child a solid academic background so that he or she can pursue other interests if show business or sports is no longer an option. Sasha Eden went on to study acting at many drama schools and in college; she continues to work as an actress as well as a producer. She has created and runs WET Productions, a nonprofit production company that produces media that challenges female stereotypes and advocates for equality. Through WET, Sasha has acted in and produced numerous plays written by women, developed screenplays and plays written by women, and created a media literacy and leadership program for teenage girls. Sasha was recently selected by the *Utne Reader* as one of "25 Visionaries You Should Know." Piper Weiss is a senior features editor and writer at Yahoo! Shine, Yahoo's site for women, and most recently appeared in the movie *Without,* which has made all the rounds at the major film festivals. She is also pursuing a career as an author—her book, *My Mom, Style Icon,* has been featured in media all over the world. Chemmy Alcott has started working as a sports commentator and adventurer inbetween training for her comeback at the 2014 Winter Olympics in Sochi.

HARMONIZE BLENDED FAMILIES FINANCIALLY

Perhaps no one is more hopeful and more wary than a mother who marries a man with children of his own and thereby creates a blended family. She is not alone. We have learned that 43 percent of all marriages constitute a remarriage for at least one member of the couple, and that 65 percent of remarriages involve children from a prior family.[24] Today, more than 40 percent of Americans have at least one "step" relative, according to a report released in 2011 by the Pew Research Center.[25]

It is sobering to note that an unhappy 60 percent of all remarriages involving children will end in divorce.[26] In order to avoid the financial consequences of divorcing a second or third time, as well as to prevent emotional chaos for yourself and your children, it is paramount that you devote your time and resources to evaluating the wisdom of remarriage before you commit.

Once you are married, it is critical that you and your husband have a game plan to make your new blended family work.

Creating a blended family raises the stakes in a marriage. Both sets of children have been uprooted by divorce, and now you are proposing a new family configuration that will deeply affect their lives. We believe that good financial discussions and planning before you remarry will greatly increase the odds that your blended family will thrive. According to a study by Marilyn Coleman and Lawrence Ganong from the University of Missouri at Columbia, only 20 percent of couples planning to remarry discuss finances before they walk down the aisle.[27] This noncommunication may account for the high failure rate among stepfamilies, since we know that 60 percent of divorces are caused by financial problems.

Before you remarry, we recommend that you follow the same guidelines and take the same precautions as you would before you marry for the first time—that is, ensure that you're making a good financial match as well as a good emotional one. As we discussed in chapter 2 (see page 64), you need to look at each other's credit reports and go over each other's financial habits, assets, and plans in detail. Make sure his divorce was not caused by an out-of-control addiction—if this is the case, chances are extremely high that you will not succeed in "curing" him where his last wife failed.

In addition, it is advisable to determine whether your new husband will be a good financial role model to both sets of children. How does he handle money around them? Do his kids have an allowance? How does he handle the kids' requests to buy them things? Do you agree with the money lessons he will teach them by example?

Age Matters

Realistically, much of your thought process about whether to remarry will be driven by how old both sets of children are. We spoke with Fredda Herz Brown, principal of Relative Solutions and a top family enterprise and wealth consultant with more than thirty years of experience. Fredda's consulting firm specializes in helping wealthy families manage the intersection between their economic and emotional lives. She notes that the younger the children are at the time of remarriage, the more the families' finances tend to be blended. It is easier to remarry when most of the child-rearing years are past. When there are younger children involved, the remarriage may be easier if children go off to boarding school rather than stay home for most of the year. She says that if children are teenagers or older, there is more of a tendency for each partner to take care of his or her own children first. The easiest remarriages in terms of parenting occur when couples are older and their children are already grown. Although there can still be a sharing of assets, the emotional issues of child rearing are not present to strain the marriage.

Who Brings More Money to the Marriage Matters

A lot depends on who brings more financial wealth to the marriage. When there is a great deal of money involved on both sides, it is more likely that each of you will come with financial advisers, legal structures that hold your wealth, and a host of estate-planning issues. In this case especially, you may wish to work with consultants who can help you formalize a decision-making process. The traditional situation is that the man brings more money to the marriage, and if that is the case, it is important to discuss how his money will be shared with you and your children. Will he support your expenses while you stay home with the children? Will you be expected to cover the costs of your own children? All these issues should be understood before you marry. If you are not used to being around a great deal of money, you may wish to hire a consultant or an estate-planning lawyer to help you.

Increasingly, however, women are coming into their second marriages with more wealth than their new husbands. Wilmington Trust and Campden Research, in association with Fredda's firm, released a comprehensive study on women and wealth in 2009. The study showed that women who bring more money to a second marriage than their new spouses often feel a bit unsure of how to deal with the difference in economic power. She notes, "Often a woman feels uncomfortable about taking power and managing the family and figuring out what kinds of decisions she includes her husband in and what kinds she excludes him from . . . the more she participates in raising his children, the more of her money and her power she feels like sharing."

Fredda notes that wealthy women view money very differently from wealthy men, in her experience. Wealthy women see money as a means to freedom, a way to help society and help their children, rather than a way to accumulate status or power. They are very concerned about fairness and want to break the silence around money that they may have experienced growing up. Educating the children in financial matters is extremely important. "I think the hardest subject for people to talk about, the most taboo subject in our culture, is money," says Fredda. "We talk about sex more easily than we talk about money. There is no easy way to talk about it . . . talking about it places you on a continuum of more or less. It gets really hard for people to deal with because they have to place themselves in relation to you. Money means more than cash or investments. It means love, power, control. Affection. When you are getting married, these are the issues, and money just magnifies them, especially if you add kids into the mixture."

Fredda explains that when one spouse has more money, it is important for that person not to be too controlling of the other spouse and to make sure that there is a balance of power for them as a couple. It is better, for example, to give your spouse a regular sum of money in a separate account that he or she has control over rather than to dole out money for requests, as if he or she were a child. If not, resentment can poison your union. She says, "There needs to be a sense of both people having control over their lives. Not just for the individual but for the marriage."

Reveal Child Support Obligations Before You Remarry

If you are remarrying, chances are good that both of you must make payments for child support, alimony, or both. Sit down with your future spouse and figure out what your joint child support obligations are, how long they will last, and how they will be paid. One of you may have higher child support payments than the other. How will you handle the financial discrepancy? For example, if your husband has to put most of his money toward child support, does that mean you need to shoulder the cost of the mortgage yourself? Are you each responsible individually for your prior obligations, and if so, do you plan to split joint costs? Or are you planning to just split all costs evenly, even if one of you has more children than the other? There is no right or wrong answer, but a little time spent with a spreadsheet prior to marriage will make these financial issues clear.

Discuss Children's Lifestyle Issues

Some parents believe in giving their children private-school education and sending them away to summer camp; others believe in public school and summer jobs. When you are blending two households, you will need to establish one standard for all the children in order for there to be a perception of fairness. This can be an extremely emotional topic to discuss; parents are often very passionate about their style of child rearing. Tread gently, but make sure you come to an agreement. Do you have enough room to house all the children fairly? Will the new siblings need to share bedrooms? Will your children's standard of living be raised or lowered? If it will be lowered, are they okay with that? It is always easier for children to get used to an easier lifestyle, less discipline, or more toys than it is for them to get used to reduced circumstances or fewer privileges, so be sensitive if you have to cut back on their fun in order to blend.

Protect Your Assets and Your Children's Inheritance

Many people enter into remarriage with the assumption that their family homes and other ancestral assets will pass on to their blood relations rather than to their stepchildren. But if that is your wish, you must have your will written in a way that carefully spells out the disposition of real property upon your death. One good vehicle to use prior to remarriage is a QTIP trust, or a qualified terminable interest property trust. It allows you to leave certain assets for the use of your spouse during his or her remaining lifetime, while the ultimate beneficiary can be your children. This type of trust is often used, not surprisingly, to bequeath a family home. If you would like the home that you inherited from your grandmother to go to your children from your first marriage rather than to your stepchildren, you can place the ownership of the home in a QTIP trust, which will allow your husband to use the home while he is still alive yet make sure that your children ultimately inherit the property.

A QTIP trust is attractive because the assets in the trust will be taxed upon the death of your spouse, and not upon your own death. That means that if you die first, there will be no estate taxes to pay on the property at the time of your death. Since tax laws are constantly changing, it is important to work with a trusts and estates attorney to figure out if a QTIP trust would be the best vehicle to protect your property.

Another protective document to consider using when contemplating remarriage is a prenuptial agreement. As we discussed in chapter 2 (see page 72), a prenup makes the financial division of your assets crystal clear in case the marriage does not work out. Having two sets of children involved makes signing a prenup an even more important step to take before a second marriage. Fredda says, "I advise couples to get really, really clear on what it is they are bringing into the marriage and what they want to take out of it if it ends. . . . I don't care what the legal structure is as much as I care about getting women to realize what will happen to them if they give up ownership of their assets."

Realize that when it comes to inheritance, you may have three sets of children to consider—his, yours from your former marriage, and then any children you may have together. If there are uneven amounts of wealth brought into the marriage, it is common that these sets of children may inherit different amounts. Your trust for your own kids may include property from your previous marriage, for example, whereas a trust for your husband's kids will not.

QUESTIONS TO ANSWER BEFORE YOU SAY "I DO" AGAIN

1. How much alimony and child support are you each responsible for?
2. How much is the monthly budget for each of your children?
3. What are your credit scores?
4. Where will you live and what will you do with the homes you are currently living in?
5. What is your annual income and what are the monthly expenses for running your family?
6. What expenses do you consider necessities and what do you consider luxuries—especially where your children are concerned?

7. What is your financial involvement with your former spouse, and how will it affect your family?

8. What will be the visitation obligations and living arrangements for each child?

9. Are there any extraordinary costs associated with any of your children— that is, do any of them have special needs, or is one of them pursuing a career at a young age?

10. Do you have enough life insurance to cover everyone's expenses in the event of your death?

11. Is there any large financial challenge you need to overcome, such as bankruptcy or a business that is in trouble?

12. Who will be responsible for paying monthly bills?

13. How will you divide expenses?

14. How many and what types of accounts will you have—single, joint, or both?

15. How will you decide to handle financial requests from the kids?

16. How will you measure whether or not you are fair to all the kids?

17. How will you fund college tuition?

18. How will you handle disagreements on financial matters?

19. Will you have separate accountants?

Have a Plan to Support All Children

When you remarry, you are assuming responsibility for a new set of children, and you and your fiancé need to agree on how these responsibilities will be met. Even though there may be a child support plan in place, the death of your former or intended husband could throw those plans into disarray. It is a good idea to assume that you might end up having to support all the children, including his, and to make sure that you have enough life insurance, disability insurance, and savings to cover this scenario should a tragedy strike. We will cover this topic further in chapter 5 (see page 188).

It is a fact that, should your second marriage end up to be a lifelong affair, it is highly likely that you will end up being in charge of your family's assets for some period of time. Fredda says,

Everyone acts as though we're passing trillions of dollars on to the next generation when the fact is we're passing on trillions of dollars to women. They die about eight years after men do, and with every decade that goes by, their life expectancy increases. They may not inherit money per se, but they definitely inherit the power to decide how it is dispensed, especially if they're trustees. Who is going to be the financial controller and decision maker in the future? It is going to be women. They're the ones most interested in passing it along with value.

Creating a blended family is a courageous act of love. If you approach the financial aspects of your union with an open heart and a willingness to be honest, you are likely to succeed.

WELCOME TO DOG MOTHERHOOD

We live in a time when being a mother often means nurturing not only children but also treasured pets. In some cases, people are choosing pets as their children, forgoing human offspring altogether. The idea of getting a pet seems easier and less expensive than raising children; however, the reality is that buying and caring for a pet is a major investment. For example, a dog's basic care will cost anywhere from four thousand to forty thousand dollars over a fourteen-year lifespan, and that doesn't include critical care or other problems that may come up.[28] And U.S. pet expenditures in 2011 reached an estimated $50 million, according to the American Pet Products Association (APPA).[29]

This idea of parenting your pets is gaining popularity with the animal lovers community. "The words 'dog owner' are passé; people are dog *parents,* and it's a very important distinction. Our relationships with animals must come from the heart and until we can do away with the concept of owning another living being, we will never be able to treat any animals, pets or otherwise, with kindness and respect," says Wendy Diamond, who coined the term "pet lifestyle." Wendy is an animal welfare and rescue advocate, the founder of AnimalFair.com, and the proud parent of the omnipresent rescued Maltese, Lucky Diamond. Since dogs are the most popular kind of pet—according to the PPA, there are an estimated 78 million dog owners in the United States—we'll focus on having a happy financial relationship with your pooch. Bringing a puppy or new dog into a home in a haphazard fashion, without planning, leads to animal abuse, destroyed property, vet bills, and even lawsuits from the neighbors. Adopting a dog in a suburban or metropolitan environment is best approached with the expectation that you are expanding your family. This means adding the dog to your will and investigating pet insurance.

The author Louis Sabin once said, "No matter how little money and how few possessions you own, having a dog makes you rich." We would like to take this statement one step further and say that although it may appear that being a dog parent is an expensive hobby, you do get a major return on your investment, a return so valuable that it can't be quantified.

Studies show that dogs can increase your productivity at work, encourage personal integrity, release relaxation hormones in the brain, improve your general health, and enhance your children's health, self-esteem, and capacity for empathy.[30] A dog provides hours of free entertainment for you and your family. The dog's walking schedule can create structure and organization in the family. Certain dog breeds, such as German shepherds and Doberman pinschers, provide increased security in the home at a relatively low cost. Having a dog may be one of the few instances in which a human being experiences unconditional love.

Imagine the financial rewards of caring for an animal who brings down your risk of heart disease, reduces the need for treatment for depression, and even takes the place of your gym membership. Erin Kennedy, a proud mom of two toy poodles, Teddy and Simon, says, "They've become my support system and my family; and I'm at an age when I'm not necessarily ready for a support system or a family in a more conventional manner."

Costs of Parenting a Dog

According to the 2011–2012 APPA National Pet Owners Survey, basic annual expenses for dog in dollars include the following:[31]

Surgical vet visits	$407
Routine vet visits	$248

Food	$254
Kennel boarding	$274
Vitamins	$95
Travel expenses	$78
Groomer/grooming aids	$73
Edible treats	$70
Toys	$43

Because veterinary bills constitute such a high percentage of the cost of owning a dog, you may want to consider purchasing pet health insurance, especially if you have a low tolerance for risk. Erin Kennedy, besides being a mom to Teddy and Simon, is also a sales and risk consultant in the Private Client Services division of Marsh Inc., a global insurance brokerage. She was able to take advantage of a corporate benefit that offers discounted rates on pet insurance, which is payroll deducted. These types of benefits are becoming more widespread in U.S. corporations and are well worth investigating. It's important to note that pet insurance still operates on a reimbursement basis. Until a pet insurance brokerage emerges, the ASPCA can be an excellent resource for coverage comparisons.

Advances in medicine are now helping dogs live longer, healthier lives. Unfortunately, this can sometimes mean that dog parents will have to cope with a pet's serious illness in its later years. For dogs older than ten, approximately 50 percent of deaths are cancer related.[32] This is where pet insurance can come in (more than) handy. Yes, pet insurance can be expensive. But, as Erin Kennedy says regarding the risk of massive veterinary bills, "If I were looking at thirty thousand dollars in vet bills because my dog had cancer, would I be glad that I purchased this coverage?"

Traveling with your dog also adds an extra expense, although it is becoming increasingly popular as more hotels begin to allow pets in rooms. Investigate any additional fees before taking your dog on the road. Many hotels have restrictions on the sizes and breeds of dogs that are permitted, and charge nonrefundable fees ranging from ten to seventy-five dollars per day.

Kimpton Hotels has one of the best pet-friendly reputations in the United

States. The nationwide chain prides itself on not charging additional fees or deposits, and does not restrict the size, weight, breed, or number of pets you can have with you. Loews Hotels also has liberal pet policies and offerings.[33]

Also, it's important not to be duped financially by the new trends in dog breeding. According to Babette Haggerty, a dog trainer and owner of Haggerty's School for Dogs, "There was a time when purebreds would cost you more money. Now there are all these cool designer breeds, such as the doodle dogs—labradoodles, goldendoodles, sheepdoodles—and puggles. People are spending two thousand dollars on a mutt. The puggle, in its own right, has become a breed, but it's not a long-term or established breed that has a breeding stock and a genetic history to it."

Deciding whether to buy a purebred dog or a mixed breed can be like buying a lottery ticket—you never know. Over the course of three decades, Haggerty has seen dogs from top breeders, bred from championship bloodlines, succumb to serious health and behavioral problems. On the other hand, people who spend forty dollars at the local shelter often end up with a healthy, lifelong companion. Of course, the reverse can also be true. If a shelter dog has not been properly socialized early in its life, it can cost more to rehabilitate him or her than it would cost to buy a well-socialized dog from a breeder.

Schooling Your Dog Saves Money in the Long Term

If you decide to parent a puppy, one of the best financial investments you can make is obedience school. A wild, badly behaved dog could cost you dearly during a single afternoon's destructive rampage. It's also an opportunity to get your "gnawing" questions answered if you're worried about your puppy's early behavior. At the Haggerty School for Dogs in New York City, the puppy-training class enrolls puppies between ten and twenty weeks old. It runs one hour per week for all three weeks. The price in Manhattan is around $175. The class teaches you how to best handle your puppy's nipping, destructive chewing, and house training, and the best procedures to follow when leaving your puppy alone. This class also covers name recognition; paying attention to an owner around distractions; commands like "sit," "down," and the sit-stay and down-stay; jumping prevention; teaching puppies to greet people politely; walking on a loose leash; and teaching your puppy to come when called.[34] Haggerty says if you hire a private trainer and you don't see a huge difference in that dog after that first lesson, then you need a different trainer.

Providing for Your Dog After Your Death

Too many dogs and other pets are sent to the pound upon their owner's death. The family dog should always be mentioned in your estate planning, and the lifetime cost of his or her care should be estimated and taken into account. It's wise to choose a dog guardian in advance and make sure your dog's care is properly financed, so there is no question what will happen to your dog after your death.

When Ashley Dobbs turned thirty-five, she ran out of room to take in any more rescue dogs and decided it was time to put her passion for pet protection into law. By the time she was forty, Dobbs was practicing at a large law firm in Washington, D.C., and now uses her pro-bono time to advocate for animal issues. Dobbs educates people on the importance for arranging for their pet's care when they can't be there and provides tools for setting up pet trusts through her nonprofit organization, Keep the Promise to Pets. She believes that "once we've domesticated animals, we have a responsibility to care for them." She has outlined several important considerations to take into account when planning your pet's future. After your death, or if you become incapacitated, your pet's fate should not be left in limbo.

First, a dog parent should calculate the expenses associated with caring for his or her dog over the course of its lifetime. Then, money for that dog's care should be placed in a trust. The trust can be funded either with savings you have allocated for that purpose or through a life insurance policy that you purchase. Legal fees to structure such a trust usually start at about two thousand dollars.

"We are fortunate that, in the last ten years, most states have passed laws that make it possible to have a legally enforceable pet trust," notes Dobbs. "That is, you can leave money to a third-party trustee, who in turn gives it in accordance with the trust instructions to a named caretaker who will care for your pet after you die. That arrangement can be enforced in court." After witnessing many cases where a person was willed both the animal and the funds and abused their responsibilities, even pretending the dog was still alive when it had long been deceased, Dobbs recommends structuring the trust so that one person is named the caretaker of your pet and another individual is named the trustee.

If you choose to purchase a life insurance policy to fund a trust for your pet, you need to designate the trust as the beneficiary of the policy. A life insurance policy is a great option if you don't have a lump sum of money to fund a trust but are able to pay an annual premium. If you buy a hundred-thousand-dollar policy, and if there is money left over after your pet's death, you can make provisions for the remainder to go to another beneficiary. If you create a revocable trust, you can change the beneficiary of the trust at any time.

In addition, it's very important to not overfund the trust, especially if other parties are being left out of the inheritance pool. "Leona Helmsley's trust for her dog was considered to be overfunded," explains Dobbs. "Whatever that dog's lavish lifestyle was, it couldn't possibly have needed twelve million dollars in its lifetime. So the court deemed the trust to be overfunded, reduced it to two million, and disbursed the other money to Helmsley's charitable foundation."

In addition, be sure to name your dog's guardian well in advance of preparing your estate planning. You should explain the dog's care routine and the source of the funds to the guardian in depth, and inform your family and trusted advisers of your wishes. One of the reasons for setting up a trust, rather than giving your pet to the guardian as a bequest in a will or through other informal means, is the well-being of the pet. "A will has to pass through probate. There is a significant period of time that passes between your death and the distribution of your assets," says Dobbs. "That's a really long time for a pet to go without having your wishes known and without being cared for."

If you're considering handing over the care of your pet to an animal sanctuary rather than a specific individual, you may want to think twice. Dobbs points out that the sanctuary may not be in existence anymore at the time of your death, and that the sanctuary's reputation or funding status may also have changed in the interim. Alternatively, if you've set up a trust and chosen a trustee, you could ask that individual—or someone who knows your dog well, such as a longtime dog walker—to decide where your dog should go in the event of your death. The goal is to create a life for your dog that will allow you to rest in peace.

CHAPTER 4

POWER

THE FOURTH PEARL OF FINANCIAL WISDOM:
A Woman Must Exercise Her Power in Life

As WE MOVE INTO AN ERA when women have the opportunity to build their own wealth, choose their mates wisely, and continue to nurture their prosperity in motherhood, it also becomes possible for women to step up into the next level: to become truly powerful. Our fourth pearl of wisdom, a woman must exercise her power in life, recognizes this opportunity. We often shy away from this word, "power," and insist that we don't want it, don't need it. Power feels like something we leave for men to fight over. Yet the dictionary definition of power is "the ability or capacity to perform or act effectively," and don't we want to be able to do that?

Something is happening to the notion of power in society—it is becoming more fluid, less centralized. Women no longer have to occupy the roles that men call powerful in order to *be* powerful. We women now have more freedom to become leaders than at any other time in previously recorded history, and we have the freedom to do it in our own way. Whether we choose to assume traditional roles or to forge a new trail, the world needs us to step up and bring our wisdom and influence to the forefront for the benefit of our children, our communities, and the planet.

When we women shrink from power, when we refuse to stand up for ourselves or for what we know is the right and prudent choice, others can suffer. The opposite of power is *helplessness*. This is often the grain of sand that irritates us in our shell, forcing us to grow a pearl of true feminine power.

THE GRAIN OF SAND IN THE OYSTER SHELL

Do you know a woman who . . .

- Hates her job but does not make the effort to develop a network that could help her find new opportunities in her industry—and then is fired?
- Does not pursue a corporate promotion even though she is highly credentialed and ready to rise to the next level?
- Refuses invitations to appear in public because she does not think she is a good speaker?
- Spots an irregularity at work but refuses to blow the whistle?
- Suspects that her water is tainted but doesn't do anything about it, even as her child becomes ill?
- Is appalled at how her local school board is run but doesn't bother to vote or run for office?
- Is passionate about animal welfare and tears up at commercials for the humane society but does nothing to meaningfully help the cause?

Fear often keeps us silent; fear, along with a feeling of helplessness or hopelessness, leads us to the conviction that we cannot act effectively. In this chapter, we will explore the new ways that power is available to all of us. We'll focus on learning how to say yes to a world that is inviting us to come forward and contribute.

EMBRACE FEMININE LEADERSHIP

Today, a new type of feminine power and leadership is emerging, one that embraces a woman's desire to express her nurturance as well as her decisiveness. Women are ready to shed their male-copying power suits and leadership styles. Presenting our authentic selves and maintaining our integrity in all situations allows us to be truly powerful. We are adopting a decidedly feminine approach, combining work and personal time into a satisfying, more holistic life. We are changing the world in significant ways as we bring our visions into the most powerful corporations. Here, we'll explore ways to be an effective leader today that play to your feminine strengths.

Understand Power Today

We spoke with Moira Forbes, president and publisher of Forbes*Woman,* a multimedia platform dedicated to women in business and leadership, which includes Forbes's well-known franchise, the Forbes 100 Most Powerful Women list, on the changing nature of female leadership. Moira joined Forbes in 2001 and has developed the strategy for the company's women's initiatives, including the Forbes 100 Most Powerful Women list. She has keenly watched the traditional definitions of power morph as the Internet and social media make it possible for more and more individuals to have a voice and influence even the outcome of country revolutions from Facebook. As Moira observes,

> The whole dynamic of power has changed today, regardless of gender. Power today is more about the ability to influence and to impact, and to move people and to effect change, and shape minds. That is true whatever the platform, whatever the issue, whatever the realm. There's democratization, if you will, of influence, meaning it's much easier to access influence and "power" today, but it's much harder to maintain. So we at Forbes continue to spotlight the women who wield power in traditional roles, whether that be through running a corporation or taking very high political office; but we also have seen that women are achieving influence and attaining impact in very unconventional ways, ways that no longer demand those traditional dynamics and those traditional paths to positions of leadership.

The new power is very good news for women. Historically, women have been shut out of traditional leadership roles; today, women are becoming hugely influential thanks to the ability to be heard and to build an audience via the Web. We have discussed how moms can capitalize on this trend as mommy bloggers in our third pearl. Our first pearl spoke about the fact that the best way to build our own wealth is to start a business; the reduced costs of running a business thanks to Web-based resources and the ability to develop a strong following for your company for virtually no cost via Facebook and Twitter are all ways in which this new form of power can help women achieve their dreams.

For young women growing up on Facebook, social media is as much a fact of life as electricity; for those of us over forty, it is time to learn about this new form of engagement and to harness its power for our projects. We can find our tribe online and develop an influential following on issues that we care deeply about. It is up to us to step forward and interact; the online world is completely open to us. Later in the chapter we will spend more time examining how to be effective through personal branding, networking, and developing a sphere of influence. This new form of power is just six years old (Facebook was started in 2004, Twitter in 2006), and we are just beginning to learn how to maximize it.

Communicate Your Authentic Self

One of the most critical new requirements of leadership is the need to be truly ethical and to authentically express who you are in the social media world and in the real world. There can be no gaps between your public image and private life. When you are genuinely interested in a cause or engaged in an issue you care about, this comes across to everyone you encounter. It really is impossible to express one set of values today in your business or your blog and to act in another way—eventually you will be found out and lose all credibility as amateur videos of your misdeeds are tweeted around the world.

Due to her fiercely authentic style, American pop singer-songwriter Lady Gaga topped the Forbes annual list of the 100 Most Powerful Women in 2010. Moira notes that Lady Gaga exemplifies the ways in which

> technology has generated new paths to influence through virtual networks, so much so that Lady Gaga is the number one person followed on

Twitter. With just one tweet, she has the power to move millions across the globe. She is not just doing it to promote her brand . . . she's a huge advocate for gay rights. Mega-businesses and mega-personal brands influence everything. Everything—from what we talk about at our dinner tables to the social issues we debate. Power today is defined by connectivity and authenticity. That is, the ability to build a community around you as a person, as a brand, as a professional.

Authenticity and consistency of self are requirements for good leadership. It comes back to trust—how can we trust someone who is not who they say they are? We can't. So if we want to step into leadership, we must make a strong commitment to truth in advertising—we need to be who we say we are. We can become a powerful leader only to the extent that we are willing to have the discipline and caring to maintain our character and our moral stance.

Ask yourself:

- What type of leader am I?
- Why do I inspire others to follow me?
- How have I revealed my character to others through my actions?
- Am I worthy of the trust others are placing in my leadership?
- Where do I fall short of my own expectations and how am I correcting these shortcomings?
- What can I do to further develop my authentic character and then lead from a place of truth?

As Moira notes, "Authenticity allows true leaders to build commonality. Sharing builds trust, even when it means sharing our vulnerabilities and our personalities beyond the boardroom. Remaining true to yourself allows you as a leader to connect and engage with those around you, build a team, and achieve lasting influence."

Have a Bias for Action

One of the hardest and most rewarding things to do is to be a leader of your own life. It is important to take the time to really sit down and make a strategic life plan, including specific goals for the future. It is critical to be realistic about what you want to achieve when. You will most likely have to make short-term sacrifices to achieve long-term goals. Your goals may conflict with the goals or plans that the company you work for has; you might need to change jobs or start a business that does not yet exist to achieve your goals.

That being said, without a strategic life plan, many of your goals will never be realized. Moira notes,

> The first small step for lasting influence, to achieving our goals and ambitions, is planning. Yet we often define "planning" as our checklist for the week or the countless business plans and strategy sessions at work. It is critical, though, to take this same approach with your life goals, identifying your true priorities, and confronting both what you have accomplished and what you still want to achieve. Life will throw inevitable curveballs, but if you don't have a plan, how can you even begin to get to that place that you hoped to?

Model an Integrated Life

One of the best trends we have seen is that women today are no longer willing to sacrifice having a full life to be a successful leader. The arrival of job sharing, working from home, and access from anywhere means that more and more women are combining work, family, passionate hobbies, and philanthropic activities to create a life that is more satisfying. Many women are refusing to settle for a corporate life that leaves no time for family and outside interests, especially since they are routinely paid less than males for making this sacrifice.

As a leader, your ability to model an integrated life to your employees makes it more likely that they, too, will stop putting in needless hours at the office. Your example of including friends, family, pets, and projects in your life as well as work means that they will feel freer to follow suit. You are much more likely to create a sustainable life and leadership style if all parts of yourself and your employees are being expressed.

Change the World with Your Vision

Women often underestimate what the power of their innovative ideas can do to help the world, especially if they can harness the power of major global corporations. Women in traditional corporate roles who engage their corporations in a new vision can impact millions. We spoke with Bonnie Wurzbacher, Senior Vice President at the Coca-Cola Company, who has been with the company for twenty-seven years in various senior leadership roles and is currently rolling out a new global initiative to economically empower 5 million women by the year 2020, called 5 by 20. Bonnie's story is inspiring because she is using her authentic self and vision to bring an entirely new initiative to life, which fulfills the commitment of her corporation to the United Nations Millennium Goals. Equally important is the fact that she views her work as congruent with her personal faith and life plan.

Bonnie's strong Christian faith is the cornerstone of her authentic self and informs her actions. She feels strongly that being a businesswoman and working at Coke for the last twenty-seven years has been aligned with her personal values and goals.

> I often surprise people by explaining that my work as an executive with the Coca-Cola Company is exciting and purposeful, because I'm part of a 125-year-old global wealth creation machine that creates millions of jobs and contributes to the sustainable economic well-being of thousands of communities in 206 countries. I feel God's pleasure in both the product and the process of my work because of the way it enables so many people throughout the world to use their gifts and skills for good and for God. With that being said, I also believe that the ultimate purpose of business is to advance the economic well-being of communities and, as the only creator of wealth in the world, business enables every other institution to exist. Schools, colleges, hospitals, churches, missions, every 501(c)(3) organization in the world would not exist without ethical and sustainable business.

Bonnie earned the trust of her company and rose through the ranks for twenty-seven years. She has been active in building new teams and helped to lay the groundwork for this exciting initiative. She was a founding member of the Women's Leadership Council, an advisory group that reports to the Chairman, whom she credits for championing this initiative, among other things. "We use that council to influence the global leadership of our company in a lot of different ways. We've influenced them in terms of what we measure and track relative to women in leadership. We've used them to influence more flexible work–life programs, and their importance today for both men and women. We've influenced the business case for why we need more women in leadership roles. Our Chairman really gets this and he's a huge proponent of it."

When coming up with the 5 by 20 plan, they focused on how to use Coca-Cola's pledge to support the UN Millennium Goals (read about them at www.un.org/millenniumgoals) by engaging the corporation in more intentionally using its global reach to empower the poor with a special emphasis on women. Coca-Cola has significant business in the developing world, and sells products in both hard-to-reach rural and urban areas, through its local bottlers, to millions of small retailers, many of which are run by women. Bonnie explained that Coca-Cola is the largest private employer on the continent of Africa, where for every one job it creates directly, another sixteen jobs are created indirectly. This fact has given the company an enormous opportunity to impact women in Africa through job creation. Coca-Cola has more than five hundred brands and three thousand packages that are sold around the world. Active corporate learning is taking place by launching this initiative in several large countries, developing programs to build new capabilities and seeing which programs work best. The company is now crafting metrics to measure the effectiveness of this new program.

Bonnie radiates a "bias toward action" and has successfully demonstrated her ability to lead the company into new territories on several occasions. Crafting initiatives that dovetail into the corporation's commitments, strategies, and capabilities is crucial, and committing to make it happen is critical to success. Bonnie says,

> My experience has been that there are few people in large companies who are willing to take on starting up and then leading a new initiative,

because it can be risky and it's uncertain whether it will succeed. But I love to do that. My favorite roles at the company have always been ones that involve starting up something new that solves a problem or creates a new growth opportunity. This project will be successful because it is right in our sweet spot and we have the capabilities to do this better than just about any other company in the world.

Having a vision to economically empower 5 million women by 2020, while working at one of the largest corporations in the world, is an example of how women are using their authentic leadership to create meaningful social change in unexpected ways. As we all step into our power and put forth our visions for change, backed up by our skillfulness and history of success, there is no telling what we will achieve. As Bonnie says, "There's this relatively new concept called authentic leadership, which involves bringing who you are, your values and your life experiences, to the purpose of your leadership. This is the type of leader that people want to follow and that many leaders want to be. For me to be an authentic leader requires that I bring my faith to it, too. To be an authentic leader requires connecting who you are with the work that you do and the way you work with others."

DEVELOP YOUR BRAND OF ONE

This is the greatest era for immediacy in consumer and business communication in history. Now your personal and business information is available online, in emails, and in social media, and all that information is creating a public image of who you are that is available to anyone who Googles you. Taking control of that information means creating your own brand consciously, and it has never been more important. It is time to learn how to exercise the power of your brand. Although it's impossible to control all the content that circulates about you, you can structure your communications to create a positive, directed image of who you are and what you're about. If you've created a Facebook, LinkedIn, Twitter, or Foursquare page, or if you've created a website or blog: Wake up! You have just put out your brand to the world.

How you present yourself and your brand promise is the most important factor in establishing power and unseating the competition in this frenetic world of tweets, spam, on-demand programming, virtual workforces, and Internet lifestyles. Digital and offline revolutions are everywhere, whether you're in a corporation or work for yourself, so you must become aware of the ways in which new technologies are shaping your image so that you can control how you are perceived.

What is branding? Branding, at the corporate level, is marketing "the sum today of a company's value, including products, services, people, advertising, positioning, and culture."[1] Branding at the individual level means creating a clear message of who you are in all aspects of your life, and acting—both professionally and personally—in ways that are congruent with your message. Consciously creating your brand allows you to tap into your power and create the opportunities of your dreams.

According to the *Oxford English Dictionary,* the word "brand" was first used in the 1500s to denote the "identifying mark made by a hot iron." Similarly, we like to say that you should think about your individual brand as though it were a series of tattoos. If a woman wears a butterfly tattoo on her arm with the word CHANGE beneath it, what is she signaling? That she has blossomed from a caterpillar into a glorious thing of beauty. She is messaging "evolution," and when we see her, we identify her with that message.

Creating Your Brand Promise

Nancy Mendelson is the Founder and Chief Advisor of NEM Global: a branding and communication consulting company. As a senior executive in the corporate world, she has been creating messages and developing branding for major clients like CBS and Loews Hotels for more than thirty years. "Loews Hotels was around for sixty years before it embraced the concept of becoming a brand," says Nancy. Today she considers everything the corporation does in terms of how it affects the brand. It's the same for individuals. You may not have thought of your actions this way, but it's true: how you behave can be thought of as your brand promise. Corporations like Loews actively create a brand promise and then attempt to live up to it. "If you're asking people to connect with you, to give you money, to entrust their lives with you for a certain number of nights," says Nancy, "you have made a brand promise. Loews promise is: 'At Loews Hotels, we provide a four diamond and MORE experience.' MORE to Loews is a supremely comfortable, vibrant, and uniquely local experience."

When Nancy first arrived at Loews, she met with all the directors of marketing and tried to get them to understand the brand mentality. "I had them each look at themselves as a brand and I said, 'If you were a brand, what do you promise? If I shake hands with you, what can I count on? What are your values? Who are you? Try to give me a sense. Try to give me a tagline that encapsulates who you are.'"

When you are trying to uncover your brand and design your brand promise, you need to identify the market for your skills, your strengths, your values, your style, what makes you unique, and your most effective channels of communication. Although this may sound daunting, don't worry—the key is to look at the situation objectively, and make sure that everything you are doing and communicating is in line with your goals and your vision. If it isn't, now is the time to close the gap. You may find that you are much more accomplished than people realize. Or you may find that you have changed, and it is time to let the old messages go.

Discover Your Assets

To begin, first make a list of your assets—your positive qualities. What are your skills? What are the tools in your tool kit? What are the characteristics that make you attractive, likable, and useful? Think about the assets you have both in your personal life and your professional life. Engage an honest friend, colleague, and a former boss to describe why they picked you to be part of their team. Professionally, maybe you have a keen eye for detail, excellent creative talents, or you are a superb communicator. As a friend, perhaps you are funny, loyal, and always willing to help out in a crisis.

Define Your Values

Move on and list your values. What is important to you about the way you conduct your life? Your values should be the same whether they relate to your personal or professional activities. You may have learned your values from religious tradition, from your family, or from your friends. If you're struggling to define your values, look at your close friends and ask yourself why they're your friends. Look at the things you do with your money and how you spend your free time. Ask yourself, in observing the world around you, Do I agree with what I see? Are these things in line with my values? Is that what *I* value or is that what my *family* valued? Have I outgrown my childhood values? It's important to be present and mindful in every moment, says Nancy: "Some of the most interesting things you can learn about yourself can be identified while you're watching a movie or walking down the street."

Outline What Makes You Unique

Once you understand your assets and your values, the next thing you should do is list what makes you unique. What's different about what you're saying versus what your neighbor is saying? Why should I connect with you? What are you passionate about? What do you really love and why do you want to move in that direction? For example, a woman might say, "I am a Venezuelan-American raised in Chicago. I studied foreign relations in college and I am trilingual in Spanish, Mandarin, and English. I lived in Beijing for three years working on developing new products for my company. I love to tweet about what's happening at the orphanage I support in Cambodia." One could picture this woman dressed in a vibrant red silk designer coatdress that she had made in China, excitedly discussing China–Venezuela trade relations. When she looks at her life experiences, she realizes that she's unique. She's interesting. She stands out.

Understand How Your Personal Brand Affects
Your Professional Brand

We all have at least two brands: a professional brand and a personal brand. Due to the fluid nature of the Internet, it is critical to remember that what you communicate about your personal brand will be seen online by people who know you professionally. This doesn't mean you can't have passionate beliefs and interests that have nothing to do with your job. When it comes to Twitter, you may end up having two handles: one for personal tweets and one for professional tweets. However, be aware that your employer is most likely monitoring your personal postings. Also remember that your personal followers could retweet your message to your boss, so think twice before you type. Make sure you are familiar with your company's social media policies—in some places, you can get fired for making inappropriate remarks about your employer online. In addition, it is well known that colleges are now looking at the Facebook pages of students to determine whether their values match up with the school's. In the same way, realize that even your most personal posts on secure Facebook pages can make their way into the public domain, so always think twice before you write anything. Keep things positive and productive on all communications.

Remember that what you and your friends consider funny others may consider offensive, racist, or ignorant, so watch what you tweet, videotape, or comment on. It goes without saying that you should never send revealing photos of yourself to anyone electronically. All these things will come up when someone searches for you online. Things that you do when you are young may have seemed harmless then, but they may harm your career and make people question your character, values, or judgment later in life. If you become famous, everything you ever wrote will be dug up by zealous journalists and fans, and you want to make sure that you are not ashamed of your past. Be aware that background-check companies are now permitted to screen job applicants by reviewing all Internet photos and postings.[2]

On the professional side, you can advance much more quickly if you make a competitive analysis of your field and decide how you stand out. Think about the leaders of your company and the rising stars in your field. How do you differ from them? What do you bring to your firm and your industry that will add value? This will be the thing that you choose to highlight when you communicate about yourself.

Create Your Style of Delivery

What differentiates a brand or a person within a given public space is his or her style of delivery. It is critical today that you develop the skill of communicating well to the media and through the media. Whether you write a post on Facebook, tweet an opinion, or deliver a PowerPoint presentation, you must be able to get your message across clearly and directly. As you rise through the corporate ranks or start a company, you may be interviewed by journalists for print articles or on television, and you must know how to speak concisely to the press.

One of the most valuable gifts you can give yourself in this regard is media training. If you work in a corporation, you may be able to persuade your company to pay for a course. Even if you have to pay for it yourself, you will be making a wise investment that will pay off for years to come.

During these training sessions, often conducted by top public relations firms, you will learn how to answer questions on camera and to deliver clear and focused messages that cannot be easily manipulated. You will learn how reporters are trained to trick you and to throw you off guard with troubling questions, and how to think on your feet. Once you see yourself on camera, you will also be able to correct unconscious habits like nodding your head too frequently or playing with your hair.

Be sure to take advantage of sales training courses, presentation courses, and public speaking courses offered at work. Organizations like Toastmasters International or even acting classes can help you develop a clear communication style.

If you are communicating via email or social media, think carefully about what you're about to share. Do you have a tendency to be verbose? If you take too long to come to the point, you will lose your listener. Do you send hundreds of emails on topics that are important to you? You may turn off people on the other end because you are communicating too frequently. Do you reflect carefully on the power of the words on the page? Ask yourself if your message is consistent with the person you are and the person you want to be. Make sure your style is not getting in the way of your message.

Conduct a Gap Analysis of Your Brand

Now that you have taken a hard look at your personal and professional presentations, it's time to be honest and conduct a gap analysis of your brand. Where do you fail to live up to the promise of your brand? Are there certain things you do online that are not helping you? You can't easily erase anything that's already in cyberspace, but you can commit to conducting yourself in a different way going forward. Are there strengths that you have in your personal life that you could apply to your professional life? Maybe you love speaking French; perhaps there is a way to weave this skill into what you do for a living. Your awareness of your brand should make it easier to tweak your message so that it becomes even more powerful and unique.

Seek Out Your Audience

If you are planning to develop yourself as a brand, you must identify the audience with whom would you like to communicate. This is your market. Make a list of the people in your profession whom you would like to reach. Make a list of the people in your personal life whom you would like to reach. Study the social media audience of the people and companies you admire. How many Twitter followers do they have? What are they saying? What needs are they fulfilling in the marketplace? What are they delivering and what is the dialogue between these people or companies and their audience?

Master Your Channels

When you're building your brand, make sure that all your social media messages are effective—that is, they are meaningful, not empty; they have content, and aren't sent just for the sake of meeting a quota. Especially if you are not a celebrity, you need to guard against audience fatigue—make sure what you are communicating is interesting and useful; otherwise, your audience will "unfollow" you eventually. Making it meaningful means setting aside time in your schedule to carefully craft your emails and updates, whether you're participating in a public-speaking tour or a charitable event. Make a list of all your channels of communication and what you want to say in each of them. And don't forget the power of individual phone calls and face-to-face engagement.

If you're publicizing anything about yourself or your work as a new entrepreneur, it's not only content that matters—it's consistency, too. For example, it's absolutely critical to have a website and business cards ready to go before you enter into any brand-related communication. All your visuals, taglines, and logos—across your websites, social media accounts, invoices, and stationery—should be consistent.

Finally, show your gratitude to people engaging with you. Thank them on Twitter, follow them, or send out thank-you notes. In a technological world that tends to flatten the emotional impact of communication, hit them with your humanity. You will gain more followers and more loyalty.

Whatever the channel, you need to make sure that each and every communication you make fulfills what you promised as a brand. As Nancy Mendelson says, "Create a dialogue with your audience and diligently keep up that dialogue. Any smart marketer or branding executive needs to be informed by their customers and constituents."

PUTTING IT ALL TOGETHER

Now that you have taken a hard look at what your brand stands for, it's time to write a short brand statement that you can use for inspiration and to keep yourself "on point" with every communication. We created the example below for a woman we'll call Pauline Power, a San Francisco veterinarian.

Pauline Power Brand Statement

My Personal Brand
I am a loyal friend to animals, committed to animal rights, and committed to promoting the vegan lifestyle.

My Professional Brand
I am a rising-star veterinarian whose groundbreaking research centers on equine diseases.

My Assets
Personally
- Funny—my friends beg me to do stand-up
- Loyal—I am still in touch with my friends from high school
- Vegan—I have been vegan for the past five years and love it
- Green—I drive a hybrid car and have solar panels on my house

Professionally
- Collaborative—I am working on joint research projects with a colleague in Utah and another in the United Kingdom

- Cutting-edge—I regularly publish my research papers in the most forward-thinking professional journals
- Caring—I help find homes for retired racehorses
- Ambitious—I would like to write a successful book on equine genetics and raise funds to stop the hunting of wild horses
- Entrepreneurial—I would like to eventually open my own international research center and get grants from major universities

My Values
- Thrift
- Generosity
- Responsible stewardship of the planet
- Rationality
- Simplicity
- Humor

My Uniqueness
Personally

For a person with such an "out there" sense of humor, I am very serious about my work.

Professionally

It is unusual for someone to have achieved as much in the veterinary research field as I have at my age, and it is also unusual for someone who has achieved such wide recognition for her research efforts to still be a working veterinarian—to care for animals every day.

My Audience
Personally
- I am a member of three vegan groups:
    Don'tEatMeat.org
    KillLessHugMore.com
    AnimalsAreNotOurProperty.org
- I am a member of People for the Ethical Treatment of Animals.
- I am a member of the local Democratic club.
- My blog has 39 subscribers.

Professionally
- I want to attract the attention of top universities, so I have been speaking at major conferences of veterinary organizations and scientific institutes.
    - XYZ Organization
    - ABC Organization
    - DEF Organization

- I then follow up with meetings with other researchers I meet to see if we can combine our efforts.
    - Joe Smith, Ph.D. at GHI Organization
    - Mary Jones, head of research at JKL Hospital
    - Jane Doe, professor at MNO University

- I write three major grant proposals a year. In the past those have included
    - PQR Foundation
    - STU Award for Innovations in Biological Science
    - WXY Institute for Applied Medicine

My Gap Analysis
- I could be using my sense of humor more in my professional work. Although I want to be taken seriously, my field could benefit from occasional lightheartedness to alleviate some of the pressure I and my colleagues feel. I plan to start adding elements of humor to the beginning of my presentations.
- I might also be able to use humor to make my vegan ways more understandable to some of my friends who don't get it.
- I need to stop sending out really angry tweets about animal rights violations. If I want major universities to sponsor me, I need to soften my message and become more professional in all my communications.

Succeed with Brand Integrity

What are the odds an Israeli-born classically trained female violinist would engage the hearts and minds of the White House, the greatest rap stars and musicians of our age, and nearly a billion people in China? One woman and one small violin. Yet Grammy-winning hip-hop violinist Miri Ben-Ari performs over one hundred times a year and helps to sell millions of records worldwide. She is the ultimate example that one person with excellent handling of her tools, a unique offering, strong values, consistent remarkable performance, and a stunning appearance can create the ultimate brand.

When it comes to branding, Miri says, "It is important to choose something that you believe in and is an authentic match to who you really are. It will convince others to believe in you and your story. Don't try being someone you are not." While she was raised as a classical musician in Israel and recognized early for her potential by the legendary Isaac Stern, eventually Miri's spirit took her to America and her performance took her in a very different direction.

Hip-hop became her muse. *Rolling Stone* describes the pioneer's style as bringing "highbrow musicianship to the street, integrating everything from classical to R&B, klezmer to dancehall, and jazz to gangsta rap." Her strings are a vibrant musical voice and commentary alongside the tracks of some of the greatest artists of our time. When asked what part of her unique musical talents plays the biggest role in her identity, Miri says, "That would be the connection to a real art. Although my music is considered as commercial music, it is indeed complex. Sometimes it is arranged and orchestrated for over one hundred parts of orchestral instruments. The fact that I play the violin and grew up playing classical music helped me combining both worlds of classical and commercial."

The Grammy-winning violinist has performed and recorded alongside Britney Spears, Wynton Marsalis, Doug E. Fresh, Kanye West, Lil Wayne, and Akon. She has performed live in collaboration with Mariah Carey and Britney Spears. In 2011, Miri Ben-Ari joined Wyclef Jean onstage for a dazzling performance to honor former President Bill Clinton at the first annual Urban Zen Stephan Weiss Apple Awards for Donna Karan. The Urban Zen Foundation is guided by three initiatives: well-being, empowerment of children through education and the preservation of culture, and curator of several programs including Hope, Help & Rebuild Haiti. While Miri has played at Carnegie Hall for Clinton, she says she didn't practice for the standard Carnegie Hall audience. She practiced for her hip-hop fans, once again reinforcing this is a performer who has always had a clear vision of her audience.

Miri also understood how she had to master her channels to succeed and there was more than one way to approach the market. "My performance is definitely the driving force of my career," explains Miri. "I am not an artist that was created in the studio. I was introduced as a performer, as an act, and my job was to win over the audience. Because I am doing something different, I had to perform lots of shows in order to introduce myself and create room in the music world and industry."

With a rising awareness of her unique style, she attracted major sponsorship deals. "Your brand should represent you," she says, "your talent and your style. For example, I have done campaigns with companies such as RBK, Coca-Cola, and Pepsi that tried to capture the essence of me as an original artist.

"Yet we can't always control the message entirely," explains Miri. "Sometimes you learn about your brand from the perception of others no matter how hard you work to brand yourself in a certain way. It is important to know what you would like to accomplish as a brand but also to go with the flow and let things happen organically."

In 2011, Miri embraced her role as a Remarkable Woman Mentor, an honorable title bestowed by the First Lady of the United States, Michelle Obama, and in recognition of her support to numerous admirable causes around the globe. She was also invited by Yue-Sai Kan, the Oprah Winfrey of China, to perform at the Miss Universe China Reignwood Pageant—a nationally televised event watched in 900 million homes (over 90 percent of the country).

When performing, Miri always tries to deliver on her own brand promise, taking advice from an expert communicator by engaging and honoring her audience. "My friend, the legendary Donna Summer, told me one time something that I will always remember: she said that most people will meet you once in their lifetime and so you should make sure to make this one time very special."

BANK ON YOUR APPEARANCE

When you are a powerful woman, your appearance sends messages about you to your company, your clients, and to the world around you. In an era when moving images often replace still photography, and when meetings are held on camera via Skype or videoconferencing, your signature style can make or break the next opportunity. It's essential to make your looks support your brand and work for you in your chosen career.

Neither conventional beauty nor dress size is the game changer when it comes to winning hearts and minds through your appearance. Banking on your appearance comes down to creating a sense of personal style, one that fits and supports your feelings of confidence and control. When you radiate self-assurance, you naturally increase the power of your delivery and support the message of your brand.

Clothes Make the Woman

In the area of personal appearance, we would all do well to follow the example of two of the most influential women in the world, both of whom make themselves appear relatable, modest, and extremely elegant during the recession. The U.S. First Lady, Michelle Obama, has mixed couture pieces from Jason Wu and Jean Paul Gaultier with affordable ready-to-wear items from companies like J.Crew and Tory Burch, which makes her approachable to the American people. The Duchess of Cambridge, Catherine Middleton, mixes High Street items from Zara and Reiss with couture pieces by Alexander McQueen, Prada, and Ralph Lauren, garnering kudos for her frugality and down-to-earth nature in the first few months of her marriage to Prince William. Both women beautifully demonstrate that a contemporary and age-appropriate look, one that's dignified yet fashionable, will only enhance your brand.

Breaking the Masculine Style Habit

One of the most significant shifts in female fashion since the 1980s has been the fact that women no longer have to dress like men to earn respect in the hallways of power. Today, dressing like a man—in styles that hide our figures and our femininity—sends a disempowering message, and is often inauthentic. As we step into our power, we are permitted to express that we are women in charge. We are not aiming to be women "fitting in" to a man's world.

Beckie Klein and Martina Gordon, founders of the firm beckiemartina, re-stylists, which restyles women's closets and their wardrobes, have seen a great change in the way women approach dressing for work. "There's a huge shift from ten to fifteen years ago for the corporate woman and the way they had to dress and present themselves in order to be taken seriously," says Beckie. "The clothes were 'harder' and more masculine. We see these suits over and over again in our clients' closets. But we encourage them to let these outdated pieces go—there are more choices available today, which are feminine, flattering, and affordable while still appropriate in a business environment."

Even in the most conservative environments, it is now normal for clothing to follow the line of a woman's body. Whether you are a size 2 or a size 20, you look better when clothing follows your natural curves. The welcome addition of stretch material into most business suits means you can be comfortable and appropriate at the same time. We want women to seriously consider removing boxy jackets from their wardrobes.

Many women over thirty-five are often still trapped in the dress-for-success mentality of their early career days and are hesitant to break out and try a more stylish look at work. However, thinking you can wear clothing more than a decade out of fashion is unwise—this may send the message that you are out of touch with current reality. If you want to wear older pieces, take them to a great tailor and have them recut to reflect a contemporary silhouette. "Hopefully, we have left the corporate uniform back in the eighties and early nineties, when it was very prescribed," says Kathy Reilly, who owns the award-winning company Lifestylist Advisory, which focuses on building up lifestyle management platforms, private wealth institutions, and connecting them with luxury brands. "Now we can have our own new way to communicate the confidence and intelligence that we bring to our particular roles and not feel like we are wearing an outfit that someone else has picked out for us."

So how do you express your femininity in a very conservative business environment? "I think it's through jewelry, a shoe, a briefcase," says Kathy.

I am not a big fan of big earrings during the workday. I tend to be more conservative: gold or silver hoops, depending on what other jewelry I am wearing. With a briefcase you can communicate both luxury and sophistication through beautiful materials and detailing. There are some beautiful bags that have a bit of detail that don't look like the traditionally masculine briefcase. This adds a little bit of fashion edge. Your personal grooming also says a lot about you—beautifully done hair, well-applied makeup, and a couple of well-chosen accessories communicate that I am both appropriate and current.

Make Over Your Closet

Virtually all women who appear on television have been groomed and clothed by a professional stylist. This is because most women who appear in public—whether on camera, on a podium, or on a stage—will look more polished if they hire a professional to improve their look beforehand. Stylists are even becoming more common in the personal arena, too. For a relatively modest sum, you can hire a stylist to come to your home, review your wardrobe, and update your image. For Beckie and Martina, the best place to start is in a woman's closet, so that any shopping she does from that point on will be done with *intent*—and with the ultimate goal of building a versatile, functional wardrobe.

Once a woman "edits" her closet, Beckie and Martina find that her confidence rises tremendously. "How do appearance and power go hand in hand? A woman who looks like she's put some thought into her outfit and cares about how she looks naturally conveys a sense of confidence and power. It's important to shop for pieces that reflect the image you want to put out into the world but that also complement your personality—so that you look and feel 'in your skin.' The old adage of wearing your clothes, not letting your clothes wear you, is a good rule of thumb to go by," explains Beckie.

The team also sees their work as closet therapy because there are so many reasons women have trouble dressing, and part of their job is to get down to the bottom of these feelings. They notice that when women are challenged in their wardrobe, there is a domino effect. "Women shop for a lot of reasons, many of which have nothing to do with what their wardrobe needs," says Beckie. "And this rarely translates into a wardrobe that makes much sense. What Martina and I try to do is take the emotion out of shopping and create a wardrobe of flattering pieces that work well together."

Women don't have to have a beckiemartina restyling team to get started on revamping their looks for maximum power. The duo suggests that you ask a couple of girlfriends to come over, pop open a bottle of champagne, and invite them to go through your closet one evening for a few hours. Try on clothes and let them give you the thumbs-up and the thumbs-down.

BECKIEMARTINA'S CLOSET RULES

- Buy yourself a full-length mirror to see how outfits look.
- Start with an inventory of what you have. Do you have multiple items that look exactly the same? If so, choose one or two to keep and donate the rest.
- Make sure the fit of everything in your closet is correct and figure flattering as well as having a contemporary cut. If not, have them altered—you'd be surprised what a good tailor can do!
- Make a shopping list based on gaps from your inventory before you head out.
- Build the foundation of your wardrobe with well-fitting basics that you feel confident in.
- Create a "uniform" that works for your figure type and profession. This can be the basis of your signature style.
- To spice up your wardrobe with trendy items, we often recommend that you experiment with less expensive brands, as they are often, by definition, in this season and out the next.

It's especially important to redefine your message—and your physical presentation—when your life circumstances change. For example, Beckie and Martina have worked with women who are moving to the other coast or getting promoted. One of their clients was leaving a position at Google and relocating to California to work for Facebook. "She was a young, hip girl, and we found a lot of kind of hippy-dippy vintage clothes in her closet," says Martina. "But she needed to show Facebook a strong, cool, and in-charge look. We wanted her to look like she knew what she was doing. Her look needed to say, 'I am your boss, but I am as cool as you are.' So we had to find the nuances that sell."

Envision Your Style

Another useful exercise is to imagine yourself as you would wish to look at work and in your personal life. Keep a journal and write about what you would be wearing as your ideal self. Create a "vision board" on a laptop or a standard bulletin board: this could include clippings from magazines, books, and catalogs that reflect the styles you admire. You could also include photocopies, fabric swatches, or even paint chips—let your imagination be your guide. Look at those images and compare them with the way you see yourself today. Take a photo of the vision board and carry it with you when you shop. Arrange an appointment with a personal shopper. Share your vision board with her so that she can seek out pieces that conform to your vision but also fit your body type. As you purchase pieces over time you will be creating an appearance that enhances your brand and sends out the message you want the world to see.

Creating the Message Is Key

When you get dressed in the morning, you are sending a message about who you want to be and how you wish to be perceived. "As an executive woman, I work in the luxury space," says Kathy Reilly. "I also spend most of my days in the private wealth world, which is very conservative. Critical to my success is inspiring trust and confidence in myself and my capabilities. But I also need to inspire confidence in my taste level and sophistication, given the caliber of clientele that we work with. Every day my appearance needs to say that I understand the brands and experiences that you care about and that you can trust my judgment."

Even your hands send a message about you in a business environment. Kathy continues,

> I have a friend and client who is a very senior insurance-industry executive whose job entails having people sign significant insurance documents. So she always has to make sure her manicure is perfectly done,

because she is in front of families of significant wealth who are insuring their wine collection or cattle ranch or fine pieces of jewelry and they certainly can't be across the table from someone who has chipped nails. That would show a lack of attention to detail.

Put the Finishing Touches on Your Look

Your face and your hair are the key areas from where you're communicating if you're in leadership. "I think a lot of people underestimate the power of simple, little things like a beautiful manicure or a gorgeous blown-out hairstyle, particularly when you are going to be in a big presentation or you are meeting new people or interviewing for the first time," says Kathy Reilly. "I know those things are subtle; however, they are an investment that can yield a significant positive reaction."

Express Your Preparation Time

Rarely does a woman have the time for four to six hours of traditional high-end hair and makeup at salons before an event. In a world where Facebook and Twitter capture our every move, new services are popping up to give an instant makeover to busy women. At Vensette in New York City, which was featured in *Vogue* in March 2011, clients can pick a hair and makeup look on their website and arrange for hair and makeup artists to complete a look on location before an event in under ninety minutes beforehand for $250 for a daytime look, and $325 for an evening look. There are also classic hairstyles to choose from, including the blowout, the curl set, the chignon, and the ponytail. In 2011, Vensette took care of seventeen high-profile clients who attended the famous Met Costume Institute Gala at the Metropolitan Museum of Art in New York City, one of the most important fashion and business events of the year.

Vensette CEO and founder, former runway model turned financial analyst Lauren Remington Platt, saw a need in the market for the executive woman to get a polished, standardized makeup and hairstyle look in her home quickly before an event for a reasonable price. She explains,

We name all our looks, and one of the looks is called the CEO. The look comes with three different eye shadows of brown, gray, and black, the idea being that if you are a CEO and you have day meetings, you use the brown eye shadow. If you have a sort of after-dinner, late-afternoon-to-evening cocktail drinks, you get the gray. And if you have to go to a client dinner or black-tie event, you get the CEO with black eye shadow. It's a very conservative smoky eye but very toned down.

Embracing the Power of Your Appearance

Gone are the days when businesswomen avoided wearing eye shadow. In today's media-saturated world, we invite you to imagine the power that a polished and confident appearance can add to your brand. With some thoughtful preparation and careful editing, you can enhance the quality of your message by highlighting your beautiful assets. All women have the power to be beautiful, and it is time that we fearlessly embrace our feminine power to delight the eye.

REIGN OVER YOUR NETWORK

If you're looking for a new job, a way to enhance the status of your current career, or launching your first business, social networking is now the most important avenue to pursue effectively. Open communication across Linked-In, Facebook, Twitter, and Google+ has unlocked the gates to the ivory towers of CEOs, big business, and celebrities. Now, face-to-face networking is used to build on a foundation established in a digital world.

A Social Media Approach to Networking

In 1999, Melinda Emerson was a respected television producer with a big Rolodex who hated her job and needed a change. So she launched Quintessence Multimedia, a strategic communications and production company that creates marketing materials, videos, websites, and computer-based training. "I help people brand themselves and craft their messages so they can reach their target," says Melinda.

Melinda was named one of the top women in business in Pennsylvania and was honored by *Ebony* magazine as one of the thirty leaders of the future before her thirtieth birthday. She was invited to speak at workshops and leadership seminars on how she started her own business, and before long it was clear she needed to write a book to help get her message across. But she didn't have a platform, such as a TV or a radio show, from which to launch the book; she didn't have a blog or a Twitter account.

So eighteen months ahead of the launch for her book, *Become Your Own Boss in 12 Months,* Melinda worked with an expert who taught her how to use Twitter effectively to grow her network. She established an identity as @SmallBizLady, and she had ten thousand Twitter followers before her book came out. Thanks to her network on Twitter, LinkedIn, Facebook, and offline, her book became a bestseller and Forbes.com named her one of Top 20 women for entrepreneurs to follow on Twitter.

Today, Melinda creates content online that attracts more Twitter followers and influencers into her network. She blogs five times a week, tweets thirty times a day, and hosts the Twitter show #smallbizchat every Wednesday from 8 to 9 P.M. Eastern time. She is known as the "Oprah of Twitter" and a "social media black belt." She has even spoken at MIT about her approach to social media. Her mastery of social media has allowed her to create a safe and engaging environment in which small business owners and professionals alike can exchange ideas—and an environment in which she can fully leverage her brand.

Starting the Twitter Phase

One of the greatest advantages of Twitter is its ability to reach people of influence. The Twitter culture allows anyone to make contact with a celebrity, politician, or CEO, and an effective tweet often garners a personal response. It is one of the few platforms in which celebrities actually write their own messages. For example, Melinda has enjoyed conversations with MC Hammer, Barbara Corcoran, and Naveen Jain. With that in mind, as we said earlier, you have only 140 characters to strike up a conversation on Twitter, so craft your tweets wisely.

In addition, smart tweeters know their market inside out. As Melinda says, "I tweet the same every time. I do not waver. And I always know my customer and I tweet solutions-driven content. My customer is a professional woman, age thirty-plus, who is married with children, who wants to start or grow a profitable and sustainable small business. That's who I target and talk to consistently." And she talks to that person multiple times a day.

When you decide whom to follow, choose individuals, organizations, and groups that fall in line with your target audience and brand promise: that increases the likelihood that they will follow you back. As your audience grows, you may add five or ten Twitter followers a day—or more. Don't forget to request an RT, or retweet, which allows your audience to rebroadcast your messages to people you haven't tapped into yet. Study the tools of Twitter; if it feels terribly foreign, it's absolutely worth contacting a social media expert to help you learn the rules of engagement. Remember that the goal of using Twitter is to drive traffic and express your thought leadership and build relationships and partnerships.

Stand Out from the Noise

Although it's tempting to send mass emails to your contacts, be aware that recipients are increasingly buried in emails and that they're looking for unique and personal messages. Even holiday cards get lost in the information over-load. Melinda's approach, rather than mass emails or holiday cards, is to send Valentine's Day cards. She says, "I send Valentine's cards because I want my customers to know I love them. Holiday cards get lost in the sauce." This is an individual choice, and you will be the judge of what's appropriate, but the bottom line is that mass communication should be influential and effective—and that means choosing the occasion carefully.

Make Face-to-Face an Online Exchange, Too

If you want to grow your network online, one of the best things you can do is turn your offline contacts into online contacts as well. For example, when networking at an event, Melinda starts the process with a goal of making five new contacts face-to-face. If she has access to the guest list, she will research those five individuals in advance so that she can start a value-added conversation with them when she meets them in person. Her strategy is to "never be late for the reception, because the reception is the event. Once the reception is over and the meal begins—in other words, once you sit down—you can't network with anyone but the other nine people at your table." Then, once Melinda has made her five new contacts, she immediately connects with them on LinkedIn and follows them on Twitter.

In addition, we believe you should send your new contacts an email saying that you enjoyed meeting them and would like to stay in touch. This way, if they've already lost your business card, or don't use Linked-In regularly, they can easily save your contact information in their email accounts.

Follow Up When You Make New Contacts

When you're working on expanding the size and value of your network, you have to go back to basics. Often women attend an event and return to the office with dozens of business cards, and then drop the ball. When you get these business cards, you need to think ahead. Each new contact could represent another twenty potential contacts, and there are relationships to build with the people you just met. Don't leave a million dollars on the table.

We recommend that you load these new contacts into your email address book, create a category, and then add a note to remind yourself where you met them. It's also a good idea to add anything that was interesting in their conversation that you can use when you can connect again. For example, did the woman you met at the conference mention she has children, likes golf, raises money for breast cancer awareness, or paints in her free time? Does she serve on a community, corporate, or country club board? Make sure you write these details down, because six months later you won't remember them.

Take Your Online Network Offline

Just as you bring your face-to-face contacts into your online network, you can also bring your online contacts into your bricks-and-mortar world. This approach has worked wonders for Cynthia Greenawalt-Carvajal, a contributor to the *New York Times* bestseller *Masters of Networking* and the *Wall Street Journal* bestseller *Masters of Success*. Cynthia is a successful entrepreneur and investor, as well as a speaker, writer, and educator whose lectures are often about the power of social capital. A graduate of the Wharton School of Business, she helps entrepreneurs, community leaders, and executives develop their social capital and increase their return on relationships. Cynthia believes that the best way to accelerate a relationship, and create one in which referrals and trust flourish, is to invite your online network to offline events. "Facebook and LinkedIn get you to the door, and then it's up to you to take action," says Cynthia. "Then it's time to leverage that relationship face-to-face."

Cynthia suggests that you identify events in your calendar to which you can invite one or more of your online contacts whom you'd like to get to know better.

We can use Facebook and LinkedIn as a way to "water" the relationships we already have. The real fertilizing and heavy-duty work is making sure the seed turns into a fruit-bearing plant—so reach out and invite people to something. I sent out almost one hundred *individual emails* to women I've met over the last year saying, "Hey, I'm going to this event, want to join me?" It was an event celebrating National Women's Day, and I invited several women who really impressed me. Many of them couldn't make it, but they responded to say thanks for thinking of them and asked how I was. It was a simple thing that served as a huge investment in my social capital.

Face-to-face events also offer an opportunity to introduce your guests to one another. As Cynthia says, "When I promote one person to another, it's the ultimate way to win that person over, because you're making a personal investment in him or her." You are essentially giving your seal of approval to those individuals, helping them to move forward and create success.

When you are invited to an event, think, "Who else in my network needs me to connect them to this opportunity?" A great networker serves her community as well as creates her own opportunities.

TIPS FOR SUCCESSFUL FACE-TO-FACE EVENTS
RSVP

When people send you an invitation, reply immediately. Even if you can't go or you're not interested in attending, take ten seconds to respond. We often tell ourselves that we'll reply later, but we never do, because the invitation gets buried in our in-box. Take a moment as soon as you receive an invitation to say, "Thank you so much for thinking of me. I'm sorry I can't make it." Cynthia Greenawalt-Carvajal adds that if you want that ten-second reply to have an even bigger impact on that relationship, throw in a question like, "So, what's new with you and how can I support what you're working on?"

Wake Up the Conversation

Engage intelligently. Everyone asks, "So what do you do?" The phrase serves its purpose initially, but then you need to move the ball forward to really make a connection. Consider using the following questions:

- Where do you want to be in five years?
- What are you passionate about?
- What do you do that's really fun?

Let Your Passions Guide You

When you decide to network, start by connecting with people who love what you love. After all, networking does not have to take place at a conference or in the office. In fact, one of the best ways to start your network is by connecting with the people in your personal life. Cynthia went on a quest to find passionate people in the art world when she wasn't being fulfilled at her corporate job. She zigzagged through the art galleries near her home, adding her name to the guest book at every gallery that interested her. "Within a couple weeks of doing this, I started getting all these invitations to these art openings. When I attended these events, this put me in an environment where I was surrounded by people who loved what they were doing: the artists featured at the opening exuded passion for what they were up to. The gallery owners were having a blast being in the business of art, and the collectors were successful people doing what they loved, buying art. That experience changed my life." By default, Cynthia started meeting movers and shakers because her mission was to be energized and engaged with others who were inspired by their lives. That positive approach is also a winning one.

Whether you network online or face-to-face, remember that the strongest connections will form when you express an authentic interest in the people you connect with. You will not feel an equal level of connection to every person with whom you exchange a business card, so focus on the genuine feeling of excitement you feel when you make a true link—and follow through. Your network will go from being just a collection of names to a truly valuable resource.

MASTER YOUR SPHERE OF INFLUENCE

There is something very satisfying about the concept of mastery. It means we have gone beyond the apprenticeship stage, through the journeyman stage of working at our trade, and into the apex of expertise in our field. We know our field through years of study, trial and error, and hard work. We are now ready to step up to the next level. As a respected expert, we are now ready to be considered a thought leader, someone who can speak with wisdom and authority. How do we move into this level of mastery? How do we rise from being one of the many respected professionals in our field into being considered one of the most respected examples of excellence? As a master we no longer just learn, we also teach, inspire, and set the vision for our area of competence. We can begin to influence government policy in a way that is beneficial to our entire country. We can step up and serve on major corporate boards, thus affecting the lives of millions of employees and customers. This is another of the many positive faces of power. It's time to take things up a notch—we are ready to do it.

There are wonderful women today who have embraced the challenge of mastery of their fields, and who are having high impact on their area of expertise. We spoke to Sofia Adrogué, partner in the law firm of Looper, Reed & McGraw in Houston, Texas, where she leads business litigation and consultation matters. Sofia was born in Buenos Aires, Argentina, and came to the United States in 1975, when her father, a top physician, won a research grant to work in Boston, Massachusetts, at Tufts University School of Medicine. He was so impressed by the opportunities in the United States that the family (including her mother and four siblings) stayed when he accepted a position as a professor at Baylor College of Medicine in Houston. Sofia won a Board of Governors' Scholarship to Rice University, where she graduated magna cum laude, Phi Beta Kappa, in 1988. She then attended the University of Houston Law Center, again on a full competitive academic scholarship, and graduated magna cum laude, Orders of the Coif and Barons, in 1991. Subsequent to clerking for the U.S. Court of Appeals, Fifth Circuit, Sofia began practicing law in 1992, focusing on complex business litigation, very much a male-dominated specialty. Close to her fortieth birthday, she returned to school, this time to Boston, her first port of entry in the United States, to Harvard Business School to attend the Owner/President Management (OPM) Program. She was elected the U.S. Keynote Graduation Speaker for HBS OPM 37, ostensibly the first woman in the history of OPM, as well as U.S. Class Representative. Sofia has become a highly respected, honored, and influential lawyer in Houston. In the state of Texas, with over eighty thousand attorneys, and in the city of Houston, with more than twenty thousand lawyers, Sofia at the young age of forty-four has risen above her peers in remarkable ways. Among her many awards, Sofia is a National Diversity Council Most Powerful and Influential Woman of Texas; a Greater Houston Women's Chamber of Commerce Hall of Fame Inductee; a Texas Women's Chamber of Commerce "Blazing Star"; a Texas Executive Women "Woman on the Move"; a Houston Chronicle Channel 11 "Texas Legend"; an ABC Channel "Woman of Distinction"; a Houston Jaycees "Outstanding Houstonian"; a Texas Jaycees "Outstanding Texan"; as well as a U.S. Jaycees "Outstanding American." Most impressively, the city of Houston has recognized with a proclamation of July 10, 2004, as Sofia Adrogué Day.

Sofia has created a life that is built on her three passions: career, community service, and family. Her achievements as a fund-raiser for charity are formidable, with a focus on education, leadership, and women's issues. She has served as the president of Girl's Inc. of Greater Houston, served on the board of trustees of the United Way of the Texas Gulf Coast, the Memorial Hermann Foundation, and Theatre Under the Stars, among a litany of other Houston nonprofits. She conceived and executed the inaugural Latin American Gala for the Museum of Fine Arts Houston in 2005, which sold out and raised more than $500,000 in its first year. Now a member of the board of trustees at the MFAH, Sofia continues to assist as the Gala now raises more than $1 million biennially. She has been married to fellow Rice graduate Sten Gustafson for nineteen years, and has three children, Sloane, Schuyler, and Stefan. She reveals that making time to address all three passions has her living a life that is "caffeinated and oxygenated," as she says—"caffeinated because I consume a lot of it to do what it takes for me to prepare, perspire, and persist. But then it is also oxygenated, because it comes back to a life lived with passion."

Sofia is quick to add that pursuing a life of mastery does mean a great deal of hard work and that the concept of balance has to be seen as quite fluid. She has learned to focus on what is most important and delegate the rest.

> It requires a lot of sleep deprivation; that said, I have been inordinately fortunate to keep my triad of passions. I've been able to keep my career, my community service, and my family. I would lie to you if I were to tell you that it is always in balance. I think that is a complete misnomer. I don't think it can be a balance. I very much "balance" only in quotations. To me, it's actually about asymmetry; I prioritize as necessary, and truly outsource what I believe to be my non-core functions. A lot of less critical tasks in life must be negotiable if you are to focus and succeed with your priorities.

At forty-four, Sofia has created a very distinctive brand for herself, built on what she calls her five P's: preparation, perspiration, persistence, passion, and panache. Preparation, perspiration, and persistence speak to the need to be truly competent in your field in order to be powerful. Sofia demonstrates technical competence through her successful law practice and her prolific legal writing and speaking engagements. She notes: "It's all incumbent upon the bottom line; you have to have formidable competence. If you do not have technical competence, the knowledge, preparation, and judgment, it is a nonstarter."

Sofia's take on panache, which she calls "most equivalent to a brand," is her distinctive mane of blond hair, her perfect red lipstick, and a full-bodied laugh. She appreciates the saying "the higher the hair, the closer to God." She encourages other women to develop a distinctive appeal, their brand, even in conservative professions like law.

Now what is it about your particular panache? What is it that differentiates you from the others? It may be something that people hyperscrutinize, as it is to some degree for me. Upon first glance, they don't necessarily first associate me with someone who finished among the top of my law school class . . . or that I went to university and law school on a full scholarship. They may think I am trying to look a particular way, to look particularly feminine, or to be a bit flamboyant. I am not. That said, I think it is an advantage to have a unique brand—your panache, defined and executed as you will.

She likes to point out that her five P's are written boldly, with a big red pencil. "It is not about when you go forward and succeed in all that you learn, but it's about when you make those formidable mistakes, and that's when you need the red pencil. You want it red because they should be high on the radar, but there have to be mistakes, and they're going to be bold sometimes. The beauty is, of course, you can erase and move forward. You have faced adversity, overcome it, and learned from it."

How did Sofia go from being one of many practicing Houston attorneys to mastering her sphere of influence? Clearly she worked hard in her field and put in the extra time to publish articles in law journals, which led to speaking engagements and professional visibility. She also realized the value of working with women who were older than she and developed her passion for community involvement through her exposure to them. This exposure led to even greater visibility in the community at large, beyond the legal field. Due to her performance as a fund-raiser and as a leader generally, her influence grew.

With regard to community service, quite frankly, I got very lucky. A small group of powerful women ten years my senior were inspired by a national organization, Girls Inc., and recruited me almost from its inception to assist with Girls Inc. of Greater Houston. They heard that I had the drive and energy and was interested in the empowerment of women and girls generally. Well, I was quite young, knew nothing about nonprofits, myopically focused, working up to three thousand hours a year at a top national litigation boutique, and I was about to have my first child—a girl. Bottom line, I said, "Of course." Girls Inc. of Greater

Houston just celebrated its fifteenth anniversary. I've chaired the board, the advisory board, and the annual luncheon (several times). My most recent passion within Girls Inc. has been to assist in raising the funds for scholarships, mentor the recipients, and follow their trajectory to growth and success as we empower them to be strong, smart, and bold. The most amazing aspect is that I now share this passion and endeavor with my daughters Sloane and Schuyler, past co-chairs with me in our 2010 annual luncheon.

Indicative of her belief in self-scrutiny and reflection for further improvement and continuous growth, Sofia also likes to point out that, as she says, "Your soul is nonnegotiable." You must have an internal set of values and integrity that is not for sale or up for discussion. This bedrock must guide all your decisions and is the key to developing the respect and trust that are the basis of your mastery.

MASTER YOUR SPHERE OF INFLUENCE

- Practice Sofia's five P's
    Preparation
    Persistence
    Perspiration
    Passion
    Panache

- Develop true technical competence in your field.
- Share your knowledge by writing for professional journals and lecturing.
- Seize opportunities that are offered to you for greater exposure.
- Engage in the broader community by working with nonprofits you care about.
- Focus on your top priorities and delegate nonessential functions.
- Maintain your integrity and remember your soul is nonnegotiable.

GET ON CORPORATE BOARDS

There is exciting evidence that our entire society can begin to change when female mastery infiltrates the highest levels of corporations, at the board level. Linda Tarr-Whelan was the U.S. representative to the UN Commission on the Status of Women under the Clinton administration. She is a Demos Distinguished Senior Fellow, and works tirelessly to encourage more women to take on leadership roles in government and the private sector. She is on the advisory council of Pax World, a mutual fund family that invests in companies that promote women and advances the notion of gender equality as an investment concept. She is actively studying models of female leadership both in the United States and globally, and has written a book called *Women Lead the Way*. She runs conferences all over the world and still consults regularly for the United Nations.

Linda points out that women bring monetary value to corporate leadership. A 2007 study by the research organization Catalyst decisively showed that companies that have at least one woman on their boards generate higher returns than companies whose boards are entirely male. The study, titled "The Bottom Line: Corporate Performance and Women's Representation on Boards," looked at the financial data from the Fortune 500's largest U.S. companies during the period from 2001 to 2004.[3] Companies with at least one woman on their board of directors had a higher return on equity, return on sales, and return on invested capital than those companies whose boards were all male. This is great news for you as a shareholder: companies with women on the board will make more money for you.

Linda notes that having at least three women on a company's board seems to make an even bigger difference. "One of the areas we targeted for action is what I call the thirty percent solution. Until you have a critical mass of women, you are just not going to be able to change the way things are done. But at that thirty percent, decisions are changed because the people making them have changed." The Catalyst study confirms this fact. Fortune 500 companies with three or more female board members did the best of all the companies studied, outperforming the average company by 4 to 5 percent.[4]

Linda explained that, outside the United States, governments are mandating a higher participation of females on corporate boards, and this is leading to significant positive changes. In Norway, for example, there is a law that requires that 40 percent of all board seats on public companies go to women. In tandem with that ruling, a training program for women leaders, called the Professional Boards Program, was created to get the women ready for this challenge. France, Iceland, and Spain have also mandated that public companies have women on their boards. In Australia, companies are required to set their own goals about diversity on boards and then report on their progress. In Denmark, Finland, Sweden, and Israel, companies are directed by their government to takes steps to ensure gender diversity on boards.[5]

Interestingly, once Norway passed its law, there were immediate steps taken in the United Kingdom, according to Linda.

> When Norway changed its laws, all of a sudden some of the top execs in England thought, "We're going to lose all our best women to Norway, if we don't watch out." They were pushed by Peninah Thomson, a top executive coach who runs the company Praesta (www.praesta.co.uk), to come up with mentoring initiatives. Peninah set up a program which first worked with the FTSC 100 and has now expanded to the FTSC 250. The program is actually for CEOs of FTSC 100 or 250 companies to mentor women cross-industry and cross-company for potential board seats. And, what's most interesting to me, first of all, is that it has expanded, which I thought was really interesting because they're overcoming a lot. And when I met with her in 2010, sixty-two of the 100 FTSC 100 CEOs, no one less than CEO, were doing these mentoring programs. One of the other interesting things was that many of the CEOs said that they had learned as much from the women as they were able to teach about what women could add as board members.

It is exciting to imagine what would happen in the United States if 62 percent of the CEOs of the top one hundred public companies were personally mentoring women and grooming them for board positions. Linda notes that there are no U.S. government policy initiatives that mandate gender diversity on boards in the United States. The SEC now requires public companies to disclose their diversity practices when they hire directors, but leaves it to the companies themselves to define "diversity"—and for many companies, that may not include having women on the board.[6] However, if U.S. corporations continue to report the number of women on their boards, as companies do in other countries, this could spark change. Corporations like to see what their competitors are doing, and if it becomes more widely understood that female board members translate into an increase in corporate wealth, then nondiverse companies will get interested in taking action.

In the absence of government or SEC requirements on the issue of gender equality in senior management and on boards, some large U.S. shareholders are starting to bring pressure to bear on corporations. The Inter Organization Network (ION), which tracks the number of women on public boards and promotes shareholder activism, reported in 2011 that certain top institutional shareholders of mutual funds, as well as the state pension fund of Connecticut, are working to achieve change. For example, the Calvert Group, a mutual fund company, has created a set of investment principles focused on supporting companies that have women on boards and in senior management. They work with corporations by providing guidelines for board nominating committees, developing language for diversity policies, and launching shareholder resolutions aimed at getting public companies to add women to their boards. Pax World has created a mutual fund that invests in companies that promote gender equality and actively votes no on all-male board of directors slates.

In addition, state government officials invest huge sums on behalf of their states, and can have a big impact on diversity policies. The 2011 ION report notes that state treasurer Denise Nappier of Connecticut has actively worked to make sure that women and minority candidates are included in board searches conducted by companies in which state funds are invested.

ACTIONS YOU CAN TAKE TO GET WOMEN ON BOARDS

1. Exercise your rights as a shareholder:
   - Vote no or withhold your vote for corporate board nominations in companies that fail to include women directors.
   - Write to the CEOs, board chairs, and nominating committees and explain your actions.
   - Attend annual shareholder meetings and raise questions about the board's composition.
   - Support shareholder resolutions that seek greater board diversity.

2. Monitor the actions of all the mutual funds in which you invest:
   - Hold the fund managers accountable for their proxy-voting guidelines and for their votes in board elections that do not include women.
   - Communicate your views directly to those responsible for exercising the proxies and adopting the guidelines, as well as to the trustees of the fund group involved.

3. When making new investment decisions, consider the number of women in a company's leadership before you invest.

4. Encourage the treasurer of your state to follow the example of Denise Nappier in Connecticut and those other state treasurers who have made gender diversity a governance issue relevant to their investment decisions.

5. Encourage your colleagues, friends, neighbors, and fellow graduates of your alma mater to join you in taking action.[7]

Step Up to the Board Challenge

In addition to investing in—and profiting from—companies that have women on their boards of directors, you can also consider serving on a board of directors yourself. Serving on a board is an exciting challenge and a chance to exercise your power at the highest corporate level. If you have a strong corporate career and envision yourself one day joining a board of directors, there are things you need to do now to prepare for this unique challenge.

We know that women are not well represented on boards in the United States. The 2011 ION report states that in the fourteen regions represented by ION members, women hold between 8.3 percent and 18.4 percent of board seats.[8] Women of color are barely represented, holding between 0 percent and 3 percent of board positions. We certainly have a long way to go to reach Norway's mandated level of 40 percent female representation on boards. However, this constitutes an opportunity for women who can qualify for these openings and are available to step up as pressure mounts to include females.

Get the Right Career Experience

Currently, most corporate board positions are offered to CEOs and other "C-suite" executives of public companies, such as CFOs. If you want to get on a board, the best way to qualify is to serve as the CEO of a public company. Clearly there is an argument to be made that it is not necessary to be a CEO to add value to a board, but the reality is that most board searches start with CEOs. Male CEOs often develop friendships with other CEOs and then populate each other's boards. This can leave women out of the loop entirely, since there are very few female CEOs in the United States.

We spoke with Lee Hanson, vice chairman of Heidrick & Struggles, a top executive search firm with a strong record of placing women on corporate boards. She notes that the talent pool for board searches has expanded beyond CEOs to other types of senior executives.

> Boards have to be more open in terms of their thinking about different skill sets and backgrounds. There still is a strong preference for operating experience, either at the CEO or other senior management level. But we've also seen a lot more interest over the years for functional expertise—particularly for CFOs of public companies but also beyond that we've looked at people with CIO backgrounds, at heads of human resources or general counsel backgrounds. Chairs of nominating committees have developed an expanded view of what kinds of skill sets are valuable to a board. It just opens many more doors than it used to when there was such strong pressure to exclusively consider sitting or retired CEOs.

The first step to landing a board seat is to get the right corporate experience and to demonstrate success at your job. The more you can showcase an ability to build a strong division, the more likely it is that you will be tapped for larger assignments and eventually move up to the C-suite.

Contact Board Development Groups

Once you have the right corporate credentials, you can begin to take advantage of the mentoring programs that are springing up all over the country. Lee Hanson recommends Women Corporate Directors (womencorporate directors.com), a membership organization of a thousand female board members who serve on twelve hundred boards around the world. At least 85 percent of members are on the boards of public companies, and another 15 percent are either sitting on major nonprofit boards or are being prepared to sit on boards. Another good organization is DirectWomen (DirectWomen.org), which identifies, develops, and supports female attorneys as candidates for corporate boards. An organization with a similar mission is the Financial Women's Assocation, which helps women in finance achieve board positions. A great activist organization is 2020 Women on Boards, which wants to see the ratio of women on the boards of U.S. public companies increase to 20 percent by 2020. They are actively measuring the progress of the Fortune 1000 companies in achieving this goal, and are encouraging the use of social media to spark shareholder activism in support of the cause.

Network with Influential Male CEOs

Another great way to get considered for boards is to do what men have always done—make friends with male CEOs and ask them for their help. The CEO of your own company may even be willing to promote you for board membership to his friends. You can often interact with male CEOs by serving on nonprofit boards or by asking them to mentor you. Another great way to connect with male CEOs is by fund-raising for your college, graduate business school, or law school. Ability to be a great fund-raiser will bring you to the attention of important alumni, including CEOs. Men are often very pleased to help ambitious women succeed and can recommend you to their friends who may be looking for board candidates.

Introduce Yourself to Search Firms

It is important that you make sure that the major search firms know who you are and that you are interested in serving on a board. Lee Hanson notes that the first board seat is the most difficult to obtain; after that, it gets much easier. Make sure you are in the database of the top executive search firms: Heidrick & Struggles, Russell Reynolds Associates, Korn/Ferry International, and Spencer Stuart. Lee notes that boards may be looking for candidates outside their industry, or for an expertise not currently represented on the board. Boards need to look at the ages of other directors, the variety of experience on the board, and then—of course—diversity issues, including race and gender. As a candidate, it is up to you to use all your resources to get that first board seat. As Lee says, "It's your responsibility to make it happen."

PARTICIPATE IN YOUR COMMUNITY

One of the most satisfying ways to exercise your power is to participate in your community. We all can feel overwhelmed at times by our family responsibilities, career ambitions, and personal challenges. Yet we reap many rewards when we decide to become involved with the world beyond our immediate concerns. Society has many problems, and the only way to make them go away is to tackle them head-on. Every religious tradition urges its followers to help others and to see to the needs of our planet. The simple fact that we are alive means that we have an obligation to take care of the place where we live and the people who live there with us.

Fortunately, Americans live in one of the most charitably minded countries in the world. According to Giving USA 2011, Americans gave an impressive $211 billion to charities in 2010 through personal contributions.[9] Another $22.8 billion was left to charities in estate bequests, and family foundations contributed an additional $19.5 billion. That brings the total of individual gifts, charitable bequests, and family foundation gifts to $254 billion, or 87 percent of the total amount of money given to charities in the United States. There are now more than 1.2 million tax-exempt institutions registered in the United States receiving these contributions.

We are not just giving money; we are giving substantial amounts of volunteer time, too. According the 2010 Nonprofit Sector in Brief report, 26.8 percent of adults volunteered for or through a nonprofit organization in 2009. An amazing 7.1 percent of the adult population volunteered on an average day, corresponding to 17.1 million volunteers per day. Americans contributed a staggering total of 15 *billion* volunteer hours in 2009, which is the equivalent of providing 8.8 million paid employees to charities. At average private-sector wages, the volunteer time given was worth nearly $279 billion.[10] If we add our $254 billion in charitable contributions to our $279 billion worth of volunteer time, we find that Americans contributed $533 billion to help others in a single year.

But participating in your community allows you to receive as well as give—you will not only gain a sense of personal satisfaction, you will also increase your power. Although the simple human need to do good works is reason enough to help others, you should also consider the many additional benefits that will accrue as you focus your attention on those in need.

Widen Your Network and Scope of Influence

The first benefit that you will receive for participating in your community is a chance to meet interesting, positive, generous, and committed people—some of whom may be very powerful. Like you, your fellow volunteers are taking time from their busy lives to give to others, which make them good people to get to know. If you spend all your time focused on work, you might never meet people outside your industry, and volunteering is a great way to change that. Whether you meet them face-to-face while working on a project or connect with them through a charity's Facebook page, your new friends can open the door to many opportunities you may never have dreamed of. We know a young woman named Elizabeth who was buried in her job as a banker but decided to make time to volunteer at a local soup kitchen on the weekends. She met a retired senior executive who was so taken with her commitment and great ideas that she was asked to join the board of the nonprofit. This led to an introduction to several wealthy board members, who in turn introduced her to lucrative business opportunities not normally offered to someone her age. She was also asked to join other nonprofit boards, and her power within the community grew rapidly.

Broaden Your Skill Set

One of the greatest benefits you can get from volunteering is the chance to broaden your skill set. If you are an accountant by day but want to spend more time working with people rather than numbers, a volunteer position can provide the solution. If you would like to try your hand at managing people, you can learn this skill by offering to run a project and managing the other volunteers. If you want to demonstrate your ability to move into a sales position, acting as a fund-raiser allows you to assign a real economic value to your efforts. If you are a mom wanting to reacquaint yourself with the work world, volunteering can be the prefect bridge between home and office, and can give you great credentials for your résumé.

Renew Your Spirit

Perhaps the best reward of all is the spiritual renewal you feel when you help someone. Whether you teach a child to read, help a victim of domestic violence get a job, or comfort a cancer patient, the response that you get from those you help will surely feed your soul. By doing good in the world, you remind yourself that there are good people out there and that many times a helping hand can really turn someone's life around. The pure joy you feel when you see a child read his first sentence, for example, is priceless. If another person ever once helped you, you can feel the satisfaction of passing on help to another, of "paying it forward." Your renewed spirit of gladness will shine through all your activities; don't be surprised if people ask you why you look so good.

Participate in a Way That Makes Your Heart Sing

Although we should use these criteria for everything we do, we should particularly choose to participate in ways that we are passionate about and bring us joy. The world is full of causes that cry out for volunteers, so we can't go wrong no matter which way we choose. We will find ourselves much more energized if we choose to participate in a way that we are truly interested, rather than because it is the popular cause of the moment. Look for opportunities where your skills, time availability, and interests match the requirements. We'd like to share with you the story of two remarkable women who are participating and making a huge difference in their communities.

Tell Your Story and Heal Hearts All Over the World

Rita Cosby is an Emmy Award–winning journalist who has interviewed world leaders and famous celebrities. She was the host of her own television shows on Fox and MSNBC, but the most important story she ever broke was solving the mystery surrounding her estranged father. Rita's father, a Polish immigrant, left the family abruptly when she was a teenager. She lost contact with him, and her mother never discussed his mysterious past. After her mother's death, Rita and her brother made a life-changing discovery in a storage locker. She writes,

> We discovered an old tattered leather suitcase containing war mementos from another time and place: a worn Polish Resistance armband, a rusted metal tag with a prisoner number and the word, "Stalag IV B," stamped into it, plus a card with secret code names on it, and the identity card for an ex-POW named Ryszard Kossobudzki. At that moment, I was overcome with emotion, and wept, realizing who my father really was and imagining what he had endured as a starving POW. I knew that whatever pain I had suffered, not having a father present in my life for decades, was nothing compared to the pain he must have suffered at the hands of his brutal Nazi captors in WWII.

Rita then reunited with her eighty-five-year-old father, who finally told her his amazing tale. He had been a child resistance fighter in Poland against the Nazis starting at the age of thirteen. He was captured and endured brutality and starvation in a Nazi prison camp, later escaped, and was finally rescued by the Americans. He and his surviving compatriots swore never to speak about their experiences. He had felt that his story was too upsetting to share with her when she was a child. Rita wrote her father's story in the moving *New York Times* bestseller *Quiet Hero: Secrets from My Father's Past.* She gives a percentage of the profits to benefit the USO's Operation Enduring Care, which benefits wounded soldiers returning from Iraq and Afghanistan and their families.

Rita travels around the country and the world speaking to military families, veterans groups, and active-duty soldiers. She inspires them with her father's story and uses her celebrity to help fund-raise for military causes. Rita says,

> I'm a big believer in our troops. For example, I met with the 77th Sustainment Brigade in New Jersey out of Fort Dix right before they took off for Iraq, and they asked me if I could come and speak at a farewell

breakfast. I helped raise money for that breakfast for the troops and their families to be able to have a send-off right before they were going off to the battle zone. I felt as an American, it was the least I could do to try to help to bring some much-deserved attention to these men and women. I spent the morning with them, and it may have been one of the last breakfasts they'll spend with their families. I try to do things which I hope make a difference, and with causes that are near and dear to my heart. I think the key is finding ones where you feel that you can make a real impact, and also that have personal meaning to you, like for me the USO and helping our wounded warriors.

Rita's mother died of lung cancer, so she also gives time to cancer causes and to causes related to children. She realizes that her celebrity is one of the best things she can offer, because her presence brings media attention and often a bigger crowd turnout to the charities she visits.

Rita challenges us to think creatively about not having enough time to help out.

It's funny, but if you really look at it, you can do a lot in a day. There was one time I went to six events in a night . . . and I felt like I spent at least some substantive time with each. I just looked at the map and said, "Okay, I can go to this one first and then make it to this one and next go to this one," and I told each event organizer about the tight time frame. I literally clocked my time and said, "Okay, I've got to be here. I can only be a half an hour at this one, half an hour at this one, half an hour at this one." I started, I think, at five o'clock, and I even got on stage at two or three of them and spoke. So you'll find that if you set your priorities, you can actually get a lot done.

Rita feels strongly that by giving to others, she gives to herself.

I think that you could be a rich and successful person but poor in spirit if you don't give back. To me the most gratifying moments of my life have not been in front of the camera lights. They have been helping others and trying to give back in the community. I think there's a lot of ways that you can do it. Whether you're rich in the pocketbook or rich in spirit, it doesn't matter. I always try no matter how crazy my schedule is and how demanding my schedule is; to me it's not a gift to the group that I show up. It's a gift to myself. Some of the greatest people I've met in my life are the people you'll never hear the names of on the news, but who have done extraordinary things. Every day I feel like it's a reminder of how blessed I am and how fortunate I am to be able to give back.

Lauren Bush also talked to us about the joy she feels participating in her community. For Lauren, a former model, fashion designer, and a granddaughter of former president George H. W. Bush, the focus has been on creating a simple message that will move millions to act in behalf of hungry children. Lauren created FEED Projects, an organization whose brand promise is this: Buy a FEED bag and you will ensure that a hungry child in the developing world gets one nutritious meal in school every day for one year.

The FEED website explains that school feeding is one of the most effective solutions to stopping hunger and breaking the poverty cycle. So the charity has partnered with the UN to provide a solution. In seventy-four countries, the UN World Food Programme (WFP) offers a nutrient-packed meal to children in school. And for many children, a school lunch is the only meal they will eat all day. FEED Projects' goal is to support this program through the sale of FEED bags.

So far, FEED has raised more than $50 million for this worthy cause. Partnership is a key ingredient to its success. The group interacts with donors via Twitter and the Web, where people post pictures of FEED bags that they have spotted in their travels. There is an active Facebook page, where FEED posts successes and members share their stories. The group has partnered with major corporate retailers to distribute FEED bags throughout the country.

Lauren says that, for her, simplicity is the key to the success: "My whole philosophy is to keep things as simple as possible. There's too much stimulus in the world: I think one of the reasons people respond to us is that we keep our message as simple as possible. This bag feeds one kid in school for one year. Done. If you want to learn more, we have more information, but it's not overwhelming."

She also spoke to us about the personal satisfaction she receives from meeting the children whom her project is feeding.

When I travel, I'm able to visit many different kinds of programs that are happening on the ground. And the kids are just so universally great. They're so innocent and curious, and even though there are language and cultural barriers, it's so much easier to interact and break through those with kids. When you visit, you see the hardships that people are living with, and as a fellow human being, you can't help but be empathetic to those plights. It makes me want to do more. I feel so blessed to be born where I was born and when I was born. Because of that I never had to worry about where my next meal was coming from.

Lauren notes that many of her friends are involved in charity work, but they would rather give to an online appeal than attend a charity gala. Charitable giving, for the younger generations, is moving to the Web, where the goal is to get smaller donations from larger groups and individuals, which also ensures that most of the funds go directly to the cause. She adds, "Young people who may not have a large check to write to a massive humanitarian agency still can feel active and involved in many different ways. They don't have to dedicate their lives to serving in the Peace Corps. It can be as simple as running an online fund-raising campaign with their friends or throwing little fund-raisers or get-togethers of their own creation."

Participate in the Political Process

We would be remiss if we didn't mention the opportunity we have as women in the United States to vote in elections and run for office. It is important to remember that women got the right to vote as recently as 1920, thanks to the tireless efforts of our foremothers, who endured ridicule and jail time in order to get us the right to go to the polls. Whether we choose to serve on a school board, canvass for the local city councilperson, or volunteer for a presidential candidate, we are very lucky to be able to exercise our political power.

It is encouraging to learn that women are becoming extremely effective in our national government. Linda Tarr-Whelan told us that a study published in 2010 titled "The Jackie (and Jill) Robinson Effect: Why Do Congresswomen Outperform Congressmen?" demonstrates the power that women are bringing to the U.S. Congress.[11] The study covered the period from 1984 to 2004 and found that, on average, women in Congress introduce more bills, attract more cosponsors, and bring home more money for their districts than their male counterparts do. The study also found that women deliver roughly 9 percent more discretionary spending to their districts than men. This is great news for you as a taxpayer: if you vote in more women, your district will get more money and your government will work harder for you. As this book goes to press, 17 percent of congressional representatives are female, up from 3 percent in 2009.[12]

These statistics constitute just one more piece of evidence that women can increase their power by participating in their communities. Whether it's as local as reading to children in a homeless shelter or as global as fund-raising online to protect women from sexual slavery, pick an area you are passionate about and dedicate some time to helping others. You can run for office in your hometown or travel the world to speak out in behalf of those who have no voice. Your voice matters, your power can help, and your contribution will definitely change the world.

CHAPTER 5

CRISIS AND LOSS

THE FIFTH PEARL OF FINANCIAL WISDOM:
A Woman Under Pressure Must Act with Grace

THERE IS AN OLD ADAGE we call to mind when the going gets tough: "Fail to plan? Plan to fail." That adage, and this chapter, are about readiness.

We want you to be prepared for the inevitable crises in life. We can't avoid challenges, but we can move through them with dignity, grace, and the best financial plans possible. We all need to plan for the worst, to make ourselves as safe as possible, and protect our families effectively. Our fifth pearl of wisdom—a woman under pressure must act with grace—channels the power we've learned to use in chapter 4. We can now face life with an renewed sense of purpose and security.

When we mimic the chaos around us, when we appear desperate or fearful, we put ourselves in further jeopardy. The opposite of a powerful woman is a woman burdened by discomfort, fear, and indecision. These are the qualities that are like sand in the oyster shell, out of which a pearl will evolve.

THE GRAIN OF SAND IN THE OYSTER SHELL

Do you know a woman who . . .

- Is a caregiver to children or elderly parents but doesn't take care of her own health?
- Is underinsured—or, worse, doesn't know whether she's underinsured?
- Has a genetic predisposition to a serious illness or disorder?
- Does not have an alarm system for her home?
- Wants a divorce—at any cost?
- Travels on business to areas where there is political unrest or violence?
- Has not created an escape plan for her family in the event of a fire or natural disaster?

It is often said that women are natural caregivers. But it is also true that we are the first ones people turn to in a crisis. We are recognized for our dependability because we so often confront domestic emergencies and lead our families through them—whether it's a trip to the hospital, handling funeral arrangements, or researching new treatment protocols for a serious illness. In this chapter, we will help you chart a course for preparedness in many areas of your life—from health care to insurance to divorce and personal protection.

CREATE A HEALTH-CARE STRATEGY

One of the biggest risks to building wealth is the rising cost of health care and home medical support. If you find yourself caring for aging family members, or if someone in your family falls critically or chronically ill, having a health-care strategy in place will increase your odds of navigating the crisis successfully. In a comprehensive study published in the *American Journal of Medicine,* illness and the inability to pay medical bills were identified as the cause of 75 percent of all bankruptcies in 2007. Researchers saw a 50 percent increase from 2001.[1] Although you may think you can go without health insurance or settle for catastrophic coverage only, this is a major financial mistake. For example, recent studies show that young cancer patients are at a higher risk for bankruptcy than their older counterparts, possibly due to their lower incomes and ineligibility for Medicaid.[2] The same goes for disability insurance: if you cannot work, you must ensure that you will have an income.

If you need help managing health care, you can hire help. If you feel overwhelmed handling your medical claims and insurance processing, you can outsource this function. You can also hire medical professionals to assist you in remaining healthy by working with medical concierge companies.

Health Insurance Facts

The first bullet point in any health-care strategy is insurance, and the first person you should purchase insurance for is yourself. Remember the airlines' guidelines: Put the oxygen mask on yourself before assisting a child. We are told to do this because we cannot care for others if we are not healthy ourselves. But because health insurance is expensive, some women are going without it.

The Kaiser Family Foundation reports extensively on the state of health and health insurance coverage in America.[3] Its survey covers the 96.2 million women in the United State between the ages of eighteen and sixty-four. Based on 2008 data, the survey reported that 35 percent of women have a chronic health condition that requires ongoing monitoring, such as diabetes or hypertension. The report also found that approximately 20 million women, or 59 percent, receive health insurance through an employer-sponsored program, whether it's from their own employer or a spouse's. Another 6 percent, or 5.7 million women, purchased individual policies. Ten percent were covered through Medicaid, and another 6 percent have either Medicare or another type of coverage, such as military benefits. Despite this patchwork, though, approximately 20 percent of women between the ages of eighteen and sixty-four, or 19.2 million women, are uninsured.[4]

In another survey, the Commonwealth Fund's 2010 Biennial Health Insurance Survey found that nearly one in three women between the ages of nineteen and sixty-four—about 27 million of them—did not have insurance in 2010; nearly double that number, 45 million, said they delayed or avoided buying health-care coverage because of the cost.[5]

Keep a Strong Health Insurance Policy

"The first piece of wisdom is make sure you have complete health-care coverage," emphasizes Helen Jonsen, director of digital media at *Working Mother* and a mother of four. Jonsen's youngest daughter was diagnosed with a bone cancer called osteosarcoma when she was nine years old, in 2007. The tumor in her leg grew to the size of a wine bottle. The surgeon had to remove 80 percent of her femur (thighbone) and her knee joint. "Five months before she was diagnosed with cancer, we didn't even have a prescription plan," reflects Jonsen. "We were relying on a catastrophic health plan that had very limited coverage. So make sure you have full coverage. That you're working for someone who supports that coverage or, as a small business owner, you are buying the appropriate coverage for the emergency. You never know when that emergency is going to hit, and you never know how far it's going take you. In the course of eighteen months, my daughter's on-paper cost of care was a million and a half dollars." The family was responsible for 20 percent, because the company she worked for had an excellent policy. Today Clare is doing great. She has a bionic leg that has been lengthened noninvasively to make up for the discrepancy in growth with her other leg. She has caught up with her peers in height and size and is looking forward to high school. "We're looking forward to passing the magic five-year mark—disease-free from cancer."

If you are self-employed, health-care coverage can be prohibitively expensive. The best strategy for you is to join a group rather than to purchase individual coverage. Consider joining the Freelancers Union, for example, which specializes in insuring freelance workers. Some alumni organizations also offer health insurance. You may also be able to join groups that offer insurance based on your expertise; for example, the Authors Guild offers health insurance programs for writers.

You can also research new state initiatives that make it possible to purchase coverage at a reduced cost. In March of 2010, Congress passed the Patient Protection and Affordable Care Act, which makes coverage available until

January of 2014 for legal U.S. residents who have a preexisting medical condition or who have not had insurance for six months.[6]

If you have COBRA and it is running out soon, you need to apply for new individual or family coverage a few months in advance of your end date so you do not experience a gap in your coverage. Read the fine print on hospital stays and coverage limits. While you are waiting for your new policy to kick in, be aware that in some states, such as New York, you can get major medical coverage immediately for less than two hundred dollars per month from providers like Empire BlueCross BlueShield. This will at least cover you in a hospital emergency situation. In New York, the Empire TraditionPLUS Hospital program covers your hospital expenses in full starting with the first day. Benefits include maternity care, hospital care for newborns, outpatient physical therapy, radiation therapy, home health care, and care in skilled nursing facilities.[7] There is no lifetime maximum and no limit to the amount of days you can stay in the hospital.[8]

We suggest using your coverage to get regular checkups, mammograms, and other preventive tests, which are often covered at no cost, and that you take advantage of alternative medicine options now covered by most insurers, including procedures such as acupuncture. Finally, if you work for a corporation, make sure you get to know your human resources health-care liaison well. This individual may become your advocate and negotiator over billing issues during a health crisis.

Disability Insurance

Many people think that workers' compensation will cover them if they should ever contract a disability. This is an inaccurate assumption. Workers' compensation assists you only if you are injured on the job; but according to the Social Security Administration, nearly 90 percent of disabling accidents and illnesses are not work related.[9] Even if you do qualify for workers' comp, the payout is not that large. In June of 2011, according to the Social Security Administration, there were 10.4 million disabled workers and their families receiving benefits; the average benefit was $1,816 per month.[10]

In spite of these numbers, fewer than half of all workers are purchasing disability insurance. The U.S. Bureau of Labor Statistics reported in 2009 that just 46 percent of full-time workers had short-term disability insurance, and only 39 percent had signed up for long-term disability insurance.[11] In the Live to Work survey, conducted by the CIGNA insurance company in 2010, only 36 percent of workers said they had taken steps to prepare for a disabling injury or illness; of those who had, 51 percent said they would rely on increased personal savings to carry them through, while only 32 percent had purchased new or additional disability insurance.[12]

We feel strongly that this is one type of insurance you cannot afford to live without. Make sure your policy is noncancelable and provides guaranteed eligibility without a medical examination. If you are a business owner, you can buy a policy for your employees and yourself. You should also purchase disability insurance for the key members of your organization. If you are a sole practitioner just starting out, you can purchase disability insurance through the Freelancers Union at reasonable rates. The price you pay will depend on your age, health, and the types of disabilities you want to protect against, as well as the percentage of your income you want to replace.

Get Your Insurance Claims Paid

If you have a sick child, parent, or spouse, it may be overwhelming to care for him or her and make sure that insurance claims are handled properly. It can be exhausting to appeal denied claims or investigate charges for expenses not covered by your insurance company. A good place to start is the Patient Advocate Foundation, which assists people with debt problems brought on by medical insurance costs, as well as providing other vital support services. Another great resource is Advocacy for Patients with Chronic Illness. You can also hire a medical billing advocate, who will either charge a percentage of the costs recovered or an hourly fee. A list of such advocates can be found on the website of the Medical Billing Advocates of America.

Concierge Medical Services

A number of services are springing up to help busy people navigate the health-care system. One such company is PinnacleCare. Founded in 2001, the company provides a medical advisory service that helps clients find the best doctors for their medical conditions. The company also offers to upload and maintain an online database of all a patient's medical records. For busy professionals who need to monitor the medical care of aging parents, a PinnacleCare patient advocate will keep on top of medications and attend doctor visits on your behalf. The company also offers medevac services for clients traveling abroad. For those clients, they will prepare a dossier in advance of an international trip that gives the name and phone number of a good local doctor to consult in case of an emergency. A slimmed-down version of the full PinnacleCare service is offered as an employee benefit in some companies.

Create a Caregiving Plan

If you or a member of your family becomes seriously ill, set up a budget and care plan. First, find out exactly what the medical treatment plan will be. We advise you do not take these meetings with health-care providers alone. Have an advocate—a friend, a family member, or another professional—with you who can take effective notes, ask proper questions, and go over all the details with you after the meeting.

Next, develop a strategy to support the sick individual and the other members of your family. "We were looking at a ten-month treatment plan, possibly a year if everything went well. There were no guarantees," remembers Helen Jonsen.

> And with a self-employed person, my husband, running a small business in media with crazy hours and clients to serve, and me being at a larger company with all of the benefits attached to my job, within twenty-four hours, we made the decision that my husband would stop working to become the full-time caregiver so I could keep a job going that had all the benefits attached as well as the salary. We were placed in a unique position. The dad who had never been the full-time at-home caregiver would become just that. It was the right decision. It was not an easy decision, but people have to understand somebody has to work.

Review your overall financial position in case you need to consider dipping into savings, taking out a loan, or taking out a second mortgage. If possible, this is not a decision you want to rush into during the care process. It's best to give yourself time to investigate options. There are extra costs to consider, including transportation back and forth to the hospital, airfare to visit specialists, the high cost of parking in a garage for a week, the price of take-out food for caregivers and visitors, and caregiving costs for other members of the family like children or the elderly. In a family, you're often losing one person's income, as Helen Jonsen did, and costs like ongoing physical and psychological therapy may continue long after critical care is complete. Where cancer or a transplant is involved, large-scale tests, including bone scans, X-rays, CTs, echocardiograms, extensive lab work, clinical visits, and the like are scheduled every three to six months. The cost of ongoing care and the time it takes need to be considered.

"People will often say, 'Oh, you can take time off. You have FMLA.'" Reminds Jonsen,

> The Family [and] Medical Leave Act does not pay you to be out of work. The Family [and] Medical Leave Act only says that your job can be held for a certain period of time. So when I went to human resources and said, "Do I need something legal here because I'm going to ask for more time than my normal personal days or my normal vacation time?" HR basically said, "Let us work with you to keep you in the job where you will continue to be paid." It was explained that the minute you put FMLA in place, you are now officially asking for an unpaid set time off. It doesn't necessarily protect your job. It protects *a* job, but it doesn't pay you. There's no money attached to the Family [and] Medical Leave Act. There are no mandated paid sick days in America [with the exception of a limited law covering state workers in Connecticut passed in June 2011]. There is no federal law that enforces paid sick days or paid maternity leave of any kind in America. It's extremely important for people to realize that. So while protecting your job sounds good on paper, it does not support you.

But the company you work for may have other practices in place.

Nurture the Emotions

Set out a communication strategy on when to share information with family and friends when an illness strikes. Their reaction is often overwhelming.

Prepare yourself also to cope with the patient's own grieving period over their diagnosis or your own. Seek professional and spiritual support. Use experts to educate you on mood swings and changing behaviors.

Create Your Network

Tap all the available resources and seek others who have survived similar situations or whose families have shared the experience. Accept and encourage support from outside organizations like the Make-A-Wish Foundation and community support.

Get Organized

If there are multiple family members engaged in the care or support of the individual, organize commitments on charts with reminders and positive reinforcement. Caregiving can be enjoyable and bring you closer together if it's well organized. Shared calendars that can be accessed by friends and family, or special sites like CareCircle.com or CaringBridge.com are personal websites that will allow ease of communication, taking stress off the family.

Jonsen says the most important word is "yes." Say yes when friends, community groups, and others offer to help, and tell them what you need, whether it's meals, transportation, babysitting for other family members, errands, laundry, or a little cleaning help.

Arrange for medical powers of attorney, wills, and get ready to manage the patient's affairs. Create a binder, a CD-ROM, and a flash drive with medical information and documents that may be shared with experts, caregivers, and facilities.

Be Tenacious

Tap into your drive at work to accomplish your goals when you're the caregiver. The patient may require an adjustable bed, an extra nurse, a doctor's note, or need help with a medical claim. Rest assured, it will often take every sales and negotiating skill you know to get the treatment and care you desire.

If you need an advocate or can't be present to represent the patient and chart the course of treatment effectively, you may want to consider using a service like PinnacleCare, which is a leading private health advisory company.

Establish Quarterly Goals

Review methods to improve the day-to-day life experience of your loved one. It can be simple tasks. We know a husband who writes love letters to his wife who has Alzheimer's so she can reread them when her memory falters.

Create a Positive Environment for Yourself

Family and friends may disagree or criticize you over a patient's care. Remember their opinion is often just an opinion.

Joining a major association that focuses on a patient's condition may support you. It is often empowering to focus your leadership skills toward the issue. It also can keep you abreast of new treatments, top specialists, and developments in the medical field.

Schedule Personal Time

Caregiving consumes extensive emotional and physical energy. It's important to schedule therapy/self-care and exercise into your regime on a calendar. Make a twenty-minute commitment to take exercise, meditate, enjoy a relaxing bath, or a positive companion.

INSURE YOUR FAMILY

One of the best ways to handle crisis and disaster is to be prepared before they occur, and a key element of being prepared is making sure you have enough insurance. The topic may seem daunting or even boring. But think of it as protection. If you have valuable belongings, you want to protect them from theft, fires, and other misfortunes. You want to defend yourself against lawsuits if a mishap occurs on your property. You want to protect your business, employees, and your directors from the consequences of litigation or a natural disaster.

What Is the Best Way to Buy Insurance?

There are generally two ways to buy insurance: either directly from an insurance company or its agent, or from a broker who represents multiple insurance companies. Generally, you are wiser to work with a broker—this way, you are exposed to a number of possible products. We spoke with Diane Giles, a business development executive at Marsh, one of the world's largest insurance brokerages. Diane has been an expert in the insurance industry for more than thirty years, having worked directly for insurance companies and for brokerage firms. She now works in the private client division at Marsh, where she handles the often complex insurance needs of wealthy families. She explained to us that although it may be fine to buy insurance from some of the large companies that sell directly to the consumer, especially if you have very simple needs, a broker is especially desirable if you have a large number of assets. "In those cases," says Diane, "you need someone who is going to give you independent, consultative advice."

Diane also emphasized the importance of understanding where a salesperson's or broker's potential conflict of interest might lie. For example, a broker is usually paid a commission based on what you purchase. If she sells a great deal of insurance from one company, she may get an additional bonus called a contingent commission. Some brokers are paid on salary rather than on commission, which reduces some of the potential for conflict of interest. A good broker should disclose to you how she is getting paid.

In addition, not all insurance companies are created equal. An insurance company needs to be able to pay the claims you make, which means that it must be financially solvent. Luckily, insurance companies are rated, and before buying any insurance product you should ask your broker for that company's ratings from the two top agencies, Standard & Poor's and A.M. Best. Diane says, "The company should carry an A rating or higher. If a company's rating falls below A-minus, Marsh will not sell their insurance and we would contact clients to discuss replacing their insurance with new carriers."

Insure Your Belongings

The first item on your insurance list, after health insurance, should be property and casualty insurance. You need to make sure that you have enough insurance for your home, automobile, and valuables, such as jewelry, art, fine wine, and antiques. There are even specialized insurance companies that will provide you with insurance for classic cars. A good broker can help you know who the best carriers are in each category.

A good broker can also help make sure that your home is covered specifically for the types of natural disasters most likely to occur in your geographical area, whether they be wildfires, floods, earthquakes, or hurricanes—to the extent coverage is available. Your policy should provide coverage for the replacement cost of items rather than the actual cash value, which is the replacement cost minus any depreciation.

As soon as you buy insurance, you should create a detailed inventory of your belongings. You can have the insurance company take a video of your belongings that is kept outside your home. You can also hire consultants to do an inventory of your belongings for you. This inventory can include a private, secure website that contains photos of the items, original purchase receipts, and insurance policies. If you have a large jewelry collection, for example, you should have a catalog created that includes a photograph of each piece, especially if you have one-of-a-kind items. You may also want to purchase a fireproof in-home safe to hold jewelry and other small valuable items.

Buy Excess Liability Insurance

In addition, you want to buy plenty of insurance to cover the possibility that other people may suffer an accident while on your property. This excess personal liability coverage protects you in the event you are sued under these circumstances. Your need for this insurance increases as your children begin to drive, as you become wealthier, and if you become famous. Diane says,

> You're working very, very hard to accumulate wealth so that you can have a wonderful retirement and perhaps leave a legacy beyond that. It could be gone in an instant if there is, for example, a horrible car accident,

there are injuries, and you end up being sued for several million dollars. The absence of proper liability coverage could result in you having to liquidate your assets and, potentially, your business to pay for a judgment in a lawsuit. Ten million dollars in excess liability coverage could cost you only two thousand dollars per year—a very small expenditure against a potentially devastating blow to your financial well-being.

Hiring Household Staff Creates Insurance Needs

If you hire a nanny, housekeeper, or gardener to work directly for you, state law may require that you provide workers' compensation and disability insurance for these workers. In addition, if you are hiring people to work in your home, you have a need for excess liability insurance—if a worker is injured on your property, he can sue you. You also need to protect yourself against employment-practice lawsuits. Unfortunately, some domestic workers are now filing lawsuits as a way to make money. You do not need to have this insurance if you hire a service that employs your workers, but you do if you are their direct employer. Diane says, "You could have a domestic worker allege that you discriminated in hiring or firing her. Or she may allege that your husband made sexual advances. This is now a very common lawsuit. Clients need to be aware of the coverage available and make a conscious choice about whether or not they want to pay for this coverage."

Maintain Proper Life Insurance

If you have children or other dependents, or if you are married, you should have life insurance. A good place to begin educating yourself about life insurance is the website of the LIFE Foundation, a nonprofit organization that provides information to consumers about insurance. The site gives a good basic explanation of the kinds of life, disability, and health insurance policies that are available. It also provides a calculator to help you figure out just how much life insurance you need, depending on your age, how many children or other dependents you have, your income, savings, and so forth.

In order to figure out how much life insurance you need, you need to answer two questions. First, how much money do you need to clear your debts? Second, how much capital do you need to provide an income for your spouse and children in the event of your death? Once you have an amount in mind, you can discuss this with your financial planner or find an insurance broker to help you look at various options.

There are two main types of life insurance, term and permanent. Term insurance provides a death benefit only during a specific period of time, whereas permanent life insurance provides a death benefit no matter when you die, and allows you to build up a cash value in the policy based on your premium payments. It is best for you to discuss your individual situation with a fee-only financial planner before you approach a life insurance broker to get quotes on a policy.

If you have substantial assets, your financial adviser may counsel you to use life insurance trusts to reduce certain estate taxes. Many small business owners hold life insurance in a trust to provide the cash necessary to pay tax bills if their business is valuable but not very liquid. Your accountant should be involved in these discussions. Rules for using life insurance inside of trusts are constantly changing, so go to top experts rather than relying on Internet articles to help you understand this area of advanced estate planning.

Get Your Name on Insurance Policies

All your personal insurance policies need to reflect the way your assets are held. For example, with homeowner's insurance, Diane notes that many policyholders might think that they are protected by policies in their spouses' names—but the fine print may indicate that the policy covers only "the spouse who resides in the home." So if you move out of your home because of a trial separation or divorce, you would no longer be covered by the policy. Your belongings left in the home or belongings you take with you to a new apartment would not be covered, either. In addition, if your house is put into a trust, such as a revocable living trust, you must make sure that the name of the insured on the policy is the title of the trust rather than your personal name.

Insure Your Business

If you own a business, you need to make sure that the business carries proper insurance. A broker of business insurance should be able to help you determine your requirements. If you are unsure what you need, ask your accountant to give you a hand. In general, a small business needs property and casualty insurance, disability insurance for key workers, and liability insurance—at the very minimum.

There are four types of liability insurance that are appropriate for business. First, general liability insurance protects your business from injury claims, property damage, and false-advertising claims. This insurance is also known as commercial general liability (CGL), and it may be the only type of business liability insurance you need, depending on your situation. Second, business owners providing services should consider professional liability insurance, also known as errors and omissions insurance. This protects your business against negligence and mistakes. Depending on your profession, it may be a legal requirement to carry such a policy. Third, small businesses selling or manufacturing products need product liability insurance to protect themselves in the event that someone is injured as a result of using one of their products. Finally, if your company has a board of directors, they will most likely require you to purchase directors and officers insurance, which protects them in the event they are sued as a result of their actions while serving on the board.

In addition to these main types of business insurance, there are several industry-specific insurance policies that you may need. For example, doctors are required to have malpractice insurance before they can practice in certain states, and technology consultants often need coverage in independent contractor situations. Your accountant should be able to help you determine the type of business insurance that is right for you.

INVEST IN YOUR SECURITY

Crime is one of the greatest disrupters of financial and emotional stability there is. The legal and medical costs associated with battling the aftermath of an event like a robbery, a mugging, a kidnapping, or a rape can literally bankrupt a family, leaving us unable to work—or, worse, it could cost us our lives.

We women can take actions to minimize the chances that we or our children will fall victim to a crime. We consulted top security experts about the practical, useful steps we can take to improve our safety. We wanted to know which strategies are worth our financial investment and which are simply ineffective. Our experts had a strong message—you must invest both your money and your time in planning, preparation, and prevention. If something does happen, the combination of preparation and presence of mind may be the key to your survival.

Get a Security Review

We spoke with Betsy Blumenthal, senior managing director at Kroll Associates, one of the largest research and investigations firms in the world. The company specializes in risk assessment for corporations and wealthy individuals, including everything from complete IT systems to home security systems. Betsy stressed the need to first understand the level of risk you are facing. Since this may change over time, you must always be aware of your surroundings in order minimize the chance of being attacked.

One of the best ways to prepare properly is to hire a professional firm to perform a security review. Wealthy families often purchase this service. A security review first examines what is called your "threat environment." This involves looking at the public profile of you and your family. If, for example, you or your husband has just been made the CEO of a public company, your risk level has increased. You are now more of a public person and there is more opportunity for individuals to learn about you through documents available online, or through published articles about you. If you decide to run for office, your risk level has just increased. If you are the head of human resources at your company and are in the process of cutting staff, your risk level has just increased.

Your threat environment is also influenced by the physical security of your home or homes. If you live in a large house in an isolated area, you are at greater risk. A security review determines the physical security of your home or homes, your recreational or corporate vehicles, such as large boats or private planes, and evaluates your routines when moving from place to place. The review will also examine the ways in which you access information online, the backgrounds of the people around you (including your employees and household staff), and your travel patterns and habits. A security review can cost well over ten thousand dollars, but if you consider the consequences of a possible security breach, the price may be a relatively small one to pay. "I think most people want to live their lives as normally as possible, but a review can reveal some gaps that can easily be plugged in without being intrusive, and that's our goal," Betsy says. She also suggests that families should update their security reviews every two years, or more often if their circumstances change frequently.

Secure Your Home with an Alarm System

According to Betsy, when it comes to home security, a good alarm system and external lighting are key factors in safety. The best reason to buy an alarm system is that it provides deterrence. A thief who sees the alarm system sticker in your window or the sign on your lawn may decide to pass your house by in favor of a less guarded home. Your alarm system should also be set to go off if there is smoke or fire. Make sure it is simple enough for everyone to use, including children. The cost of an alarm will vary widely depending on the size of your home, your geographic location, and the size of your yard, so it is best to get several quotes from reputable companies in your area.

In addition, make sure you don't leave your spare key outside the front door in an obvious place. Be aware of your surroundings when coming in and going out of your home. Cameras outside your home may be useful as a deterrent if they are obvious to criminals. They are also useful after a crime as an investigative tool, but are almost never watched and therefore aren't useful in preventing a crime. Motion detectors, too, may be set off by animals, making them less dependable than other security devices. Everything depends on your location, your habits, and your lifestyle.

Perform Background Checks on Employees

One good way to prevent crime is to perform a thorough background check on all household employees, including nannies, maids, and gardeners. If a potential employee has a very poor credit record, for example, he or she may be more likely to steal from you due to immense personal financial stress. When you hire domestic workers through an agency, it may say that it has done such a background check; in that case, you should ask to see the documents and review them yourself. Background checks can cost anywhere from one hundred to five hundred dollars. This may be included in the fee paid to an agency, or it may be offered as an additional option.

In addition, you need to make sure that all your workers are eligible to work in the United States—even if you hire employees through a service, the financial and legal consequences of hiring undocumented workers are huge due to recent changes in immigration law. Make sure any service or agency you hire adheres to the standards you are comfortable with, including drug testing. And if you are a business owner, you must apply the same strict background check requirements on all employees uniformly—you cannot discriminate and perform a background check on one person but not on another.

If you have fewer than ten employees, you may want to consider having them employed as outsourced contractors through an agency. The same employment rules apply whether you have ten or one hundred employees, and it can be very expensive to remain in compliance with all requirements. Even large corporations are moving to this model in order to standardize and manage payroll and compliance issues, as well as to improve security.

Don't Invite Strangers into Your Home

Try to be careful when you invite strangers into your home. Make sure all contractors are licensed and that you investigate them before they come over. Even a nationally well-known company may have a poorly supervised franchise system, and they won't always screen the people they allow to work under the corporate name. Also, if you do charity work and have direct contact with indigent people, don't bring them into your home—this, tragically, is how Elizabeth Smart was targeted and captured. If possible, do not have workers in your home when your children are present—you don't want them to become targets of an unstable person who would never have met them otherwise.

Take Care of Cybersecurity

It is becoming increasingly difficult for nonprofessionals to protect their home computers and laptops from hackers, malware, and spyware. Technologies are always changing, so if you're not a tech expert, the best thing to do is to hire an IT firm with a good reputation to give you advice. A quick Google search will provide you with several local options. Ask around for referrals from people who do know about technology and check references provided by the company; you can easily be overcharged or hire people who really don't protect your system. The cost for computer consulting ranges from seventy-five dollars per hour to more than two hundred dollars per hour, depending on the complexity of your situation. If you commission a security review, this service will be part of the package.

A thorough cybersecurity plan will also guard against the likelihood of identity theft, which can be an expensive and difficult problem to fix. You should regularly monitor your credit reports to ensure that no one has hijacked one of your credit cards and is applying for credit in your name. You can also sign up for services that will alert you to suspicious activity through the major credit bureaus.

Store Your Valuable Documents Securely

Often we wonder where and how to store important financial documents in a secure manner. It is critical to have a centralized location for our wills, trust documents, medical and legal powers of attorney, and financial statements. We spoke with Dr. Tania Neild, founder and CEO of Infograte, Inc., a consulting company specializing in information technology solutions for the financial services sector. Tania has established successful Web-based information exchange solutions for clients from the Fortune 100 down to start-ups. Tania began her career as an applied scientist for the National Security Agency, which awarded her the prestigious National Physical Sciences Consortium Award to fund her research in heterogeneous database integration. She earned a Ph.D. in computer engineering from Northwestern University and a bachelor's degree in mathematics and computer sciences from Emory University. We asked Tania to help us devise a simple, secure way to store sensitive information.

Although there are a growing number of online encrypted digital vaults, Tania also believes that sticking to an offline solution is the best way to go. There is no online solution that is 100 percent secure. Tania says,

> It appears people really don't have time to organize their documents. They say, "This isn't something I want to do. I barely want to clean out my closet and I'll get lots more day-in and day-out value for having my closet cleaned. Now you're asking me to clean out my legal documents." Almost no one has a capacity for that. Are things really secure? Not much is really secure. Downloading your documents and putting them on an external encrypted, password-protected thumb drive in your own vault happens to be one of the cheapest, most secure ways to go. It is easy for people to do, secure from others and secure from disasters.

Tania notes that it is important to give copies of your documents to several individuals to make sure your information is available in the event of an emergency. It is best to get the information out of your house. You may want to have your information both in electronic format, in a file stored on a server, and in an encrypted format on a thumb drive or burned on a DVD in your vault. Have it in at least two places. Sometimes if you die, a safety deposit box will be sealed, and then all the papers that everybody needs have to go through a trustee. It is important to have your information in a place where your friend or your spouse can get to it, so that they can figure out what needs to happen quickly.

Personal Self-Defense

You may want to take a self-defense class. To find a class near you, contact your local police department, do a Google search, or talk to the YWCA. A good class will help you spot potential criminals, move with confidence, and develop a greater awareness of situations that might be dangerous.

Although self-defense training can be effective, keep in mind that it needs to be maintained on a regular basis. A one-week course will fade from your memory within a few weeks, even though you may feel a false sense of security. Therefore, you must make a truly dedicated decision to train regularly—meaning every week—if you really think you will need to counter a physical attack. Otherwise, you might be quickly be subdued and make the attack worse than it would have been. Indeed, Betsy emphasizes that the best thing to do if you are robbed—whether you have self-defense training or not—is to hand over your money and jewelry; don't antagonize the thief.

There are two nationally available self-defense programs that you might want to consider. One is Krav Maga, the official self-defense system of the Israeli Defense Forces. Police and military personnel around the world use this award-winning training. Another program to consider is IMPACT Personal Safety Training, a system developed in the 1970s that focuses particularly on the self-defense needs of women. The system is taught by Prepare, Inc., a training organization. Donna Chiaet, president of Prepare, Inc., is on the board of the nonprofit organization Emerging Strategies for Leadership and Learning. She is a nationally recognized speaker on issues of women and violence, and has written eight books on violence prevention for young women.

The question of whether you should own a firearm or carry a weapon raises some tough issues. Women may think that carrying a knife, pepper spray, or Taser is a good way to protect themselves, but it is often more effective on television than it is in real life. Unless you are a highly skilled combatant, an attacker can take a weapon away from you and then turn around and use it on you. Betsy points out that a good alarm system, background checks on employees, and good self-defense training are generally more effective than weapons. Owning a gun also adds the risk that children could find it in your home, a discovery that could result in a tragic accident. Keeping the ammunition separate from the gun minimizes that risk, but it also means that you won't be able to use the gun in an emergency situation—say, when you're surprised by an intruder in the middle of the night. Betsy says, "Unless you are incredibly well trained and you're prepared to shoot, there's really no good reason to be wielding a gun."

Security for Your Children

From the time children are very young, they should be taught basic security procedures. Everyone should know how to get out of the house in case of a fire or another type of disaster. Your children should be taught to memorize their address as well as your name and phone number at as young an age as possible. You also want to make sure that your children will not go off with anyone whom you have not sent to pick them up. We spoke with Tam St. Armand, Executive Vice President of Ventura Insurance Brokerage. Tam has been a licensed property and insurance broker and risk manager for more than twenty-five years. She is also a mother, and she devised a simple but very effective security plan with her two sons. Says Tam, "I instituted a family code word, so that no matter who came to pick them up, whether at school or anywhere else, they would know to wait for a code word, which I would have given to the person picking up my children in advance. I taught my children to be very firm about this. One time, a friend of mine came to pick up my son from school because he was feeling ill, but he refused to go with her, even though he knew her, because I had forgotten to give her the word."

You should also familiarize yourself with the security procedures of places your children frequent outside your home, especially those of their school. Do your children know what to do in case of an emergency in the school building? In addition, when your children go to their friends' homes for sleepovers, you should familiarize yourself with the environment there. Does the family keep guns in the home? Do the parents drink excessively? Do they allow violent video games that you have forbidden in your home? It pays to ask lots of questions of other parents before you let your child stay over at their house—you can always have the children's friends come to your house, where you control the security of the environment.

Online Security and Identity Management for Your Kids

Keeping up with the latest things kids want to do online is a daunting task for most parents. There are two organizations that can help. One is Common Sense Media, a nonprofit organization that provides specific advice to parents about how to handle all media and online issues with their children. Another good resource is SocialShield, which monitors your child's Facebook page for the presence of profanity, friends of inappropriate age, and other worrisome signals, like posts of the word "suicide." You have peace of mind while not having to read every post your son or daughter initiates or receives. They may grumble about the "intrusion" now, but thank you when they're older; inappropriate Facebook posts can come back to haunt them, seriously damaging their college admission chances. Children are forced to begin branding themselves in the media from the time they are old enough to go online, and protecting their online identity is a critical element of your job as a parent.

For your own part, although you may love to brag about your children and post their photographs on Facebook, you should think twice about how much information you place in the public domain about your children. You may notice that most celebrities do not release lots of photos of their kids for public consumption—learn to protect your children in the same way. If you do put photos of your child on Facebook, make sure you have not accepted any invitations from people you do not know well—you may be exposing your children unknowingly to predators or kidnappers.

We also recommend that you create and keep an up-to-date identity kit for your children, now required by many schools. The kit should be digital, so it can be quickly emailed to law enforcement authorities should anything happen to your child. The kit should include a recent digital photo, a copy of your child's passport, and a description of him or her. You may also want to include fingerprints. One such kit is the McGruff Safe Kids Total Identification System, which is licensed by the National Crime Prevention Council.

Domestic Trafficking of Children

Children in the United States are being kidnapped and sold into the sex trafficking trade at an alarming rate. All parents should confront this horrifying possibility. An estimated 100,000 to 300,000 children in the United States are kidnapped and forced to work as prostitutes each year. Most of these children are runaways who are quickly picked up and exploited. The average age of entry into the domestic sex trade is thirteen.[13]

A child does not need to be a runaway to be kidnapped. A very scary story, featured on the *Today* show in 2008, is that of Shauna Newell, a teenager who went to sleep over at the house of a new friend. Although her mother met the friend's father and allowed the sleepover, the man was a convicted felon and his "daughter" was another abducted teen. Shauna, age sixteen, was beaten, raped, and drugged. In the wake of the police's refusal to conduct a search for her until she had been missing for seventy-two hours, her parents launched their own independent search; fortunately, she was found alive.[14]

The problem is so serious that in June of 2003, the FBI, in conjunction with the Department of Justice Child Exploitation and Obscenity Section and the National Center for Missing & Exploited Children, launched the Innocence Lost National Initiative, aimed at addressing the growing problem of domestic sex trafficking of children in the United States. By 2010, the initiative had resulted in the rescue of more than 1,600 children. Investigations have successfully led to the conviction of more than 719 pimps, madams, and their associates and the seizure of more than $3.1 million in assets. However, many underage prostitutes are treated as criminals, and there is still a need for services to help them return to their families and to a normal life. The sex slavery industry has become an increasingly important revenue source for organized crime because each young girl can earn between $150,000 and $200,000 each year for her pimp.

Parents should make their teenage daughters aware of the sex-trafficking trade in the United States and the steps they can take to avoid becoming victims. Teenage girls and young women in their twenties can also be targeted if they travel abroad. Because teenagers move around much more independently than younger children, you will need to teach them to be alert, trust their instincts, and avoid dangerous situations. The movie *Taken* covers the subject of a young woman kidnapped on a European vacation and may also help to underscore the seriousness of this risk.

Kidnapping by Noncustodial Parents

The vast majority of kidnapping of children in the United States is done by noncustodial parents in a divorce situation. A 2002 Department of Justice report states every year, more than 800,000 children are reported missing. Of the approximately sixty-nine thousand American children who are abducted annually, 82 percent are abducted by a family member.[15] A kidnapping occurs when a noncustodial parent takes a child across state lines without permission and in violation of custody arrangements. This is both a state and a federal crime. When the noncustodial parent is a foreign national, children are sometimes taken out of the country; sadly, it can be virtually impossible to get them back. There are no international courts to handle these matters, and foreign courts usually side with their own citizens rather than with the American parent. Tam St. Armand notes that if you feel your children are at risk of being kidnapped by your ex-spouse, you can obtain insurance that will reimburse you for the costs incurred in recovering your child. However, this is a reimbursement policy only—you still have to come up with the money initially.

Fighting for the return of a child who has been taken abroad can be very expensive. In the famous case of David Goldman and his son, Sean, David's wife, Bruna, took four-year-old Sean to Brazil in 2004. She called David and said she wanted a divorce and would not allow him to see his son. She then obtained a divorce in Brazil and married a well-known lawyer from a powerful Brazilian family. Bruna, unfortunately, died in childbirth in 2008; David fought for the return of Sean through the Brazilian courts, using the rules from the Hague Convention on Child Abduction. But Sean's Brazilian stepfather refused to return him to David and even petitioned the court to have a new birth certificate issued, naming him as Sean's father. According to his website, David spent more than $360,000 fighting for custody of his child.[16] Sean and David were ultimately reunited when the Brazilian Supreme Court ruled in his favor in December 2009.

According to the Bring Sean Home Foundation, there are approximately 1,793 open abduction cases involving more than 2,488 children who have been abducted by a parent or legal guardian and taken from the United States to other countries.[17] In countries that are party to the Hague Abduction Convention, the government is supposed to represent the parent from whom the child was taken, and pay all court costs. This was the case for David Goldman; however, this rule doesn't cover the cost of traveling abroad for court appearances or any of the other assorted costs of finding a child. If the child is taken to a country that is not party to the treaty, all legal costs must be borne by the petitioner. Success rates are very low.

Group Travel Overseas

When your child wishes to attend an academic program in another country, or joins members of her church on a philanthropic mission overseas, it is essential that you investigate in detail the security protocols that the program plans to employ. You may wish to hire a top security firm to assess the safety of the program for you. It is also a good idea to get kidnap and ransom insurance (see page 217).

Just because a top university has created the program, don't assume that a detailed security plan is in place—insist on seeing one in writing. It is generally more risky to send children to developing countries than to Europe or Canada; however, don't be lured into a false sense of security just because your child will be staying in a major Western city. Here are some of the questions you should ask when your child plans to travel overseas with an institutional program for any length of time. If you don't get good answers, say no to the program.

- What are the recent crime statistics for the area where my child will be staying?
- What kind of training are you giving the students to prepare them to live in this area?
- Does everyone participating in the program speak English?
- If my child is staying in a rural area, how far is the nearest metropolitan area? How far is the nearest medical facility?
- How will the children be transported once they land at the foreign airport?
- What type of housing will they be staying in?
- If they are in hotels, will there be adult supervision?
- If they are staying in private homes, please show me the background security report on the family with whom my child will be staying.
- What are the emergency procedures in case of a terrorist attack or a natural disaster?
- Do all the children have access to a satellite phone in case they are in areas with no cell phone coverage?
- What type of identifying information are you collecting about the

children to help quickly locate them in the event of an abduction or accident?
- Who is your local law enforcement liaison?
- How often are they in contact with you once they get to their destination?
- What will you do if something goes wrong and my child needs to come home?
- What type of medical supplies are you carrying on the journey?
- How will you notify me of problems?
- What are the rules regarding drinking, smoking, and socializing?

Kidnapping

Kidnapping is psychologically terrifying; what's more, paying ransom in a kidnapping case can be financially devastating. Because the kidnapping of Americans most often occurs when they are traveling overseas, you want to be especially careful when you leave the country for any reason. Again, prevention is the key to avoiding this deadly problem.

According to Tam St. Armand, there are three types of kidnapping common today: traditional kidnapping for ransom, "express" kidnapping, and politically motivated kidnapping. Kidnapping hot spots change according to the political and economic conditions in various countries. Currently, Mexico, Colombia, Brazil, and Venezuela are the spots where you are most likely to be kidnapped for ransom. According to AIG's crisis management division, there are more than twenty thousand reported cases of kidnapping per year, and 48 percent of them occur in Latin America.[18] It is believed that up to 80 percent of kidnaps go unreported, so the actual number may be closer to 100,000 per year.[19]

During kidnap-for-ransom events, you are held against your will while your kidnappers demand that someone pay for your release. The ransom demand may range from a few thousand to millions of dollars. In an express kidnap, you are held usually for twenty-four to forty-eight hours, during which time you are forced to withdraw money from an ATM; then you are released. While being held, you may also be beaten or raped. Mexico City is the current hot spot for express kidnaps. The third type of kidnapping, politically motivated kidnapping, is now prevalent in Middle Eastern countries, such as Pakistan and Iraq, as well as in countries where Muslim militants are known to operate, such as the Philippines. In these cases, the kidnappers' motivation may be to achieve the release of terrorists held in the United States, to extort money, or simply to gain media exposure.

HOW TO PREVENT A KIDNAPPING

Before you travel, check the State Department's travel website to review the current state of stability or unrest in the country that you plan to visit. You should also consider registering online with the U.S. Embassy when you travel to other countries. If you are traveling for a corporation, make sure they have a security protocol in place and request a confidential security report on the country you're visiting; many corporations have a security firm on retainer and can get this report for you. If you are going to a particularly dangerous place, make sure they purchase kidnap and ransom insurance in your behalf.

In addition, Tam St. Armand shared the following points that are especially important for women:

- Choose a hotel with strong security.
- Before you travel, learn the customs of the country and the expectations for female guests.
- Do not draw attention to yourself by wearing expensive jewelry, driving an expensive car, or acting in a conspicuous manner.
- If you are in a Muslim country, observe the local dress code for women.
- Do not hail a cab on the street; arrange with your hotel for an airport pickup. Have the driver's name, phone number, and preferably his photograph with you before you arrive in the country.
- Do not speak to strangers about your itinerary or give details about your location.
- In the hotel, do not hang a card on the door indicating that you are ordering breakfast for one person; this will make your room a target for criminals who may work inside the hotel.

- Do not speak to strangers, especially men, in a bar or restaurant; you could be stalked or targeted for crime later.
- Do not go to deserted areas.
- Do not go to ATMs at night.
- If you hire security personnel, make sure they speak English; endeavor to establish a rapport with them.

HOW TO SURVIVE A KIDNAPPING

If you are kidnapped, your main goal is to stay alive until your ransom is paid or until your kidnappers are apprehended. Not all kidnappers are alike: their behavior depends on where you are in the world, what your captors' goals are, and their level of experience. Here are some tips that could save your life if you find yourself in this horrible situation.

- If you are being held for ransom, realize that you are considered a commodity for sale and therefore your kidnappers want you alive.
- Manage your own behavior. Do not scream, cry, or yell; this will only make your situation worse and may endanger your life. Remain as calm as you can.
- Try to stay clean and ask for small comforts such as a blanket or pillow, which increase your psychological strength.
- Do not antagonize your kidnappers.
- If you know your kidnappers' language, try to use it when you speak to them.
- Try to become a human, not just a commodity. Try to engage in small talk with kidnappers around topics like families, hobbies, and sports, which are universal interests.
- Do not argue against your kidnappers' views or religious beliefs—agree with them and try to make them see you as sympathetic.
- Although you should appear to be sympathetic to your kidnappers, resist bonding with them and remember who you are.
- If there is an attempt to rescue you, hit the floor and let the rescue team do their work.

- During a rescue, do not pick up a weapon, as you may be shot by accident.
- Try to remain calm; the more time that passes, the more likely you are to survive.

Kidnap and Ransom Insurance

It is wise to obtain a kidnap and ransom insurance policy if you are traveling to countries where kidnapping is prevalent. Tam says,

> Remember that a kidnap and ransom policy is a reimbursement policy. The policy provides access to a specialty response or consulting firm. If you are kidnapped, the response firm will be contacted and will negotiate your ransom with the kidnappers. It is important not to let many people know that you have a policy; ironically, you may be more of a target if you have one. Also, when the kidnappers realize that a response firm is handling the negotiation, the price of the ransom goes up. The insured person has to come up with the payment of the ransom, which is later reimbursed by the insurance company. If the insured does not have cash, someone can take the policy to a bank and may be able to get a loan against the policy to raise the cash.

If your company takes out the policy, they will receive the call for ransom and transfer it to the response firm. If you take out a policy privately, you will need to designate someone who can take the call and contact the response firm on your behalf. In addition, make sure that the policy you have covers all countries, since some policies exclude countries that are known to be dangerous. The cost of the policy depends on the length of your travel, your destination or destinations, the number of people covered under the policy, and the amount of the ransom covered. You also want to make sure the policy does not set a cap on the fees that the response firm charges, in case you have a drawn-out negotiation.

MAKE YOUR DISASTER PLANS

Few families have a real plan in place in the event of a natural disaster or terrorist attack. A 2011 Harris Poll of more than two thousand Americans revealed that only 56 percent of those surveyed say they are ready for a natural disaster or long-term power failure with enough supplies for three days. Older Americans were much better prepared than Gen Xers (ages 35 to 46) and echo boomers (ages 18 to 34).[20]

Extended hotel stays and last-minute flights can ruin your finances in the blink of an eye. The devastation from Hurricane Katrina was calculated at more than $100 billion. In 2011, the tornadoes that ripped through Alabama and six other U.S. states caused insured losses of between $2 billion and $5 billion. And according to the director of the Center for Research on the Epidemiology of Disasters, there has been a "dramatic" rise in natural disasters over the past decade.[21]

In this section, we'll discuss the basic disaster and emergency preparedness plan we all should have in place with the help of FEMA regional administrator Nancy Ward. Ward's region encompasses California, Nevada, Arizona, and the Pacific. Ward has worked in social services and disaster response for over thirty years. Lieutenant Erica Arteseros, who is a first responder for the San Francisco Fire Department and the program coordinator for the San Francisco Neighborhood Emergency Response Team (NERT) program, will share her expertise on community preparedness and training programs. Their expertise offers excellent preparedness information for any climate and region. (Camilla, who coordinated embedded TV crews in Kuwait and Iraq on the ground and managed news teams in New York City during 9/11, as well as coordinated coverage for multiple hurricanes, is also an expert in this area.)

We want to strengthen your confidence in your ability to manage a crisis, especially when it comes to preparedness. According to at least one expert, as women, we already have the excellent critical-response skills so vital to managing an emergency. "Women deal with at least one little crisis every day," says Nancy Ward. "We're still the primary caregivers for school-age children, for elderly parents and relatives, so crisis management is inherent in our makeup. I am a firm believer that this very quality helps us be decisive, to be able to multitask, and to maintain our wits about us in crisis. Most women emergency managers don't get flustered."

We would like to begin by posing some questions regarding your emergency preparedness:

- Do you know what to do when the power goes out?
- Do you know the location of the fire exits at work and at home, and do you practice exiting through them regularly?
- Do you have a phone connected to a landline in your home—one that will still work when the power goes out?
- Do you have cash on hand in case ATMs are unavailable?
- Do you have a predetermined central meeting point for your family if you have to leave your neighborhood due to a natural disaster or terrorist attack?
- Do you know what to pack if you had only five minutes to gather your belongings?
- Do you have a basic emergency supply kit?

Prepare to Communicate

After securing your immediate safety during a disaster or attack, your next action should be to call a friend or family member outside the state. You and your family should determine beforehand who that individual should be, and all members of the household, if you've become separated, should call the same person. "Having your communications plan in place is critical," emphasizes Lieutenant Erica Arteseros. "Don't choose someone local, because cell phone towers will be jammed. Use a pay phone to place that out-of-state call—pay phones often continue to work during earthquakes and other incidents, so part of your preparation should involve learning where they are." Tell the person you call about your physical and mental condition, your location, the time of day, and your plan of action. If your mobile phone is still working, change your greeting. Record a message that says you are okay, and state your location, the time, and the day of the week. Now you have set up a system so that people in a safe location can support the communication and rescue effort.

Prepare to Be Self-Sustaining

In the event of a disaster, it's essential to maintain a level of independence. "One of the things we all take for granted is that, in an emergency, the police, firefighters, EMS, and the National Guard are going to respond immediately. But that's often not the case. They're going to be affected by the disaster as well," explains Nancy Ward. "So acknowledging that you may be on your own for a bit of time will help you get through." In fact, in a major disaster it's likely that you will need to take care of yourself for a week to ten days. FEMA suggests having enough food, water, and other supplies on hand to last for at least three days. Its website is an excellent resource; it contains ideas for items to put in an emergency kit as well as in-depth suggestions for ensuring your survival.[22]

We recommend that you purchase supplies well in advance and store them in waterproof containers packed in lightweight backpacks that you can carry in the event you need to move. In the midst of a disaster, make sure to tune in to an AM/FM radio station. The radio and all your communications tools are your best friends in an emergency, says Lieutenant Arteseros. "NOAA's emergency alerting service lets people know where resources will be set up, where they can go for help, and what hospitals are open or closed."

WHAT TO STOCK IN YOUR EMERGENCY SUPPLY KIT

Basic Items—Have Enough for Three Days at the Minimum

- Water—one gallon per person per day, for drinking and washing
- Food—including nonperishable items such as canned goods and energy bars
- Battery-powered or hand-cranked radio and a NOAA weather radio with the tone alert feature
- Flashlight
- Extra batteries for your radios and flashlight
- First-aid kit
- Whistle to signal for help
- Dust mask, to help filter contaminated air
- Plastic sheeting and duct tape to shelter yourself in place
- Moist towelettes, garbage bags, and plastic ties for personal sanitation

- Wrench or pliers to turn off utilities
- Can opener
- Local maps
- Cell phone with chargers (including an inverter or solar charger)

Additional Items

- Prescription medications and glasses
- Infant formula and diapers
- Food and water for your pet
- Cash or traveler's checks and coins
- Important family documents, such as copies of insurance policies, identification, and bank account records in a waterproof, portable container[23]
- Emergency reference material, such as a first-aid guide
- Sleeping bag or warm blanket for each person; add additional bedding for cold-weather climates
- Complete change of clothing, including a long-sleeve shirt, long pants, and sturdy shoes
- Household chlorine bleach and a medicine dropper[24]
- Fire extinguisher
- Matches in a waterproof container
- Sanitary napkins, tampons, and other personal hygiene items
- Mess kits—including cups, plates, and utensils
- Paper towels
- Paper, pencil, and permanent marker
- Books, games, puzzles, or other activities for children

Lieutenant Arteseros warns that there is a tendency to buy nothing if you don't like the food or supplies on the list. Find an appropriate exchange. "I always tell people to buy food that you actually eat," she explains. "High-energy bars of any brand are good; they have a long shelf life."

It's important to create a comfortable environment and buy things in advance that you want. We recommend that all supplies in your kit should be in waterproof containers, such as plastic bags, and should be in portable backpacks that you can carry in the event you need to move.

Prepare to Move

If you live in a seasonal climatic danger zone, everyone in your household should have a set of sensible all-weather clothes and shoes packed and ready to go. If possible, medications should also be packed in your family vehicle. Your vehicle should have enough room for the emergency kits of everyone in the family. It should also contain a separate emergency kit of its own—flares, a hand-cranked radio, water, phone chargers, a flashlight, snacks, bad-weather gear, a towel, five dollars in coins, ten dollars in singles, and a laminated list of emergency contacts in the glove compartment. You should keep a spare can of gasoline in the garage as well.

Studying maps of the area and designing an exit strategy in advance is also essential. Maps should be printed out, laminated, and added to your emergency kit. Avoid roads in flooding zones and close to forests in case they fall victim to fire and high water. If you live in a hurricane-, tornado-, or earthquake-prone area, practice your exit routes to potentially safer ground on a regular basis.

Disaster preparedness takes thinking outside the box. Nancy Ward was visiting a disaster center in Sonoma County, California, in 1995 to make sure it was running effectively.

> I sat down with a young girl who had just moved to California about a month before the state declared a fifty-eight-county flooding emergency. She was driving in an unfamiliar place with her two-month-old baby boy and she turned down the wrong street and got into some pretty high water, which caused her car to die. She was sitting in the middle of the street, with a two-month-old little baby, and the water was rising in her car. Before she was rescued, she was having to hold her son up in the air pocket in the car's ceiling.

With that story in mind, write out possible scenarios that could happen to you in your neighborhood and find a safe exit strategy.

Preparing Your Children

Teaching your children basic survival skills and training with them is essential, especially if you get separated. "If you're talking about natural disasters and terrorist attacks, it starts with having age-appropriate dialogue about events, their emergency plans, and their communication plan," says Ward. FEMA's Ready Kids website is an excellent place for kids to learn about emergency preparedness with you.

You will need to work out a simple procedure that kids can memorize. Decide now whom they should call and who will pick them up if they're at school or another location. Emergency numbers should be stored in their cell phones, in their lockers, and in their school bags. We encourage you to make a game out of locating pay phones near your home and other places your children frequent.

One of the best ways to engage children and make them feel safe is to share the task of building the emergency kit with them. Make sure they know how to use all the items in the kit, such as the radio. That way, they will know what to do when Mom and Dad say it's time to put the plan in motion.

"I cannot emphasize enough how preparing yourself and your family is key to how you will be on the other side of the event. The more kids know, the more they are involved in the preparation, the better off they will be in the long run," says Nancy. But she warns, "We still have to keep an eye on them, because kids have a way of internalizing crisis, especially depending on how their parents act." Taking your families on an outing to the American Red Cross to go through first aid training and CPR training is a great exercise for the family. Ward and Arteseros say the kids in their communities are loving it.

Prepare Your Business

Getting your business ready for a disaster or emergency is a crucial part of protecting your investments, your employees, and your future. The record-breaking tornadoes, floods, wildfires, and other natural disasters that plagued the United States in 2011 added up to more than $15 billion dollars in economic losses.[25] Businesses are vulnerable to non-weather-related disasters as well: your team could be exposed to dangerous chemicals during construction; they could handle packages contaminated with anthrax; or there could be a serious viral epidemic that affects a high percentage of your employees. Educating yourself and your workforce, and holding quarterly meetings with management, especially if you're in a dangerous weather corridor, will keep your business running and your workforce protected. Create an ongoing dialogue with your staff about their concerns.

Make sure you review the natural disaster and terrorism clauses in all your insurance policies, especially as they affect personnel, real estate, and equipment. Review the language of contracts that commit to delivery of goods and services to find out if you're covered during emergency situations. The FEMA Plan to Stay in Business checklist is a good place to start.[26]

CONTINUITY OF OPERATIONS PLANNING FROM FEMA

1. Carefully assess how your company functions, both internally and externally, to determine which staff, materials, procedures, and equipment are absolutely necessary to keep the business operating.
   - Review your business process flow chart, if one exists.
   - Identify operations critical to survival and recovery.
   - Include emergency payroll, expedited financial decision making, and accounting systems to track and document costs in the event of a disaster.
   - Establish procedures for succession of management. Include at least one person who is not at the company headquarters, if applicable.

2. Identify the suppliers, shippers, resources, and other businesses you must interact with on a daily basis.
   - Develop professional relationships with more than one company in case your primary contractor cannot service your needs.
   - Create a contact list for existing critical business contractors and others you plan to use in an emergency. Keep this list with other important documents on file in your emergency supply kit and at an off-site location.

3. Plan what you will do if your building, plant, or store is not accessible.
   - Consider if you can run the business from a different location or from your home.
   - Develop relationships with other companies to use their facilities in case a disaster makes your location unusable.

4. Plan for payroll continuity.

5. Decide who should participate in putting together your emergency plan.
   - Include coworkers from all levels in planning and as active members of the emergency management team.
   - Consider a broad cross section of people from throughout your organization, but focus on those with expertise vital to daily business functions. These will likely include people with technical skills as well as managers and executives.
6. Define crisis management procedures and individual responsibilities in advance.
   - Make sure those involved know what they are supposed to do.
   - Train others in case you need backup help.
7. Coordinate with others.
   - Meet with other businesses in your building or industrial complex.
   - Talk with first responders, emergency managers, community organizations, and utility providers.
   - Plan with your suppliers, shippers, and others you regularly do business with.
   - Share your plans and encourage other businesses to set in motion their own continuity planning and offer to help others.
8. Review your emergency plans annually. Just as your business changes over time, so do your preparedness needs. When you hire new employees or when there are changes in how your company functions, you should update your plans and inform your people.[27]

Prepare Through Training

Catastrophic events such as Hurricane Katrina, the earthquake in Japan, and the tsunami in Thailand demonstrate that you may be on your own for a week or longer in the event of a disaster. Fortunately, there are nationwide programs like FEMA's Community Emergency Response Teams (CERT) that provide you with the skills and tools you need to support yourself and others in an emergency. Communities in twenty-eight states have conducted CERT training since 1993, when FEMA made it available nationally.

CERT training for community groups is usually delivered in two-and-a-half-hour sessions, one evening a week, over a seven-week period. It educates people "about disaster preparedness for hazards that may impact their area and trains them in basic disaster response skills, such as fire safety, light search and rescue, team organization, and disaster medical operations."[28] The price of training varies depending on the location. Some programs are fully funded and available free of charge.

Lieutenant Erica Arteseros, who has been a firefighter since 1997, highly recommends these programs, which also teach you how to protect yourself in a fire. She suggests that you sign up for the training in conjunction with a neighbor or friend. One of the most important skills that women can learn is a technique called "cribbing and mechanical advantage." Instructors demonstrate how a small person can raise a heavy object with this technique, thus making it possible to effect a rescue that at first might seem impossible.

The Future of Preparedness

One of the biggest transitions that FEMA has gone through, according to Ward, one that is really starting to get traction, is Whole Community Planning.

> We need to plan with private-sector church groups and universities. The private sector has 80 percent of the infrastructure. We shouldn't be distributing food and water out of the parking lot of a Walmart, if all Walmart needs is security around their perimeter to get open. FEMA is not the cavalry who is coming over the hill to save everyone. FEMA is not a first-responder organization. And we're not the *team,* we're just part of the team! For FEMA to assist and support our first responders we need to include everybody.

We hope you'll prepare yourselves and your families and engage with your community to get ready for the next major weather event or incident. Your actions could just save your life.

SURVIVE YOUR DIVORCE

We all walk down the aisle with the best of intentions. We say "I do" and hope it will last a lifetime. But with heartbreaking frequency, it doesn't. One day a woman may wake up and realize the thing she wants most in life is to divorce her husband. Or she may think everything is fine and wake up to find that her husband has served her with divorce papers. Either way, going through a divorce is like losing a limb. There are no emotionally easy divorces. What there can be, however, are divorces that are handled with grace and dignity, so that a year or so from now, when you calm down and regroup, you won't regret how you behaved during this extraordinarily difficult process. What follows is our strategy for facing this hurdle and coming out with the best possible result for you and your children.

May the Best Team Win

At this crisis point, you must hire the best team you can possibly afford in order to achieve the best outcome. We know many women who are tough business negotiators but who end up folding and shouldering all the costs of a divorce just so they don't have to fight with their husbands. We know women who skimp on lawyers, accountants, and custody experts who could help them but who binge on designer shoes to ease the pain. Decisions you will make around your divorce settlement will affect you for the rest of your life. It's completely understandable that you cannot think rationally or straight during the divorce process—that is why you must hire a good team and take their advice.

One good way to assemble a good team is to ask friends for referrals. Make it clear that you're looking for lawyers who are at the top of their field, and accountants who are experienced in valuing assets for a divorce. You can also call the American Bar Association and get a free referral to an experienced attorney in your area if you don't have a good referral source. Do your research online as well: look for people who have published articles on the topic, who have won professional awards, and who are active in their specialties. When you are going to meet with your potential team, come with a brief written summary of your case, which you can send in advance. This will allow the professionals to review your basic situation quickly and will save time—you don't want to have to tell your upsetting story repeatedly. Don't be afraid to ask for references if someone you know did not introduce you.

Although it may be extremely painful to fight for a fair settlement, you must be willing to bear the short-term pain for the sake of the long-term gain—the right financial outcome. If there are children involved, remember that you are also fighting for them. When asked what it takes for a woman to get a good settlement, Vikki Ziegler, a top family law expert, says, "The first component is having top advisers, including a top attorney, accountant, and custody expert, if necessary, to make sure all the *t*'s are crossed and *i*'s dotted. A woman has to be in the right emotional state of mind to listen to expert advice and to make an informed decision, rather than an emotional decision that is not a smart financial decision."

Stay Informed About Family Finances

The best way to get a fair divorce settlement is to always be informed about your family finances, long before the subject comes up. We spoke with Mela Garber, a principal at Anchin, Block & Anchin, a top accounting firm in Manhattan. Mela specializes in working with wealthy families and has encountered many divorce situations in the past twenty-five-years. She notes that the best place to start is with a document that you have to sign at least once a year—your tax return. "Many wives make the mistake of delegating tax preparation to their husbands and signing a document they don't understand or have not read. Much of a family's financial picture is revealed in its tax return," Mela says. "It is critical that you take the time to understand your tax return every year. Make sure a meeting is scheduled where you are present with your husband and the tax accountant before you sign while your marriage is going well. If you make this a regular part of your relationship, you will be informed about how much money the family has that affects you jointly."

In addition, make sure you keep copies of all financial documents that you sign, whether they are insurance policies, tax returns, or trust agreements. Get copies of bank statements, brokerage statements, and other financial statements. If you still don't understand them after meeting with your family accountant or lawyer, take the documents to another lawyer or accountant and pay for a consultation. Ask a friend you trust to refer you to his or her advisers.

Another great habit to get into is to do an annual review of both your credit report and your husband's credit report. There have been cases in which a husband will take out credit cards and send them to his business address so his wife does not know they exist. By looking at his credit report, you will be able to see all his accounts and make sure there are no outstanding debts that may come back to haunt you in a divorce. If your husband has nothing to hide, he should be willing to share his credit report with you, especially since you are legally responsible for debts incurred jointly and may end up paying for debts in his name only. Remember, if your husband ran up large credit card bills and defaulted, the credit card companies have a right to seek assets that are held jointly to repay his personal debts.

Do whatever it takes to make sure you understand what is going on now. It would be very unfortunate if your husband were to die suddenly or become incapacitated and you did not understand how to take over management of the family finances. You certainly have every right—and, frankly, some real responsibility—to understand what is going on.

Keep a Separate Checking Account and Credit Card

While your marriage is still fine, we urge you to open a separate checking account and take out a credit card in your own name. Don't keep everything in joint accounts. Mela points out that your husband could decide to empty or close those accounts before he tells you he is filing for divorce, and you would have no ability to function. You will need to pay a retainer to an attorney or accountant, and you may find your access to your funds cut off. Similarly, if you announce a desire to divorce and have no money in your own account, he could close all joint accounts quickly, leaving you stranded. Or he could owe large sums of money and a judgment could suddenly allow a creditor you are unaware of to go after assets in your joint name. It is never a good idea to be unable to function as a separate person, just in case something happens that you are not planning for. As Mela says, "We know marriages end one way or another. They either end up in divorce or a spouse dies. So to have cash available is very comforting, and it can help in any of these situations, even if a husband gets sick and the wife needs to handle the monthly bills. A woman needs to have an account in her own name and unrestricted access to funds."

Keep Your Nonmarital Assets out of the Marriage

You may come to your marriage with family assets that are protected for you inside of trusts. Sometimes, in the early part of your marriage, you may feel guilty, or your husband may begin to get moody, because he doesn't feel "equal" to you financially, since you have assets over which he has no control. For example, you may be living in a home that is owned by a trust, and your husband may ask you to take the asset out of the trust and put it into a joint name. But the reason that these assets were placed in a trust is to make sure that you would have them no matter what happens in your marriage. If possible, resist his requests to take assets out of your trust. This is a red flag and you may be heartbroken if he files for divorce shortly after you give in.

Handle Your Husband's Requests for Money Carefully

Similarly, if your husband knows you have a large trust, he may ask you for money from the trust so he can start a business. This can be especially tricky if you are a successful professional and your husband is struggling—you want to believe in him, but he complains that he is feeling "emasculated" because he is not as successful as you are. If you comply with his request for money, you've lost all control over it. Your husband may not be willing to give you regular updates on the business, and if it fails, you will lose a substantial amount of your assets.

Rather than remove assets from the trust, Mela suggests that you discuss this request with the trustees and allow the business to be owned by the trust, with the trustees overseeing what your husband is doing. This way, you are not going to be directly overseeing his activities, which could make him feel highly controlled. But you are making sure that the trustees manage these activities. The trustees can keep you informed about the business. If the business goes really well, your husband can eventually do a management buyout of the company and return the money to the trust while keeping the business. You will have helped him get started without putting yourself at undue risk.

Get a Postnuptial Agreement

If your marriage is difficult, but you are not ready to divorce and you did not have a prenuptial agreement, consider signing a postnuptial agreement. This is the same as a prenuptial agreement (see page 72), except that it is created after marriage. A good attorney can draft one for you. This document can then be used as the basis of a divorce settlement if the marriage does not improve.

Asking for a Divorce

Most women do not ask for a divorce lightly. If you have come to the end of the line and want to divorce, Mela counsels that you spend up to one year getting prepared for the divorce. This long wait time may be extremely hard to tolerate, but depending on your financial circumstances, it may really help you get a fair settlement. If your husband makes a great deal more money than you do, or if you are a stay-at-home wife, it is critical to take the time you need to gather all your financial information, make sure you have accounts in your own name, and save some money in your own name before you broach the topic of divorce. During this year, it is also wise to go to a counselor or therapist and get mentally ready to make this very big life change. Vikki Ziegler says, "I believe that everybody who goes through a matrimonial litigation should go through some form of therapy, because it is a life-changing event."

Before you announce your desire to divorce, you should assemble your top team, including, at a minimum, your divorce attorney and accountant. Keep in mind that a divorce lawyer is not enough. If your family has complex assets or if either one of you has family money, an accountant will be needed to make sure your financial settlement is correct. The lawyer will negotiate for the assets, but the accountant will figure out what they are worth.

Understand the State You Live In

You may have gotten hitched in Vegas, but the state where you and your husband have lived for the last six months will determine how your assets are divided in a divorce. Some states are community property states, which means that assets acquired and income earned during the marriage will be split equally between the partners. The other states are called equitable distribution states, which means that a fair formula for distributing earnings and assets is derived after considering many factors, including the age of the spouses, the length of the marriage, who earned what, who stayed home and raised the kids, and so on. Your attorney will be able to tell you which rules apply in the state where you live.

Beware of So-Called Friends

When you are getting divorced, you are in an extremely vulnerable state. Realize that your judgment is impaired. Turning to friends or even sympathetic strangers for support, rather than to tough-minded professionals, can lead to true disaster. Do not seek legal or financial advice from a friend who is not a highly reputable divorce attorney or a highly experienced accountant with divorce experience. And under no circumstances should you allow a friend who does not meet those requirements to represent you in a negotiation. Even more important, beware of the man who suddenly shows up in your life while you are going through a tough divorce, especially if you have money.

There are con artists who specialize in preying on wealthy divorcing women and widows. They are expert at taking advantage of your weakened judgment. Mela says,

> There are con artists who prey on a woman in a stressful time. When a woman is very vulnerable, the man approaches. At first he is very helpful, very emotionally available. He spends time with her, listening to her troubles. He offers to help her for free. He begins to manage money for her, to make decisions. She doesn't like to go to functions alone and he accompanies her. The relationship may be platonic; he may just seem like a wonderful friend. I have seen several cases where the "friend" would medicate or, in extreme situations, even poison her. The woman becomes ill and then is even more dependent on her friend. This is incredibly dangerous.

If your old friends are nervous about your new friend, this is a red flag you should pay attention to. Do not turn your legal documents or your money over to a virtual stranger. Go to a reputable therapist, listen to friends or family members who have known you for years, and be cautious. You are not functioning at your best for at least one full year after your divorce is final. Rely on the right people to protect your assets and your safety.

Physical Abuse

If you are the victim of physical abuse, it is critical that you document each abuse incident. If you are afraid to go to the police, you should still go to the emergency room and get pictures taken of your injuries. Keep a diary of dates and times when the abuse occurs to bolster your case in the future. Your local YWCA can usually help you if you are not ready to contact a shelter. For example, the YWCA in Greenwich, Connecticut—one of the most expensive towns in the United States—has been providing free services to victims of domestic abuse since 1981. According to its website, domestic violence has grown nearly 420 percent in the five years between 2006 and 2011. In 2010, the YWCA responded to 9,113 hotline and crisis calls. That is more than twenty-five calls per day. The program works closely with the Greenwich police department's domestic violence unit, which sometimes receives as many as six domestic violence calls per day. Domestic abuse happens to women who are well-off; many of the women who take advantage of the services in Greenwich are wives of top financial executives. Read *Not to People Like Us: Hidden Abuse in Upscale Marriages* by Susan Weitzman if you are facing this situation—you are not alone.

Be Aware of the Timing

Your goal in getting a divorce should be to remain calm and not unduly provoke your husband. Vikki points out that when and how you ask for a divorce will influence how much of a fight your husband gives you and how miserable the divorce process becomes. Vikki says,

> I always ask a woman to describe her husband's personality and to imagine how he will react. You have to be sensitive to what else your husband may be going through. Did his mother recently pass away? Did he recently suffer a failure in his business? What you actually say and how you say it is important. This should be planned out. Should you say it face-to-face

or through an attorney? Should you ask for a divorce in a public place? All these considerations should be factored in when planning to deliver the news in a safe way.

If He Asks for a Divorce

If your husband suddenly asks you for a divorce, it is our hope that you will at least be financially prepared—that you will have your own bank account and credit card and you will understand the family finances. If so, then you will be ready to assemble your team and move forward. If you have not put anything in place, then the first step is to immediately open a bank account and put funds in the account, assuming you still have access to funds. Make sure you can function on a day-to-day basis. Even if your husband is trying to be reasonable in the beginning, this may change if the negotiation gets difficult. Immediately start to gather copies of all financial documents, as he may later hide them. Then start building your team.

Hidden Assets

Mela told us that it is much more difficult for spouses to hide assets today than it was in the past. If you regularly review your tax return, including all the schedules, you will be familiar with the types of investments that your family has. One of the remaining ways that assets can be hidden is by undervaluing a privately owned company or by deducting non-business expenses from the business. If your husband owns a business and you suspect that it is undervalued, a forensic accountant can do a thorough review of all expenses to make sure that the value of the company is fairly reflected. Mela also says that even if your husband is having his friend hold assets in an account under another name, there will be cash or wire transfers out of checking accounts that a trained accountant can spot and trace. If you are willing to have an accountant do the work, you should be able to find most assets. It is much more unlikely, though not impossible, that your husband is hiding money offshore. Tax payers are required to disclose all foreign-held accounts, so it has become more difficult to conceal these accounts.

Make Sure Assets Are Fairly Valued

If you are getting a divorce, you should know the cost—and value—of every asset jointly held by you and your husband before your lawyer negotiates a settlement. For example, if you are dividing stocks in a brokerage account, two lots of the same security may have been purchased for different original prices, so in fact are worth different amounts because you would pay a different amount of tax if the stocks were sold. If there are complex investments like private equity funds or hedge funds, it is even more crucial that you thoroughly understand what they are worth on an after-tax basis before you negotiate.

Reconsider Keeping the House

Many women who get divorced feel that they should keep the family home. This may be an emotional decision that truly does not make financial sense. Can you really afford the upkeep without your husband's income? Whether you are going to receive money and assets from your ex-husband or distribute them to him, you should sit down with a financial planner and assess whether or not you can afford to keep the house. It may be too large for your needs: if your husband did a great deal of business entertaining and you do not plan to do so, you may be better off with a more modest house and extra cash to take care of your children's needs.

Earnings from Trusts May Be Marital Income

If you have an income-producing trust that was set up for you by your family, you may be surprised to learn that the earnings from the trust may be considered marital income. Although the assets of the trust are not marital property, the earnings distributed to you during your marriage are considered marital income if you are involved in the investment decisions. Therefore, this income would be taken into consideration when deciding how much your husband should pay you or you should pay your husband in a divorce. Consult with your attorney to see if this rule would apply to you.

Alimony Now Goes Both Ways

You may be chagrined to learn that if you have been a high earner and your husband has not been, you will have to pay him alimony. We know a corporate investment banker named Susan who earns $500,000 per year. Her husband, Jake, is an artist who earns money only sporadically by selling paintings; his income is about $30,000 per year. When they got divorced, Susan was dismayed when Jake's attorney asked for alimony; she was shocked when she learned she would have to pay. Susan's trust from her family, which pays her three thousand dollar per month, was included in a calculation of her income because she helped select the money managers who supervise the investments.

Child Support Doesn't Cover the Extras

Keep in mind that child support payments are intended to take care of essential needs, not extras. Your kids will still want lessons, trips, toys, and electronics, and all the other "stuff" they were accustomed to when you and your husband were married. If possible, hammer out in your divorce agreement how extras will be paid for; otherwise, this will be a source of ongoing friction with your ex and will cause pain for your children. Vikki says, "There's always an argument about what's included in child support—camps, college, tutoring, day care, soccer, ballet. If nobody wants to come up with the extra money, there are fights."

Take Out Insurance to Cover Support Payments

Mela points out that it is critical to make sure child support payments and alimony are covered by a life insurance policy on your ex-husband's life. A policy may be agreed to in the settlement, but then it will lapse if he does not make payments going forward. The solution to this is to purchase a "single-premium" policy if possible. One premium is made at the time of the settlement, so you don't have to worry whether or not he will keep up payments. It can be very difficult to make a claim against an estate later; if the husband has remarried and started a new family, there may simply be no money left. A good insurance policy takes care of this issue.

Reduce Costs by Settling

The reason that most divorces become so expensive is that the negotiations turn into a war. Spouses drag out the case just to ruin their exes financially, preferring to enrich their attorneys rather than give one extra cent to their former spouses. Children are often the victims of this war. Even if you are furious with your ex, try to take the high road. Listen to your advisers and accept a fair, reasonable settlement as quickly as possible. This will allow you to move forward in the next chapter of your life with as little psychological damage and as much money as possible.

ANALYZE YOUR DNA

We go to the doctor when we discover a lump in one of our breasts, when we have an anxiety attack and have trouble breathing, when we just can't overcome that cold with rest alone. But how often, as the natural caregivers, do we give *ourselves* the preventive care we need? Imagine if you could learn your risk, based on genetic factors, for certain diseases like breast cancer, type 2 diabetes, Alzheimer's, or Parkinson's? What if you could lower your risk by changing the environmental factors you can control, such as your diet, your lifestyle, or starting on a course of medicine? Imagine if you could prevent the onset of the illness just because you had the knowledge in advance that you are genetically predisposed?

Our DNA is a contributor to our disease risk and tells us some of the key stories about ourselves. It helps map our health risks for diseases like Parkinson's, Alzheimer's, type 2 diabetes, and breast cancer. We can find out if our children (as well as ourselves) will be at risk for many inherited conditions. A person's genetics has an impact on their sensitivity to certain drugs. For example the drug Warfarin (coumadin) is used in preventing blood clots, however people can experience excessive bleeding if they have two genetic variations. Our DNA also traces our ancestral origins.

Anne Wojcicki, the cofounder of 23andMe, says the company currently provides reports covering 200 diseases and conditions including a small number that include information most physicians agree is actionable and individuals could do something to moderate their risk. "So you could find in 23andMe that you are at high risk for breast cancer by being a carrier of a mutation in the BRCA1 or BRCA2 gene. Physicians have a lot of medical literature about what you would want to do if you're a carrier for the BRCA mutation. For something like Parkinson's it's a little more nebulous because there aren't standard clinical recommendations for specific actions a person can take."

Getting your genotype is now relatively inexpensive. At 23andMe the test is $99 when purchased with a one-year subscription. It's a four-step process:

1. Order a kit from 23andMe.com
2. Register your kit online, spit into the tube, and send the tube to the lab
3. The lab analyzes your DNA in 6-8 weeks
4. Log in and start exploring your DNA
   (source: 23andme.com)

You can also order an alternative kit that may be more suitable for young children or the elderly, who might have difficulty producing the saliva required for the standard kit.

Naturally there is a concern that knowing your risks for disease in the future can cause depression, anxiety, or a sense of hopelessness, but studies show the opposite is true.[29]

Many people take a proactive approach to their health. There are now over 100,000 individuals in the 23andMe database and the numbers skew to more men than women. The company peaks with individuals in their 20s and 30s and then again in their 50s and 60s. The next step for 23andMe says Wojcicki is "we need individuals to be able to take their data to their physician and have the physicians say, 'Yes, this is what you do with the data.' So I think the next step, and in my view one of the most important things we can do, is to help educate physicians about the current state of genetics and how it can be a useful tool in providing personalized medicine. For a lot of physicians, it's been a long time since they've taken genetics, and they probably weren't trained on risk genetics. So our long term goal is to make physicians comfortable with genetics and work with physician groups to make genetics a routine and useful part of medical care."

Anne Wojcicki had herself genotyped and discovered that she has a slightly higher than average risk for breast cancer. "I also have a family history of breast cancer. So I'm definitely more religious about the things that I can do to reduce my risk. I even hold back from the casual glass of wine I used to enjoy. I just try to be a lot more aware of environmental things that are associated with breast cancer."

When Anne's husband, Google founder Sergey Brin, was genotyped by 23andMe, he discovered that he has a variant in the LRRK2 gene which confers anywhere from a 30 to 75 percent chance of getting Parkinson's.[30] Brin's mother has been living with Parkinson's disease since 1996 and now the billionaire genius is taking every preventive action available.

"Sergey definitely changed his habits in terms of exercise and diet quite a bit," explains Anne. "He's really interested in things he could do that are going to decrease his odds of developing Parkinson's. He keeps quite current with the literature about Parkinson's prevention and has been very interested in the research involving caffeine. He's been drinking a lot more caffeine as a result of what he's read. He's definitely been proactive." While Sergey Brin is taking up green tea drinking, swimming, diving, and staying at the forefront of new studies, in 2011 he and Wojcicki announced a $50 million fund-raising campaign challenge with the Michael J. Fox Foundation for Parkinson's Research. The couple will match all gifts to the Foundation through 2012.[31]

We want to empower you with knowledge and encourage those who are interested to get genotyped. Genotyping is at the forefront of personalized medicine. Wojcicki says "the health care system is not set up to empower you, and I think part of the reason why is because you're not the end payer." For example, many women take oral contraceptives that contain estrogen or oral hormone replacement therapy, both of which have been linked to increased risk of blood clots. According to Anne, very few of these women have ever been tested to see if they also carry one of the well known genetic variants (factor V and factor II) that put them at relatively high risk for blood clots, as can other non-genetic risk factors such as obesity, pregnancy, cancer, surgery, and sitting for extended periods of time. Would you take oral contraceptives without considering your genetic risk, which can be determined via a readily available test, as well as your non-genetic risk factors? 23andMe also reports carrier status related to pregnancy. Wojcicki says she is surprised at the number of people who don't get tested to find out if they're a carrier for cystic fibrosis or another serious disorder that could affect their children.

"23andMe can tell you that you have a higher probability of developing something based on the current literature. But one thing that's both good and bad about genetics is that only rarely are genetics completely deterministic." Explains Wojcicki, "Huntington's (which we don't test for) is deterministic, but very few things are. We don't tell someone that you are going to develop Parkinson's disease. We tell them that based on the literature, you might be at higher-than-average risk of developing Parkinson's disease." It's your environment and day-to-day habits that will have a massive impact on your health in the long run.

If you have ever suffered a serious medical condition, you have experienced the confusing and endless testing, the fear of the unknown, and painful, or at least time consuming, treatments. It is easy to feel like a victim, to feel lost in the mysteries of the medical field, to feel like a number, even at the best of times. "Over fifteen years I have been to several doctors and they have told me a series of things. I was just making all of this up it wasn't a true disease." says Tara Hudson of her condition, a supporter of 23andMe on her YouTube video on the company's website. "23andMe told me I could have celiac disease. All I have to do is not ingest gluten in my diet. I think if other people have the potential of finding out, they can truly change their lives and live a better life. Why not?"

While some diseases are unavoidable, we can use our DNA information to work on prevention by changing our lifestyles, avoiding certain medications, and staying informed on treatment developments.

Wojcicki sees genetics continuing to evolve in extreme and wonderful ways. The data is mined not just to discover risk factors, but also to give direction to the research and development of treatments, and to push forward personalized medicine. "There was a case of someone who was HIV positive," shares Wojicicki. "This individual had a bone marrow transplant and was transplanted with the bone marrow of somebody who has the CCR5 mutation that affects the ability of HIV to infect cells.[32] So he woke up from his bone marrow transplant resistant to HIV and he's totally medication free."

This is a new opportunity to empower yourself with the best data the world has to offer. We're just at the precipice of understanding its full potential, but wouldn't it be great to start the rest of your life with as much knowledge about your health as possible? We think so.

CHAPTER 6

RETIREMENT

THE SIXTH PEARL OF FINANCIAL WISDOM:
A Woman's Dreams and Potential Are Ageless

IN THIS CHAPTER we want to impress upon you that there is no longer a fixed age that marks the end of a woman's income and the beginning of her demise. Hence our sixth pearl of financial wisdom: a woman's dreams and potential are ageless. According to an article by William Cronin in the *Harvard Gazette,* women who live to be one hundred outnumber male centenarians globally by a ratio of 9 to 1.[1] We have many exciting things to look forward to, now that we have an expanded number of years to spend on the planet. But first, we have to remove the mental constructs that prevent us from seeing that turning fifty can be a rebirth, a regeneration, an event that positions us in the exact center between the person we're already proud of and the person we've always wanted to become.

In American culture, aging has long been treated as a leprosy of sorts, and women have been left to cope with few resources and unappealing options. Only recently, with the advent of magazines like *More,* initiatives by AARP, and the brilliant rebirth of the careers of women in their later years—such as Betty White—have we been seeing the media cast a female senior's image in a positive light, revealing her true value.

As a woman enters her late forties, it's only natural for fear to set in around the future. If she has been the primary caregiver in the family, she has probably not had much time to care for herself and plan for her future. Sometimes the plans that were made for her by her partner or her family didn't add up to much. Or she has met with some serious financial obstacles along the way—a divorce, a battle with breast cancer, a struggling child, or an ill parent who needed extra support.

In even the most secure environments, midlife is a confusing time, as kids leave for college, younger people enter our teams at work, health conditions crop up, partners change or even die, and we consider selling a house that suddenly feels too big. The future feels full of unknowns. The life we have always known is changing, and it is uncomfortable.

It can also be a time driven by fear—fear of loneliness, fear of poverty, fear of boredom, fear of frailty, fear of rejection on the job and in our personal lives. Really, it all comes down to a fear of aging. This fear rubs like sand in our oyster shell, out of which a pearl will emerge: fresh vision, new energy, a feeling of security, and a feeling of belonging.

THE GRAIN OF SAND IN THE OYSTER SHELL

Do you know a woman who . . .

- Isn't sure how much money she needs for retirement or how much income she requires when she gets older?
- Doesn't have enough money to retire and wants choices?
- Needs assistance with grocery shopping, bills, and household tasks, but doesn't want to move to a nursing home?
- Was just made redundant at her job and is looking for inspiration and support?
- Is lonely and looking for a new place to live and new people to meet?
- Owns a family business but has not organized a succession plan?
- Is recently widowed and is now responsible for the bills and the family business?
- Is over fifty but feels youthful, energetic, and ready for a new adventure?

The word "retirement" has various meanings, depending on which dictionary you consult, but they're all related to the idea of cessation. Retirement can be defined as "the action or fact of leaving one's job and ceasing to work" or "the period of one's life after leaving one's job and ceasing to work." Even worse, we've seen retirement defined as "seclusion." Don't these definitions ring of endings and loneliness? No wonder we struggle to create new thought patterns. No wonder our feelings don't match the facts.

Retirement is a construct placed by an outdated system upon the human life span. We hope if you are financially fit enough to retire that you engage in a life-enhancing activity, a charity, a project, or a job just for fun, just because you can. In this brave new world, our skills and our wisdom may have been gathered over decades, but our spirit, our ingenuity, our drive, our determination, and our passion for life are just beginning. In this chapter, we're going to encourage you to embrace a word we like much better than "retirement": "regeneration," which is defined as the "activity of physical or spiritual renewal." To regenerate is to "reestablish on a new, usually improved, basis or make new or like new." Yes, retirement can be especially exciting as new paradigms are drawn for people over fifty—including everything from business to travel to living arrangements and ways of connecting with others.

REDEFINE RETIREMENT

Often women approaching fifty think of retirement as a way of removing themselves from the game of life and sitting on the sidelines. It's time to let go of this worn-out notion. We have the ability to become fully involved in the second half of our lives. By now we know ourselves well, both our strengths and our weaknesses. We know what we have to contribute, whether it is through raising a child or grandchild, starting a company, becoming an artist, or sitting on a board. We have tremendous wisdom, gathered from the hard work of living on the planet for half a century or more. We can take all our knowledge and apply it toward creating a fantastic "second act," full of financial success and personal satisfaction.

Face the 50+ Financials and Succeed

Now is the time when we must face financial reality honestly and create a sustainable plan for living and prospering in the second half of our lives. A 2010 survey by the Employee Benefit Research Institute found that 43 percent of Americans have less than ten thousand dollars in retirement savings.[2] So it is unlikely that we have enough money to loll by the pool and sip on a fruity cocktail as we hurtle toward the century mark. In fact, we may even face destitution if we don't take action. Thirteen percent of women over seventy-five years old are poor, compared to 6 percent of men, according the U.S. Census. The terror both men and women feel over poverty in their elder years in the United States is palpable. A recent poll by Allianz Insurance asked Americans between the ages of forty-four and seventy-five which they feared more—running out of money in retirement or death. A majority, 61 percent, feared running out of money in retirement more, while only 39 percent feared death.[3]

Confront Your Financial Fears

If you are scared about running out of money, the first thing you need is to find out exactly how bad your situation is. It is true that women face extra challenges that make it difficult to save. We spoke with Vera Gibbons, a top personal finance expert who appears regularly on the *Today* show. Vera is very aware of the concerns women have.

> Women have a much longer life expectancy these days; we also earn less than men and we take a lot of time out of the workplace to care for kids and aging parents. Getting divorced often lowers our standard of living, so women have a lot of anxiety around money, particularly when you consider that nine out of ten women are going to be solely responsible for managing their finances at some point in their lifetimes. In addition, women are relying on any number of crutches. For example, one out of every four women relies on her husband's pension. This is a risky strategy, because if he dies first, you'll probably only get fifty percent of the survivor benefits. Many women are expecting to receive an inheritance, but that probably won't be there, because our parents are living longer

and therefore requiring long-term care. Others of us only have Social Security to look forward to for support. What's scary is that women over sixty-five rely on Social Security for almost half their income; yet at its current level, the average benefit for retired female workers is just $1,164 per month! Saving outside of Social Security is crucial to having a comfortable retirement.

Vera urges women to crunch the numbers to find out exactly what their situation is. You need to determine how much money you will need in order to stop working and how much you need to save now in order to get there. A good place to start is by working with online financial calculators. Vera recommends a calculator called The Ballpark E$timate on the choosetosave. org website. Alternatively, you can hire a fee-only financial planner to help you come up with a realistic estimate and a workable plan. Vera notes that "you need to replace 85 percent of your preretirement income to live comfortably in retirement."

Savings Strategies

Ideally, a woman should start thinking about retirement when she gets her first job. The most important step once you get a job is to maximize your contributions to your 401(k) plan. Put the money aside and pretend it isn't there. Don't liquidate any of it or borrow from it under any circumstances— you will need it when you are older. A disturbing consequence of the financial downturn is that people have been borrowing from their 401(k) plans, and then losing their jobs. If you lose your job and have an outstanding loan from your 401(k), it must be paid back immediately, or it is deemed a withdrawal, subject to tax as income as well as a 10 percent early-withdrawal penalty. Taking a hardship withdrawal from your 401(k) when you are young may mean a significant drop in retirement savings later.

According to Vera, you should be saving 15 percent of your earnings, including your contribution to your 401(k) plan. What happens if you crunch the numbers and they are not adding up? Vera says,

Technically, it's never too late to start planning for retirement, but you've got to play catch-up. That means boosting contributions to your 401(k), scaling back your lifestyle, and working longer. The good news is that if you delay your retirement for just three years beyond age sixty-two, you could increase your nest egg by more than a third. That's because you'll save for retirement longer, postpone your withdrawals, receive more from Social Security and any pension, and you'll qualify for Medicare, which would eliminate the need to buy costly private health insurance.

Manage Your Nest Egg Effectively

If you have saved a large nest egg for your later years and would like to live on the income rather than continue to work, careful planning will allow you to do just that. Most experts recommend that you cut back the amount of risk in your investment portfolio as you get closer to the age when you plan to use the assets. Many so-called moderate-risk investment portfolios have 60 or 70 percent invested in equities or other risky assets—in our opinion, this is too much. A better rule of thumb is to follow the advice originated by John Bogle, founder of the Vanguard Group of mutual funds: subtract your age from one hundred, and use that as the maximum percentage of equities and other risky assets in your portfolio at any time.

If your husband has been supervising your investment accounts, it is important that you discuss the investment strategy he is undertaking for both of you. We know a woman named Emily who had given this responsibility to her husband and never bothered to look at what he was doing. John had saved more than $250,000, and she thought they would have a good retirement. John, unfortunately, died suddenly of a heart attack at age seventy. When Emily finally got around to looking at the retirement accounts, she was shocked to see that 100 percent of the assets were in stocks and that the value had dropped by 45 percent during the financial crisis. John had been happy to do the investing and felt he would live a long life—his desire to trade stocks in retirement without discussing this risk with her means she is facing a much less comfortable future. Couple this with the fact that he thought he would make more money by investing in stocks than by paying for a life insurance policy naming her as beneficiary, and we can see how a very difficult situation was created. Men often do not want to think about the fact that they are more likely to die before you do, and they may take much bigger risks than they should with money you will eventually need to live on. If your husband wants to trade stocks, make sure the amount is appropriate and he is not risking your entire nest egg.

There are many mutual funds that offer to gradually decrease the equity portion of your investment while increasing the fixed-income portion as you get older; we don't recommend this strategy. The financial markets are, and will continue to be, very volatile. You will be much better off buying top-rated funds or investments in each asset category and working with a financial adviser to make changes to the asset allocation as time goes on. A portfolio that is sold to you as a prepackaged "life stages" fund cannot be adjusted for your specific situation.

It is always best to remain highly liquid and to work with a good financial adviser to create a program that is right for you. If you have a large amount of money to invest, make sure you explore other types of income-producing investments, such as master limited partnerships, which allow you to participate in the revenue streams from sources such as oil wells and gas pipelines. You should also ask for funds that invest in blue chip, high-dividend stocks—funds that invest in only the strongest companies. There also may be good opportunities in certain corporate bonds. Don't shy away from great growth opportunities, such as Asian equities—just make sure you are taking risks with an appropriate amount of money. In any case, you should get experts to help you choose wisely.

Do not think that investing in financial assets is the only way to generate passive income for your later years.

Keep Working for the Fun of It

Many women over the age of fifty are amazed at how energized they feel. They have no intention of retiring in the traditional sense. Rather, they are making plans to begin life's second act. Some intend to stop working for money, but plan to pursue hobbies or serve as unpaid experts in the not-for-profit sector. They have saved wisely and are sure that their assets can support them while they pursue their various interests. Others are launching businesses, networking with other professionals, or are ready to start job hunting in a new industry. Whether the thought of your second act inspires fear or passion, you need to realize that you're not alone.

Beverly Mahone, now in her fifties, is a respected journalist and an expert on the baby boomer generation. She was named one of the top twenty-one African American bloggers in 2011 as well as the Top 50 Fabulous Women Entrepreneurs by *SistaSense* magazine and Black Business Women Online. She focuses, in part, on supporting women who choose to evolve and reinvent themselves at midlife, having gone through the process herself. Beverly also hosts her own radio show, called *The Boomer Beat,* on WCOM Radio in Carrboro, North Carolina. She writes three blogs and is the founder of Boomer Diva Nation (boomerdivanation.org), a networking group that helps women in midlife work together to empower their second acts.

Beverly sees an attitude of excitement and creativity among women entering the second half of life. She says, "I started my business when I was forty-eight, and now I'm kind of switching off in a little different direction at fifty-three. I am also the primary caregiver for my four-year-old grandson while his mom is away at college. I have a husband working in D.C. while commuting on the weekends to be home. So there's a lot going on, but I am determined to prove that you can do it and that age should not prevent you from accomplishing your goals and dreams."

Although it may be scary to start over, Beverly points out that staying in a frustrating job just to have corporate benefits is no way to spend the second half of your life. "I would encourage any woman who is in an unhappy corporate situation to take the leap. The frustration and stress can have a devastating effect on our health as we get older. So why spend the rest of your life miserable in a job that is really doing nothing but paying bills? Go out and make yourself happy and then you can have two things: You can have money and you can be happy."

If you choose to start a new business, you will find lots of support from Boomer Diva Nation. The group offers Web-based support, networking, and the opportunity to promote your business to other members.

Another characteristic of boomer women who become entrepreneurs is flexibility—they often do many jobs at the same time, not just one. For example, Beverly blogs, has a radio show, provides consulting services, and runs a networking organization. Although midlife women who strike out on their own may not make as much money as they did during their corporate careers, their sense of personal happiness and fulfillment is dramatically higher. The chance to express all their many talents is often more fulfilling than focusing on just one outlet.

Redefining Midlife and Beyond

Another inspiring example of what's possible at midlife and beyond is Aleta St. James, a success coach and energy healer. Aleta is the author of *Life Shift: Let Go and Live Your Dream*. She fulfilled her own dream when she gave birth to twins in 2004, when she was just three days shy of her fifty-seventh birthday. Aleta started her career as an actress and then became a healer who uses sound, color, and energy to help her clients—including many celebrities and wealthy individuals—reach their highest potential.

For Aleta, the concept of retirement just doesn't resonate. "I've never ever thought that I was going to retire. I always think about winding up, not down. I'm now sixty-three, and my children are six and a half years old. So they give me a lot of reason to keep going, and to keep reinventing myself and expanding my horizons."

Aleta works with many clients over the age of fifty who are just getting going. Often they need to create more wealth for themselves because they realize they cannot rely exclusively on Social Security or savings. Reinventing themselves enables them to keep leading the fabulous life they worked so hard to create. Says Aleta, "Let's just say that you get to about fifty or sixty and you feel like, 'Oh, I really haven't achieved the things that I wanted to achieve.' That's what makes people give up and close down. But once you get sparked up again, it's like you have a whole new set of lungs, and you can start to create again, just as though you were in your twenties or thirties. You're coming in with a lot of wisdom and understanding, so you can work smarter and with less effort."

For Aleta, much of the difference is in attitude. She advises her clients not to give in to the messages that the mainstream media—and most employers—heap on women over fifty. No, we are not washed-up, irrelevant desperate housewives. Women over fifty are strong, sexy, involved, and highly creative. We can do anything we want to do. Looking at the second half of your life through this lens will galvanize you into action rather than making you feel defeated. Yes, we have to learn about the Internet if we don't understand it in order to interact with the new digital economy. Yes, we must carefully understand our finances and create a viable strategy to support the second half of life. But we have learned many things in the first half of life, and we can continue to learn. We are now masters at adapting to change and moving forward.

ALETA'S ADVICE FOR A SUCCESSFUL SECOND ACT

Take Care of Your Body

Get on a good nutrition and exercise program. You want to keep your body alive, vital, and vibrant, because if your body starts breaking down, it squelches your passion and energy.

Support Your Emotional Healing

Do emotional healing work—any kind of it—so that you're constantly giving yourself a tune-up. You want to shift to higher levels of understanding about yourself, maybe even get to the point of loving yourself.

Release Past Disappointments

Release the self-criticisms and disappointments that have previously plagued you, such as: "Oh, I wish I could have done [fill in the blank]" . . . or "I wish this relationship would have worked out" . . . "I wish I could have had children" . . . or "I wish I didn't have children" . . . or "I could have been a star . . . a contender . . . an artist . . ." Ask yourself, "What can I create *now* that's going to give me the zest to get up every morning and say, 'I'm so glad to be alive! And thank you for giving me this gift of life!'?"

Leave Discontented People Behind

If you have friends who bond with one another by complaining about their circumstances, you need to release them or you'll remain stuck right along with them.

Support Your New Goals

Invite groups of people into your life who can energize you. You want to be with women and men who are excited about life and about what they're doing. We're like marathon runners. Sometimes you hit the twenty-fifth mile and you need another runner to run beside you for that last mile so that you can make it to the finish line. The energy you get from your surroundings can be enormous. Your circle of supporters doesn't have to be religious, but it helps to have some kind of cosmic connection of love and understanding and compassion with other people.

We believe retirement is a concept that will go out of fashion because it's both unnecessary and undesirable. Women's health care is improving, which means, first, that we're going to live longer than women of previous generations. Therefore, the old recommendations about what to save and how to save it are out of date. It just may not be realistic to think about retiring at age sixty-five if you're going to live to be one hundred. In addition, women are feeling more energized and ready for new opportunities than women of previous generations. What we hear from so many women is that they finally feel they have choices; they finally have a sense of freedom. The nest is empty, the mortgage is nearly paid off. They can finally concentrate on themselves and discover what they want to work on next.

RETIRE OFFSHORE IN LUXURY: IT CAN BE BETTER OUTSIDE AMERICA

It is a stark reality that many of us will have to downscale our lifestyles significantly if we choose to retire in the United States. If we lack adequate savings and have to rely on Social Security alone, or if we do not own a home that is paid for in full, we may not be able to afford shelter, food, and health care. If you have only a moderate amount of savings, staying in the United States may mean forgoing vacation trips and luxurious extras in order to afford the basic necessities. If this is your situation, you may simply need to find a more affordable place where you can have a better standard of living—hence our suggestion that you consider retiring abroad.

It may seem frightening to consider moving to a foreign country, but you may be pleasantly surprised to learn that an estimated 1 million Americans are now living in Mexico in their retirement years.[4] Many enjoy a much higher quality of life than would be possible in the United States, due to Mexico's lower cost of living and inexpensive medical care. In Mexico, you might even be able to afford a housekeeper! We want to give you the facts and help you imagine a luxurious retirement. If you are living on Social Security alone, you can live well outside the United States. If you have solid retirement savings, you can live a very upscale lifestyle offshore.

There are many locations to choose from when you consider this option. Lunigiana in Italy, Bocas del Toro in Panama, Nha Trang in Vietnam, and Béarn in France have all been cited as great places to retire abroad.[5] However, just as an example, we've chosen to profile life in Lake Chapala, Mexico, because it's a manageable distance from friends and family in the United States, it has a large American population, English is spoken widely, and U.S. products and home comforts are readily available. In addition, residency and work visas are easily obtainable. If you're starting your retirement strategy in your forties, you should consider buying or renting a property in Mexico while still maintaining your main residence in the United States. That would allow you to slowly transition to a new community where you can eventually retire amid established friends and familiar activities.

Lake Chapala, Mexico, has become a major attraction for expatriate Canadians and Americans due to its natural charms and modern conveniences. The beautiful lake is the largest landlocked body of water in Mexico, and sits 5,200 feet above sea level. It is surrounded by the Sierra Madre, and is only a twenty-five-minute drive from the very modern Guadalajara airport. Guadalajara, Mexico's second-largest city, is only fifty minutes away. The lake is a three-and-a-half-hour drive from the Pacific Ocean. Unlike the U.S.–Mexico border, which is riddled with crime and violence, this vibrant retreat, which is ten hours away from the border, has offered an oasis of privacy to the likes of Elizabeth Taylor, Charles Bronson, D. H. Lawrence, and several former Mexican presidents.

The area is a resort destination for many wealthy Mexicans, who maintain beautiful haciendas by the shore of the lake. The temperate weather, with an average temperature of 68 degrees Fahrenheit, is a happy consequence of the triple rings of mountains protecting the area, which creates a year-round microclimate. Winters are very mild and summers are relatively cool, which is particularly attractive to boomers escaping cold or humid climates in the United States. The area was first settled in 1538 and boasts beautiful architecture, incredible gardens, a lively community of artists, many restaurants, and a large, active expatriate community.

"When you're trying to save for retirement and you can't make it, there are only two or three alternatives," explains Marian Wellman, an American resident of Lake Chapala who is now sixty-two. "You can work longer, save more, or you can live on less—those are the choices! Moving to Mexico becomes a way you can live on less and still have a decent lifestyle—a much better lifestyle, actually! Instead of spending on property taxes and heating bills, you can spend on travel and recreation, which is something I can do."

Today, Marian enjoys singing in an eighty-person choir called Los Cantantes del Lago. She is single (divorced, with two grown sons), and moved to Lake Chapala at the age of fifty-five. She estimates that there are between seventeen thousand and twenty thousand Americans living in the area.

I had a tax preparation and financial planning business in the United States and I had lived for thirty-five years in Denver. During the week I came to visit Lake Chapala, I had almost a gut reaction that this was somewhere I could really be. I loved the beauty of the place; everyone I met that week was incredibly friendly and helpful—all with very interesting personalities—and they seemed to be having a wonderful time. I just had the feeling, 'If they can do it, I can do it.' I toured around with a real estate agent, and the day before I was ready to leave, not having found anything, I discovered a great place in a gated community that was still under construction—a development of cluster homes, all with contemporary designs and all very low-priced. I put half down with the rest due in six months, when the home was scheduled to be ready, and returned to Denver having made my life decision to move to Mexico.

Part of the original idea of moving to Mexico was financial, and when I got here, the beauty, the type of people who lived here, and just "getting out of the rat race" made it the right decision for me. I had originally planned on not working, but wasn't completely in a position to do that, so I started up my income tax–preparation business again the following year. I started only with flyers on bulletin boards and doing twenty returns that first year. That has now built up to a website, reaching people all around Mexico and some other places around the world from referrals and people moving, and now is a very substantial business for me, now specializing in issues for expatriates (www.taxesinmexico .com). There are also tax advantages to working out of the country, along with lower costs for help and other expenses. If you work outside of the United States and meet certain requirements you still need to file a federal tax return, but may have an income tax exemption for "earned" income. That means, for example, in 2011, someone with an Internet business, a writer, artist, designer, a regular salaried job in Mexico, or otherwise able to work from their home in Mexico (or elsewhere outside the U.S.), the first $91,500 of earned income per person may be exempt from federal income tax.[6] This amount of exemption changes periodically, so it is important to work with a tax preparer familiar with your situation. In addition, in some states, you may owe state taxes if you move offshore but maintain a U.S. bank account. The U.S. government will send a Social Security check to a bank account in Mexico, but not to certain other countries. Make sure you check the latest rules.

If you are intrigued by the idea of moving to Mexico and want more information, you might want to check out Focus on Mexico (www.focus onmexico.com). The website is filled with comprehensive information about Mexico, and you can sign up for a free monthly newsletter about the Lake Chapala area. There are also a number of videos on the area to give you a sneak preview. You can even "test drive" Mexico by taking advantage of a Focus 8-Day Education program, created and run by Marie Dwyer-Bullock, who moved to Mexico in 1995 with her husband. The program includes seminars given by expert speakers on living, working, and retiring in Mexico, and is designed to give people everything they need to make an informed decision as to whether Mexico is right for them. "Hundreds and hundreds of people have participated in our programs over the years, and as a result, are now happily living in Chapala," says Marie.

An Active Expatriate Community

One lively center for the expatriate community is the Lake Chapala Society, which has more than 3,700 members from twenty-four countries. The nonprofit organization has been in existence since 1955. LCS offers Spanish classes, a twenty-thousand-volume lending library, a four-thousand-volume DVD and video library, free medical screenings, and a mail drop in the United States. Members offer fascinating lectures and there are classes on a wide variety of topics, from yoga to history. There are numerous volunteer opportunities, ranging from working with disabled children in a horseback-riding program to teaching organic gardening. There are extensive gardens and a beautiful clubhouse in Ajijic, one of the most picturesque towns in the Lake Chapala area. Most activities are offered for a nominal fee; introductory Spanish classes cost 150 pesos, or twelve dollars. According to the website, annual dues are 400 pesos, or thirty-four dollars. Marie explains,

> There are many English-speaking organizations to belong to on the lakeside: a computer club, camera club, a garden club, a book club, and a culinary arts society. I often hear people say I don't know what I did all day but I didn't get half of it done. There are people here who are ninety years old and still driving, who serve on boards of charity organizations and go dancing at night. There are also people moving here that are in their thirties and forties. Living in Lake Chapala is like going back in time fifty years. People love the more laid-back way of life, where they don't need to keep up with the Joneses. It's an amazingly active world. There are a few more women than men simply because that's what's happening in our world. In this area there's a huge support group among the foreign population. People just join in together. Singles and couples go out together so you don't feel like the last man out as a single person. There are so many different things to get involved in.

Lower Cost of Living

It is the cost of living that really closes the deal for baby boomers; living in Mexico can be 30 to 40 percent cheaper than living in the United States or Canada. Marie says,

Many of our clients are well traveled, and familiar with other retirement locations, but one of the reasons they chose Lake Chapala is because of the lower cost of living. Many people are concerned about running out of money before they run out of life, so if they move to a place where the cost of living is less, they can live better and stretch their retirement dollars farther.

It varies depending on lifestyle, of course, and whether you own or rent, but on average a single person can live an enhanced lifestyle on $1,400 to $1,800 a month and for a couple $2,000 to $2,500 a month. However, Karen and Bill, who work with us, lived just on his Social Security of $1,400 a month for both of them when they first moved here, but they did own their own home. Several years later they are enjoying good appreciation in the value of their home, which is their hedge against inflation.

A decent rental property in a good location, with a reasonable number of amenities, costs between eight hundred and one thousand dollars per month. You can also find very nice rental properties—a one-bedroom house with a garden—for as little as three hundred dollars per month a bit farther from the center of the expatriate community. It is always a good idea to rent for six months before you buy, just so you can be sure you like the area and the lifestyle change. Six-month rentals are easy to obtain.

If you are interested in buying a home, $150,000 to $300,000 will get just about everyone what they want: two or three bedrooms plus a den, two bathrooms, and a covered terrace. Marian says, "The great majority of people buy with cash. It's also quite possible to have a mortgage." She purchased her home rather than renting first because she preferred the feeling of security that home ownership gave her. "I had owned a house since I was twenty-six years old and it was a big lifestyle change anyway and I couldn't handle the idea that not only was I moving to another country but I was not going to own my own home," she explains. Property taxes are very low in Lake Chapala—between fifty and two hundred dollars per year.

Labor is also very affordable. To employ a maid or a gardener costs $3.50 to $5.00 per hour, depending on whether your staff is part-time or full-time. You can hire a team of maintenance workers for a whole week for around $250. Household help is usually out of range for women living on Social Security in the United States, but it is an affordable reality for women who live in Mexico. A home health-care aide to help you if you become infirm or frail is also extremely inexpensive.

In terms of transportation, many people get by without cars and use the local bus system or the readily available local taxis. You can also buy a car or bring your car from the States.

Residents enjoy a range of entertainment, from free fiestas to world-class concerts. A steak dinner with wine in a nice restaurant is around fifteen dollar. A seniors discount card is available that provides 50 percent off first-class buses all over Mexico, 50 percent off property taxes, and a long list of other discounts.

Getting Residency

There are different types of visas available for those who want to retire to Mexico; in her sixteen years of residency in the country, Marie says she has never seen an individual or a family turned down. The FM-3 (Visitante Rentista) visa is designed for someone who wants to live in Mexico at least part of the time. It is a state document, and working papers can be attached to this document. The FM-2 (Immigrante Rentista) visa is designed for those who intend to reside permanently in Mexico. It is a federal document issued by the Mexican government. After five years on FM-2, you can apply for *inmigrado* status and no longer need to renew your visa; if you are working, there is no longer a need for working papers.

Health-Care Costs

"The quality of health care in Mexico is comparable to that in the United States, and the nicest thing about it is that you can afford it. I know people who have had triple bypass surgery and it's all covered under the IMSS [imss. gob.mx]," says Marian Wellman, referring to the Mexican national health insurance system. She adds, "My IMSS health insurance premium is around three hundred dollars per month." Marian also has an expatriate health plan called IMF, which costs her about two thousand dollars per year. "As long as you're not in the United States for more than six months in any given year, you're qualified." she says. "It costs roughly a third of what it would cost to have a comparable policy in the United States."

Marie Dwyer-Bullock says her experience with the health-care system in Guadalajara has been outstanding: "It's funny—when people go to one of the hospitals in Guadalajara, they often refer to their room as the hotel room instead of the hospital room. There's one hospital that has an Italian restaurant on the ground floor and you order your food from a menu. Your spouse has a cot in the room. In a lot of the hospitals here, they encourage a spouse or a family member to come and stay with you. The doctors befriend their patients."

In Mexico, kind doctors make house calls if you are sick, and get to know each patient individually. Veterinarians also make house calls if your pets are sick. Home aides are inexpensive, as are physical therapists. If you become seriously ill, Guadalajara has an excellent hospital that can consult remotely with doctors and hospitals back in the United States. The old-fashioned idea of patient care is alive and well in Mexico—an idea that has been driven out of the United States by high costs.

Starting Fresh

We believe that creating your regeneration strategy abroad helps you launch a new lease on the next phase of your life. However, Mexico isn't for everyone. Residents say that some people who are not very flexible have a hard time adjusting. But the people who are willing to open up and embrace the culture and the people have an amazing experience there.

Living abroad offers an opportunity to discover who you truly are. "Many Americans and Canadians want to get away from the materialism and the politics and the fast pace of life," says Marie.

> When we boomers were brought up, it was all about work, work, work. Living here, you get a different handle on what's important in life. It's not about materialism and what you have, but what you do with your life and the difference that you can make. Here we learn from the Mexican people and come to appreciate their value system, where being with friends and family is more important than working overtime so you can acquire more stuff. It is living a more meaningful life, every single day, and learning to appreciate what you already have!

Living abroad also offers an opportunity for what's become fondly known as "border promotion." Instead of being known as John's daughter, Mr. Keen's widow, Bill Saunders's ex-wife, Mary's mother, sister, or cousin, wouldn't it be refreshing to be known as *you*? To make a fresh start as the person you wish to be as an individual? That's a kind of promotion we can give ourselves that no boss could ever provide.

We're not asking you to forget your past or devalue your memories and connections with home, but moving out of the country gives you a chance to live well and dump the albatross of your old life if it no longer fits. "There's something different about leaving your old world and going to retire in a new place. You can really reinvent yourself," explains Marian. "It's hard to change who you are and how you act in familiar surroundings. But when somebody crosses the border, they can give themselves a border promotion and become whoever it was they wanted to be."

BEAT THE NURSING HOME RACKET

The cost of nursing home care is becoming increasingly prohibitive. The average yearly cost is fifty thousand dollars and climbing.[7] Six out of ten women don't know the cost of long-term care; even more frightening is the fact that many people who need extended nursing home care drain their personal finances in only six months. One third of nursing home residents pay for all their expenses with their own savings. Just 5 percent are paying with long-term care insurance they purchased in advance. The majority of Americans mistakenly think that Medicare covers the cost of long-term care; in fact, Medicare pays for short-term stays only. Medicaid picks up the tab for two-thirds of nursing home residents, and these individuals have exhausted most of their savings. (Their spouses are permitted to maintain their assets under some circumstances, including a home, income, and savings.)[8]

It's no surprise that baby boomers are rebelling against nursing homes and other long-term care facilities. Born between 1946 and 1964, baby boomers are the generation that burned their bras, embraced free love, and rejected the conventional lives of their parents' generation. In 2012, when they're between the ages of forty-eight and sixty-six, baby boomers are once again forging their own paths and lashing out again at the establishment.

They're fighting the nursing home stigma and mapping out a new kind of life for their golden years, which includes liberating and life-enhancing choices within their communities.[9]

Alyson Burns runs AARP's Decide, Create, Share campaign. It's dedicated entirely to women, particularly older women, and helps them prepare for a more secure financial future and retirement. Alyson says, "This generation of boomers has always fought for opportunities to maintain their independence, specifically women, and they are the decision makers when it comes to their families. These baby boomers who are making these decisions are women who were on the forefront of the women's movement." But unfortunately, only 23 percent of women will likely be able to pay for future long-term care with personal savings.[10] Alyson's mission is to get more women to realize if they want to stay in their beautiful homes and have nursing care, they need to plan where they want to live and save for it, on top of their savings to fund their lifestyles, as early as their forties.

In AARP surveys, 90 percent of people fifty and older say they want to stay in their homes and communities.[11] "They want to be part of a strong social network; they want to stay in a place that feels comfortable and where they feel vibrant and active, a place that is part of their lives and part of their families' lives. The baby boomers are graying the suburbs because they want to stay where they live," says Alyson. Many baby boomers see retirement as a second youth and often plan to continue working. Their houses are being modified not just for aging gracefully but to accommodate home-office workspaces and lifestyles.

Staying in Your Home

Many individuals heading toward retirement are renovating their homes to increase the possibility that they can remain there even as they meet physical challenges. If you are buying or renting a new home for the next stage of life, features to consider include single-level living quarters, wide doorways (to accommodate a wheelchair), room to construct a ramp between the garage and the home interior, living quarters for a home health-care aide or nurse, and easy-access bathrooms. Forty-nine percent of people over the age of fifty indicated on an AARP survey that their homes will not be able to meet their physical needs as they age. Only 34 percent said their homes have an entrance without steps. Just 37 percent said they had doorways wide enough to accommodate a wheelchair.[12]

If you are considering renovating your home, meet with an architect who specializes in senior living design. You should plan to make your home wheelchair accessible, particularly around bathrooms and kitchen areas. Even if you are a younger boomer, still relatively young, you may need knee surgery or other medical procedures that limit your mobility. "It's not just about the later years of life. Boomers should be thinking about how they can maneuver in their homes if they have an injury that challenges their mobility in the short term, too," says Alyson. Adding or renovating a first-floor bathroom, which should include features like grab bars and an unobstructed low-curb shower room, is a good investment for the long term.[13] You can get more guidance at AARP Home Design (www.aarp.org/homede sign), with examples of award-winning full-home redesigns that are elegant yet wheelchair accessible in various locations, including Pasadena, California; Burns Harbor, Indiana; and Lakeland, Florida. Make sure to review your home's proximity to public or assisted transportation, medical facilities, and local community centers as well as the availability of delivery options for groceries and other supplies. It is especially convenient to live near a pharmacy that delivers.

Move In, Golden Girls

Many single boomer women are choosing to live together, and nonprofits like Golden Girls Homes, Inc., in Minneapolis are supporting their efforts. Their mission: To help women live in community by sharing housing, developing networks, and linking them to services supportive to women. There are resources and listings on the organization's website, www.goldengirl homes.us. There is also a growing trend of empty nesters moving into metropolitan areas, seeking single-floor homes in high-rises, a lively cultural life, and entertainment and services within walking distance.

Entering the Elder Communities

AARP has identified a number of new models for the aging communities that are not nursing homes, including niche communities, cohousing, and the village model. In niche communities, you find groups of people living together who share similar interests, goals, or backgrounds. These are very different community cultures with various price ranges. If you are purchasing a university community unit, you may invest hundreds of thousands of dollars. Rent at an artists' community for $1,700 a month or live in an RV for $800 a month with the park set.

The Village Model

The village model is suited to couples or individuals who want to stay in place but benefit from services, support, and social activities. It is increasingly popular, as aging boomers want to remain in their homes. Beacon Hill Village in Boston, which was founded in 2002, was the first of its kind in the United States. Villages can have as many as four hundred members, though many have fewer than one hundred. There is an annual membership fee that can range anywhere between one hundred and one thousand dollars. Any services are coordinated centrally and range from dog walking, medical services, grocery services, and transport. "You are creating these incorporated communities of people who can access services like a caregiver or someone who can do the housework chores," says Burns. "You are finding people who have been living together for years and who say, hey, we should pool our resources and identify other services we can tap into to benefit everyone." As an advantage of membership, many activities like movie tickets and events are discounted.

The Niche Communities

The Burbank Senior Artists Colony in Los Angeles draws artists, thespians, and musical types and offers a performance theater, creative art studios, and art walk area for residents to showcase their work alongside the more traditional facilities.

In Santa Fe, New Mexico, Rainbow Vision caters to the growing aging gay and lesbian communities. There are over 3 million gay, lesbian, bisexual, and transgender Americans. Many of them have no adult children who might serve as caregivers. The New Mexico community caters to dwellers seeking condominium, independent, and assisted living. They offer concierge services, first-class dining, Billie Jean King Fitness Centers/Spas/Tennis Centers, cabaret, and more.

One of the fastest-growing areas of this sector is university-based retirement communities. Known as UBRCs, there are over fifty on campuses including Dartmouth, Cornell, Oberlin, and Penn State. They are particularly attractive to highly educated women who can attend courses at the universities and enjoy being involved in a community spurred on by a younger generation.

Cohousing

Many Americans are entering into elder or multigenerational cohousing, which engage inhabitants in their community and their new neighbors. According to AARP, to buy in costs anywhere from $100 to $750,000, monthly anywhere from $100 to $300. Many cohousing projects offer rentals between $600 and $2,000 a month. Architects Charles Durrett and Kathryn McCamant brought the Danish living concept to the United States in the 1980s. "These are communities that are popping up among strangers," explains Alyson Burns. "These cohousing communities can be intergenerational. These are communities where there are separate units but common spaces. Those common spaces can be used for fun things like having meals together or doing recreational things together. I think that's an added bonus to boomers who want to remain in their community."

The Silver Sage Village in Boulder, Colorado, by McCamant and Durrett Architects is a great example of this growing concept and the U.S. Winner of the National Association of Home Builders (NAHB) Silver Award for Best of 50+ Housing, 2008. "The common house supplements the private houses with facilities including a public dining room and kitchen, sitting room, crafts room, media room, library, guest rooms, and storage."[14] Their design for the Oakland, California, cohousing development Casa Velasco is a conversion of a 1920 three-story building. There are "fifteen studios and five single-bedroom apartments for low-income senior singles and couples. Extensive common facilities (on the roof) serve to give seniors a place to get to know each other and to have meetings of mutual concern and activities of mutual interest."[15]

The Changing Face of Elder Care

We hope we have given you an abundant number of options to beat the nursing home racket, and even if you need nursing home care, there are improving, less institutional options like the Green House Project, in which around ten individuals share the same home. This option includes private bedrooms and bathrooms as well as individual nursing care. Residents are charged the average rate for a nursing home in their area, and Medicaid and Medicare coverage is accepted. "Green homes are a new style of nursing home, that looks and feels and operates more like a cozy home. If you truly need the care of a nursing setting, you want to be part of a beautiful place," says Burns. Now that you are ready to plan the next stage of your life, we hope the future looks brighter and more exciting.

CHAPTER 7

LEGACY BUILDING

THE SEVENTH PEARL OF FINANCIAL WISDOM:
A Woman's Legacy of Love Is Priceless

THIS CHAPTER IS ABOUT ENDINGS and beginnings. Now is it time to pause and reflect on all that we have achieved, and decide how we want things to go on when we are no longer around. As we have planned and strategized and tried to do the best for ourselves and our families throughout our lives, we have the opportunity to manage the end of our lives with the same skills—that is, we have the right *and* the ability to plan our personal endings. We can help our loved ones and ourselves by attending to our final needs in a thoughtful way, a way that reflects all that we have become. As you will discover, our seventh pearl of wisdom—a woman's legacy of love is priceless—brings the other six pearls full circle.

After you die, you may be leaving behind a business that continues to live on. You'll want to ensure that your business will produce a great return on the investment of time, money, and love that you have given it. Whether you sell the business or leave it for the next generation, we'll help you make this important transition in the most positive way possible. But in addition to our personal legacies of love, or the love we have poured into our businesses, we may also have the privilege of leaving a larger legacy, born straight from the heart.

The grain of sand that enters our shell around the topic of dying and leaving a legacy is called denial. We can't imagine not being here—running our businesses and managing our lives, so we make no plans for this inevitable future. We refuse to write a will, thinking this will make us live longer. Our denial will lead to chaos for those we love if we don't break through it.

THE GRAIN OF SAND IN THE OYSTER SHELL

Do you know a woman who . . .

- Does not have a will or an estate plan?
- Has not yet purchased a burial plot?
- Has a terminally ill parent whose doctors have suggested hospice care?
- Owns a business that she wants to sell?
- Owns a business that she wants her children to take over after she dies?
- Plans to leave the bulk of her assets to charity, but has made no designations?

We have faced plenty of challenges in our lifetimes, many of which have seeded new pearls. We may have lost a husband, we may have realized how deeply affected we were because we felt unloved and unattended in childhood, we may have done battle with illness. These personal blows seem unbearable when they strike, but they often transform us and connect us to others. Suddenly, we feel a sense of compassion for the human condition that is so strong that it drives us beyond anything we could conceive of before we were wounded. Our hurt stimulates an untapped courage, a strong sense of self, and true vision we never even knew we had. With our newly inspired actions, we can change the world. We are no longer just consumers of life experiences; we have become investors, and the returns for the world keep coming long after we stop living. It is often at that time when we change direction and set the course for giving. And therein follows our legacy—one that is nourishing not only to those we love but also to those whom we will never meet.

PLAN YOUR ENDING

Women are wonderful planners, so there is no reason not to plan the end of your life as thoroughly as you've planned everything else. The plan for the end of your life should reflect the whole of your life and allow you to leave this earth with dignity and in a way that is consistent with your values. Death is a "when" question, not an "if" question, yet it is one area that most people have not given serious thought to unless they are suffering from a grave illness or facing the death of a parent. There are legal, financial, practical, emotional, and spiritual issues to examine.

We want you to face your ending with as much power as possible. This means making sure you have put in place the legal documents that will allow your wishes to be fulfilled even if you can no longer speak for yourself. This means making sure your financial house is in order so that you do not burden your heirs with a difficult estate or a heavy tax burden. It also means talking about the emotional, psychological, and spiritual issues you've put off examining for years. Planning your final exit can be a liberating experience.

Create a Living Will and a Medical Power
of Attorney

The first piece of business you need to attend to is to put in place a living will and a medical power of attorney. The living will sets forth your wishes concerning your care if you cannot speak for yourself, and the medical power of attorney gives someone the right to act on your behalf should you suddenly become incapacitated—say, in a car accident or a plane crash. You can download a copy of your state's living will form for free from the website of the National Hospice and Palliative Care Organization (NHPCO), which strives to improve care at the end of life. Every state has different rules concerning living wills, so be sure to download and complete the one recognized by your state. You can also use the wonderful online resource on the website www.agingwithdignity.org called Five Wishes, a sample living will that is legal in forty-two states. The website helps you answer five questions about your care. The document is now in use by more than 15 million people and has been translated into twenty-six languages. The Five Wishes focus on your physical, emotional, and spiritual care when you are ill. We think it is a wonderful resource and encourage you to use it for yourself and your loved ones.

A medical power of attorney specifies who shall make medical decisions on your behalf when you are not able to do so. This document is also referred to as a health-care proxy, appointment of a health-care agent, or durable power of attorney for health care. You should have an attorney write your medical power of attorney and review your living will as well.

Complete Your Estate Plan

If you have not already done so, you need to complete a will and an estate plan. You should hire an attorney who is an expert in this area to draft your documents. Each person's estate plan is unique, and takes into account the types of belongings you have, the relationships you have, and the assets you have. We discussed the advantages of holding your assets in a revocable living trust in chapter 1, and the idea of using a QTIP trust to hold assets for your children in chapter 3. We also discussed setting up a trust to fund the care of your pets should you die before they do. Trusts are often an integral part of a comprehensive estate plan. Do your homework and get a top-notch professional to represent you. This is another time when you must find the most competent individual you can afford.

When you die, a tax is due, which is currently equal to 35 percent of the value of everything owned by you. However, this estate tax is not applied to the first $5 million of your assets. In addition, every U.S. citizen has a unified credit of $5 million, which means you can give away up to $5 million during your lifetime without paying a gift tax (35 percent of the value of the gift). This is called a unified credit because your gifts and your assets are considered together when calculating the value of your estate. In other words, the amount you give away during your lifetime is deducted from the $5 million of nontaxable assets you are allowed to have in your estate. So if you gave away $1 million during your lifetime, the first $4 million of your estate would be exempt from estate taxes.

If you die without a proper estate plan and will, the financial penalties can be severe. If you die without a will, this is called dying intestate. In that case, the state decides how your assets are divided up. This allocation depends on the state where you live, but certainly may not reflect your wishes. If you die with a will but without holding your assets in a revocable living trust, your will goes through probate, which is a public process—your assets are listed in the public record and can be known to anyone with an Internet connection. This can create a great problem for your heirs, who can become targets for con artists hoping to cash in on their inheritance.

There are many legitimate estate planning techniques that you can take advantage of to lower your estate tax burden. For example, you can give away assets during your lifetime so that you can lower the amount of assets in your estate. There are ways to give away assets that lower their value, enabling you to give away more of them. If you give one of your heirs a minority interest in your business, for example, it is considered to be worth less than a majority interest because it does not allow control of the business. You can also give shares of your company to your children when the value of the shares is low—that is, when the company is just formed. Any growth in the value of the shares is then out of your estate and into the hands of your children. A good accountant and attorney will help you do the planning that is necessary to make sure you are taking advantage of all options.

If you own a business, you must also be aware of the potential estate taxes due on the value of the business. Many businesses are valuable but not liquid, so it may be difficult for your heirs to come up with the cash necessary to pay either the gift tax (if you have transferred the business to your heirs) or the estate tax on your business that may become due after you die. In this case, there are ways to use life insurance inside of a trust to pay for the estate tax that will be due. There is also the possibility that you may be able to sell your business to an Intentionally Defective Grantor Trust (IDGT) as a way to minimize estate taxes. Consult your attorney for the latest information.

Designate Who Gets Your Personal Belongings

One of the ugly fights that often occurs after a person dies is the fight over personal belongings. You can minimize the chance of your family going to war over your jewelry, for example, if, rather than telling them to divide it among themselves, you use technology to create a digital catalog of your belongings and designate the recipients yourself. You can take a photograph of each item and name the recipient in the caption. If your children want to trade later, that is fine; at least you have done your best to prevent any bickering in advance. If you don't have children and you want your beloved objects to go to nieces, friends, or charity, a digital catalog of your things will remove all confusion about your intentions. Your will can reference this digital catalog and you can instruct your executor to distribute your possessions according to the catalog.

Plan Your Funeral

As you can imagine, your loved ones will be very sad and distraught when you die. You will be doing everyone a great favor by writing out detailed instructions on what you would like to have happen when you die. Do you want to be buried or cremated? If you are going to be buried, do you want to have a wake with an open casket or a closed casket? Do you want a certain type of casket or a particular burial plot? Do you want particular music played, photographs displayed, or a particular person to speak at the service? Do you want a religious service, a party, or no service at all? You can write down all these instructions and ease the minds of your loved ones, who can be comforted by the fact that they are doing as you ask.

In addition, planning your funeral allows you to estimate the costs and make sure enough money is available to pay these expenses. According to the National Funeral Directors Association website, the average adult burial in the United States costs $6,560, not including a burial plot or monument, flowers, or other expenses. If you decide to purchase a more extravagant casket, funeral costs alone can rise to more than $15,000. It is very difficult for your loved ones to bargain over these costs, so it is much better if you state what you want and put aside money to pay for it, either directly or through life insurance.

Make Arrangements for Your Burial or Cremation

It's not easy to envision exactly where you want to be buried, but burial plots are becoming increasingly scarce, so the earlier you can purchase your lot, the better. Some people know they want to be in the same cemetery as their families, others may be living in another country or far from home and want a local grave. The sooner you can buy your spot, the better off you will be. Given how often people move, you may be able to purchase a plot at a reduced rate from someone who wants to sell it rather than directly from the cemetery; burial plots are now sold via eBay and Craigslist. Of course, make sure it is a legitimate sale before you send any money. Headstones can cost thousands of dollars, so you may also want to purchase this in advance if you want to save money for your loved ones later on. This will also allow you to get exactly the headstone you want.

If you would prefer to be cremated, you still have decisions to make. Do you want your remains kept in an urn or scattered? If the latter, do you want them scattered in a certain place? Do you want your heirs to hold a service at which your remains are present? Again, you will make their lives easier if you set forth your wishes in as much detail as possible.

Develop an End-of-Life Philosophy

Just as you researched and sought out experts to help you with all your other major life challenges, you should do some research to help you decide how you want to handle your death. In fact, we recommend that you develop a "philosophy" of dying, which will help guide all your decisions in this area. To explore this idea, we spoke with Mona Hanford, a vibrant wife, mother, grandmother, educator, and fund-raiser who is an expert on the issues of elder care, caregivers, and end-of-life decisions. She believes that once you come to terms with the reality of death, you live better. From 1982 to 2008, Mona was concurrently a capital campaign consultant and the director of development at St. Patrick's Episcopal Day School in Washington, D.C. She has served on the boards of Capital Hospice and the Washington Home and Community Hospices as well as on the Washington National Cathedral Foundation and Philanthropy Committee.

Mona told us that her involvement with issues of death and dying began when her husband's parents became elderly.

> My husband was an only child, and his parents moved down to be near to us when they retired. They lived near us in retirement for twenty-five years. During the last ten years, we created a little nursing home in their condo for them. They very much wanted to stay in their own home. Eventually, we had hospice for the last one. They died at eighty-nine and ninety-two. And it was a very meaningful experience, so then I joined the hospice board. And there are two hospices in Washington, and I've been on the board of both.

Mona is concerned that there is so little discussion within families when one member is dying, and that no one wants to acknowledge when the end is coming. To address the need in the community, the Washington National Cathedral, one of the largest cathedrals in the world, cosponsored with Hospice and Palliative Care of Metropolitan Washington a conference called Journey of the Soul: Peace at Last in 2001. As chair of the conference, Mona worked with both the dean of the cathedral and the CEO of the hospice. They were skeptical that the conference would draw a crowd, because people don't feel comfortable talking about death. But the public responded. Fifteen hundred people attended the conference and five hundred were on the wait list. The conference is still the largest event held at the cathedral that was not an official service.

> We're all worried deep down, because we'll all die. That's the universal thing. We're all going through the same experience; no one's going to buy a lottery ticket out of this place. People have this deep hunger underneath, but it's not polite to talk about it. It's true even in a hospice. Many hospice nurses have experienced a situation in which family members will say, "Don't mention death to Mother, whatever you do. It'll kill her." And then the mother will pull the nurse close to her and say, "Honey, I'm dying. Don't tell my children. It will kill them." Death is the big elephant in the room that no one talks about.

Mona feels strongly that one of the biggest blessings you can give your family is to be the first one to talk about the elephant. If you set an example of speaking calmly about death with your family, and if you approach death with a plan, you will create an atmosphere in which everyone can have a chance to discuss his or her feelings and enjoy meaningful conversations with you while you are still alive. If you have a religious faith or tradition to rely upon, you can discuss death with your loved ones in this context. If you are not religious, you can still provide them with an example of courage in the face of the unknown. After all, you are going through a great transformation that one day they, too, will face. Mona says, "Picture this as your exit line: 'Dear, I will be just fine.' That shows no fear. That shows hope that this is a transformative chapter and we don't know what comes next. 'I am not scared to die, do not be afraid.' That offers hope, a legacy of hope that will reverberate through generations and will get passed on and on. Just as the opposite attitude will reverberate negatively."

It also helps to learn about what to expect during the physical experience of death. There are many books available that discuss the experiences of individuals who have been clinically dead and then have come back to life. There are also several ancient texts that deal with the subject, such as the Tibetan Book of the Dead, which describes death in terms of a step-by-step process of leaving the body. Most religious traditions have their own theories and approaches to death. The Hospice Foundation can provide further resources and information. Sharing what you learn with your family may make it easier for everyone to accept what is to come and what we all will eventually face.

Create an Ethical Will

One of the important things you can share with your loved ones before you die is your values. A good way to do this is to create an ethical will. An ethical will is a written document or a video that conveys your values, wisdom, and hopes for future generations. Ethical wills, or *zevaoth* in Hebrew, have been a tradition in the Jewish faith since biblical times. There are no hard and fast rules for ethical wills, and there are many wonderful guides to help you create them. You can also record your ethical will on camera, so your loved ones can hear the emphasis in your voice when you speak to them. Mona says,

Probably the most important gift you can leave to your family is a legacy of values, which can never be lost. Money can be lost. Money gets lost in divorce. Children get divorced. Grandchildren get divorced. Money can get lost in business deals or in stock market crashes. Money can disappear in a multitude of ways. Values can be given equally to everyone in your family. They can last forever and your family members can share them with however many people they want to give them away to and still have them. Values are perpetual.

As a development professional, Mona has spent decades educating donors and volunteers about leaving a legacy of philanthropy. Now, as a caregiver and elder-care activist, she is endeavoring to leave a legacy of hope through the program she is developing called Journey of the Soul: Peace at Last.

Discuss End-of-Life Care

One trend that Mona has seen in her work on death and dying is that the tendency to deny the reality of death leads to extremely intrusive and painful attempts to prolong life in a way that is not helpful to the dying person. When women end up as caregivers, they often face the task of deciding when to use extreme measures and when to switch to humane, palliative care offered by hospice. When extreme measures are chosen, the results may not prolong life but rather may make an elderly person's last days or months very uncomfortable. A better option may be to realize that the end is near and to allow patients to die with dignity, in their own homes, comfortably. These are all topics to discuss with your family. It is vital that your wishes are clearly understood.

By taking a proactive, responsible approach to the end of your life, you can inspire your family and loved ones. Mona suggests having conversations about death with your loved ones, especially with your adult children. This will be an experience all of us will face, and we have the opportunity to make it meaningful for ourselves and to provide emotional, spiritual, and financial support to those we love.

TRANSFER YOUR BUSINESS

If you have built a successful business, one of the most bittersweet issues you will face is the question of who will run your business when you no longer want to do so. You have no doubt put your heart and entrepreneurial soul into your company and are proud of the many products you have produced, customers you have served, and employees you have worked with. If you are now coming to a point where you think it may be time to let go, or at least let go of your active involvement, you should develop a strong transition plan that will serve you and your company well.

The key to a successful transition is to create a well-thought-out plan, working closely with your advisers and your management team. We'll assume in this discussion that your business is privately held, rather than a company you have taken public. Your options include shutting down your business altogether, selling your business to a third party, selling your business to the management team, and transitioning your business to the next generation of your family.

To learn more about business succession options, we spoke with Tina Albright, a New York attorney and a partner in the law firm Curtis, Mallet-Prevost, Colt & Mosle. She has more than twenty years of experience advising wealthy families on trust and estate matters and business succession plans. Tina notes that although some clients have provided for management succession in their business plans, estate planning and other life transitions lead clients to consider succession planning. Succession issues may also come up when businesses seek outside capital. Tina says, "Most people start thinking about it when they are getting married or getting divorced. Or they realize that the clients need to plan for the estate taxes on the value of the closely held interests in the business. And as companies grow, they often are looking to bring credit facilities, venture capital, or private equity or co-investing or a public offering of some of the shares of the company. Those significant financial transactions will often instigate questions about succession."

Assess Your Need for Liquidity

Tina notes that one of the first considerations is liquidity. Your business may be providing a good living but may not be generating significant savings for you, so essentially all your assets are tied up in the business. A business needs liquidity to pay out a spouse in a divorce settlement, or to pay estate taxes if the owner or owners die. Tina says, "One of my first concerns is whether the principal owner has sufficient liquidity to do what she wants to do in the next phase of her life. If she doesn't, how can we get that? If she has other pockets of funds that are going to be more than sufficient, then the question becomes, If you aren't looking for liquidity, then what are you looking for from the business? What are your objectives?"

Can the Business Survive Without You?

The next thing to assess is whether the business can survive without you. If you are a professional and your clients are purchasing your expertise, is there a real company that can go on without you? Or is your business really about what you personally provide to clients?

In the latter case, you may find that there is no market for selling your business. For example, if you are a massage therapist with a private clientele, it may not be possible to find someone who is willing to pay to take over your clients; therefore, you may need to simply shut down your business if you decide you no longer want to practice your profession. This is the simplest kind of ending.

In that case, you may want to speak to a business broker first, just to make sure it would not be possible to sell your customer list or some other aspect of your business before you simply stop operating. Your logo or brand may be more valuable than you think, so it is worth trying to sell it before you let it go. Make sure you work with your accountant to cleanly wind down operations and leave no unpaid taxes or unfiled tax returns. You should also work with your lawyer to make sure there will be no outstanding legal issues. If you have long-term employees, try to treat them fairly and help them transition to other employment.

Assemble a Team

If you think you might try to sell your business or transfer it to the next generation of family members, you need experts to help you. You will need a trusts and estates lawyer to determine the right way to sell your business in order to minimize the tax consequences of the sale. You will also need a good accountant, one who's experienced in selling businesses. You will need a firm that can provide you with an expertly determined and objective value for your business that will be accepted by the IRS as valid. You may also need a lawyer skilled in selling companies—and knowledgeable about your industry—to help you structure the right sales contract.

In addition, if you have a small company, you may want to hire a business broker to help you market your firm. If your company is larger, you should consider hiring an investment bank to represent you and find a buyer. The investment bank will be very expensive, but may get you a much better price than you would get on your own, unless you know a strong competitor who wants to buy you out and with whom you can make a friendly deal.

Moreover, you may want to add a family business expert to your team. He or she will help you deal with the dynamics of working with family members and help you groom your successors properly. Consider joining the Family Business Network, an excellent resource for advocacy, education, and advice.

Because there are many tax-planning strategies that require a long lead time, it's best to assemble your team as far in advance as possible. If you think you want to sell your business in four or five years, for example, now is a good time to talk to an estate-planning attorney. The earlier you plan, the more options you will have. In addition, the unified tax credit of $5 million may be reduced in the future, so if you think you might want to transition or sell soon, work with your estate-planning attorney immediately to take advantage of this incentive.

Read the Shareholders' Agreement

Tina notes that there are two additional important issues to consider when planning to sell or transition your business: who owns the shares of the company and whether there is a shareholders' agreement that contains any limitations on the transferability of the shares. If you are the sole owner of your company, you will likely have full control over the shares. If you have one or more other shareholders, you will need to consider the terms of the share-holders' agreement and obtain their agreement to a sale or other transfer of the business. Restrictions on transferability are important. For example, if one of your shareholders dies, you may suddenly find yourself in business with his or her spouse or children, unless the shares are subject to mandatory redemption upon the death of a shareholder. The same is true in a divorce situation—you want to make sure the shares cannot go to an angry ex in a divorce case. On the other hand, transfers to family or other related entities for estate-planning purposes are often permitted.

You should also make sure that the way shares can be transferred is spelled out in the shareholders' agreement. If one of the shareholders needs liquidity before you want to sell your company, the shareholders' agreement should contain a provision for the company to buy back his or her shares. This is more desirable than having a partial interest sold to a third party.

Valuing Your Business

If you decide to sell or transition your business to the next generation, you will need to find out what it is worth. Your accountant can help you find a firm that specializes in valuations for your type of business. A professional valuation will take several different types of value into account. First, the book value of the business is calculated by adding the value of the tangible assets—in other words, things that can be seen and touched, such as plant and equipment—and subtracting the liabilities. The book value does not include nontangible assets, such as the value of your brand, your market position, and your customer list.

A business valuation also considers a company's cash flow, or EBITDA (earnings before interest, taxes, depreciation, and amortization). A simple rule of thumb for many privately held companies is to value the company at five times its EBITDA; if your company has an EBITDA of $100,000, for example, your business may be worth $500,000 in a sale. Some businesses are worth more than just their cash flow or book value; if you have a strong brand or are in a market sector where there is a great demand, your business might be worth twenty times EBITDA rather than five times EBITDA.

Sell to Your Management Team

You may find that the best market for your business is your management team. They may have a strong interest in keeping the business going when you are ready to retire or no longer want to work actively. If you think you have a competent, ambitious team that could take over, you can structure a management buyout. A management buyout gives your team a chance to purchase the company from you at a mutually agreed-upon price. They may be able to purchase the business with a loan from a bank or give you a promissory note and pay you an income stream over time, a debt that may take several years to pay off. Clearly, you are at greater risk of not getting paid if you accept a note rather than requiring the team to get a loan. If the team doesn't do well, you may never see the note paid off; if you are paid out from a bank loan, you get your cash, and the team bears the brunt of a loss if the business fails.

On the other hand, an installment sale over time means you can spread out tax payments, and if you think the team can handle the business, you may end up with more cash over time. Your accountant needs to crunch the numbers with you to determine the best thing to do in your particular case. To reduce risk, you also may be able to create two classes of stock and to keep some control over your company by continuing to own voting shares until the note is substantially repaid.

If you think you might eventually want to sell your business to your management team, then, ideally, you need to start grooming them years in advance. Tina says, "It takes incredible foresight. Large companies are better at this than small companies. The culture within General Electric, for example, is based on grooming, on supporting careers. Large companies are typically much more disciplined about developing character, experience, and conducting milestone reviews with executives who are going to take over business lines and senior positions."

Sell to a Third Party

If you do not have a management team that wants to do a buyout or family members who want to take over your business, your best bet may be to sell your company to a third party. If you have been running your company for some time, you are well aware that industries experience business cycles. You clearly want to sell at a time when companies in your industry are highly valued, but don't try to time the peak of a market cycle. It is better to sell just before the peak rather than trying to wait for prices to move higher— industries can abruptly crash, and in that case, there might be no market for your business for another ten years or more. You can look back at the dot-com boom and bust and the real estate crash to see the effects of business cycles in recent years. If you are thinking of selling at some point in the next four or five years and your industry or sector becomes hot, consider selling quickly and moving on to the next phase of your life.

When you sell your business, usually the best thing you can get in exchange is cash, rather than stock in another company. If you sell your company to a public company that wants to give you stock, you are usually subject to a lockup period and cannot sell that stock for some period of time. This means your risk now depends on the performance of the stock of your buyer. Selling for stock is particularly risky if the stock you receive is that of a small cap company—a fairly illiquid company with less than $1 billion in sales. You may be able to hedge some of the risk of holding a single stock position by buying options that guard against a fall in the stock price. But this may not be possible or desirable in all cases.

Receiving cash is also better than accepting a note that pays over time. This way you avoid taking on the performance risk of the other company, even if you pay more in taxes. Of course, consult your accountant and make sure he or she crunches the numbers both ways. Saving on taxes may not be worth the extra risk of taking on a note from the buyer.

Sell to Your Family

If you would like to have your business remain in the family, or if you are now running a business that has been in your family for one or more generations, then usually your goal is to prepare the younger generation to take over the business. But a well-known proverb in family business circles is, "Shirtsleeves to shirtsleeves in three generations." This refers to the fact that, often, the first generation makes money, the second generation keeps working in the business, but the third generation loses interest and indeed loses the business. The statistics in the United States are not encouraging. A comprehensive 2008 study called Protecting the Family Fortune, which was conducted by U.S. Trust, Prince & Associates and Campden Research, found that only 15 percent of family businesses last into the second generation.[1]

Passing the business along to the next generation is always a source of anxiety, fear, and pride for family business owners. There are so many questions: Are my children ready to take over the business? What will happen when I give up control to them? How do I help them to be ready? Should we keep this business in the family or should we sell it? How do we have a smooth transition either way?

These questions are being asked by family business owners around the globe. In fact, we are in a period of massive business-ownership transition. Consider the following facts, reported in the 2011 Merrill Lynch Capgemini World Wealth Report[2]:

- High-net-worth individuals, or HNWIs (those with more than $1 million in financial assets), numbered 10 million globally in 2009; they hold a total of $39.3 trillion in assets.

- Ultra-high-net-worth individuals, or UHNWIs (those with assets valued at more than $30 million), numbered 103,000 around the globe; 40,000 of them are in North America.

- Women make up 27 percent of HNWIs globally and 37 percent of HNWIs in North America.

Now consider the statistics reported in the Merrill Lynch Capgemini World Wealth Report in 2006[3]:

- 15 percent of the world's population is over the age of fifty-six, but 61 percent of the world's HNW population (5.3 million individuals) is over the age of fifty-six.

- 83 percent of HNWIs over the age of fifty-six have children.

- 92 percent of those are expected to transfer their wealth to their immediate family members.

- Globally, 37 percent of these individuals derive their wealth from a family business.

- Regionally, 26 percent of North Americans, 50 percent of Europeans, 48 percent of Latin Americans, 35 percent of Asians, and 24 percent of Middle Easterners derive their wealth from a family business.

As these family business owners consider the fate of their businesses, they are seeking to understand the best practices available for succession planning.

EARLY PREPARATION FOR FAMILY SUCCESSION

The sooner you think about succession planning in your family business, the better off you are. The best time to start is when your children are born. The more information you have about the character, capabilities, and interests of your children, the better you will be able to judge whether they can succeed you and keep the business in the family. What does this mean on a practical level?

Business Owners Need to Be Involved Parents

Thinking that you are building the business for the family and that this excuses you from the job of parenting is a big mistake. If your children never see you and view the business as the "enemy" that takes you away from them, they may rebel and hate both you and the business. Absentee parenting leads to resentful, rebellious children who have problems with school, drugs, alcohol, and so on.

Get to Know Your Children as Individuals

Help them to understand what the business is and involve them in the business in age-appropriate ways. Try to nurture their sense of pride in the business, and encourage them to have fun. For example, we know a mother who brings her ten-year-old son to business meetings so he can have a sense of what his mother does.

Her father did this for her, and now her son is becoming an interested third-generation potential business owner.

Don't Overinfluence Your Children

Do not pressure your children to think that they *must* be part of the family business, especially if they have absolutely no interest in it. Help them find a path that works for them and support them as they develop their natural passions. You cannot make your children want to take over your business. We know a top family business in which the principal has four children; two are in the company, one is an accomplished artist, and one is a highly specialized veterinarian. All are happy and continue to have good relationships with the family.

CULTIVATE POTENTIAL SUCCESSORS

Let's assume that you have identified several individuals who may wish to become successors in your family business. If your business involves several generations, they may be your children or your nieces or nephews. What are the best practices for cultivating these future leaders?

Education

Insist that potential successors complete their education to a college level and obtain an MBA. It is important that children learn to compete in the outside world, where there are objective measurements of excellence. This will build their confidence that they are not inheriting the business just because they are sons or daughters but rather because they are competent successors.

Outside Experience

Insist on some years of work experience outside the family business. It is extremely valuable for children to come into your business with up-to-date know-how so that they can expand the range of possibilities for the business. Work experience in another environment will help them to prove to themselves and to the family that they can be reliable and productive employees.

Fair Treatment

Once children enter the business, give them appropriate levels of responsibility. Do not give them a corner office on day one. Give them the same level of responsibility you would give another hire of their age and experience, and let them earn the respect of other employees and senior management by demonstrating that they can add value to the company.

Inclusiveness

Inform nonfamily senior managers of the succession plan. Valued longtime employees need to feel comfortable with what their role will be when the new generation takes over. Give ever-increasing levels of involvement and responsibility to your successor, and let him or her know the succession timetable. Ideally, have a two- or three-year period during which the new generation takes over while you remain involved in an advisory capacity to smooth the transition.

GOOD OWNERSHIP PRACTICES FOR FAMILY BUSINESSES

Keep Your Estate Plans Current

You and the other owners of the business should have up-to-date wills and estate plans ready at all times, and you should draw up comprehensive instructions on what to do should there be an unexpected death or illness that causes you to become incapacitated. We know of several large private companies where the untimely death of the founder resulted in years of chaos, since the founder had no will and had preferred to keep all information about the business in his head.

Bequeath Your Shares Early

You should work with your estate-planning advisers upon the birth of your children to create a plan for giving them shares in your business as early as possible. This will allow the value of the business to grow without you or your children having to worry about facing a huge gift tax. If you wait until the value of the business increases, your children might have to pay more tax.

Consider the Distribution of Voting Rights

You should think very carefully about giving your children voting rights in the family business and come up with a plan that feels comfortable. We know of a situation where five children own shares in a very large company; their father now has dementia and can no longer make decisions, but he still retains all the voting shares. It has been very painful for the family members and difficult for them to take legal control of the business.

Prepare for Conflicts

When you bequeath shares in a business, be prepared for the possibility that your children may not always agree on the best course for the company. In that case, not all of them may want to stay a shareholder. You should plan for possible shareholder dissension by creating buyback plans, in which some family members can get out of the business by selling their shares back to the company. Paradoxically, people are usually more willing to stay in situations where they know they can exit at any time.

BE A GOOD PASSIVE SHAREHOLDER

You may be in the position of owning shares in your family business but not working in the business actively. If this is the case, you still have a very important role to play. As someone who is not caught up in the day-to-day details of running the business, you can provide an objective voice. You have a responsibility to understand what the business is doing and to cast an informed vote rather than vote as others ask you to. In addition, you should do the following:

- Make sure you are receiving at least quarterly reports. If you don't understand something, ask.

- Attend the annual shareholders meeting as an active participant. If there is no annual shareholders meeting, take steps to make sure that one is initiated.
- Work with an outside consultant if you are unsure about what is happening or uncomfortable with how the family business is run.
- Volunteer to take a turn running family meetings or chairing a committee. This will help you understand more thoroughly what is going on in the company.
- Become involved in the financial education of the next generation. You will learn something as well, and you will educate those who will directly affect the value of your shares when they take over.

Set Up or Join a Family Office

If your family business has assets worth millions of dollars, you may want to consider setting up a single family office or joining a multifamily office. A family office will look after your family's estate planning, tax, and other financial affairs. The family office can make sure you are not burdening the staff of your business with your personal needs. The office can also coordinate a program of financial education for the next generation over a period of years. The family office can make sure the annual meeting happens, taxes are filed, and all the family's administrative needs are taken care of. This frees you to focus on the business and other, more exciting activities.

SET A COURSE FOR GIVING

One of the most admirable ways that women share their legacy of love with the world is by supporting philanthropic causes. We want to inspire you to embrace the wider world in this very rewarding way. We have been thrilled to hear amazing stories of giving from so many of the wonderful women we have spoken with for this book. Here, we would like to highlight three exceptional philanthropists who exemplify our seventh pearl of wisdom: Loida Lewis, Katrina Peebles, and Doris Buffett.

Each of these women turned a personal challenge into a drive to serve others and to make the world a better place. All these women have achieved a level of mastery in which they are no longer just helping particular causes but also teaching others to be great givers. We encourage you to envision all the ways you can follow in their footsteps and leave a lasting legacy in our world.

Loida Lewis

What do we do when we are thrust into a role we never sought? How would you react if your husband passed away suddenly at the age of fifty, leaving you the owner of a public company worth more than $1 billion that was floundering without his leadership? How would you preserve his legacy and fulfill his dreams while setting goals of your own?

Sometimes, the path of destiny is shaped by events beyond our control. These events may seem overwhelming at the time. But we have been inspired by a story of turning tragedy into a legacy of success and philanthropy. The story of Loida Nicolas Lewis is the story of a woman who was forced into a leadership role and surprised everyone with her success. Because of Loida, the memory of one of the greatest African American businessmen in history remains alive and well. She has also blossomed to become a powerful philanthropist in her own right, honoring his memory as well as leaving a very personal legacy in her native country, the Philippines.

Today, Loida Nicolas Lewis is a very busy woman, a mother and grandmother, political activist, Philippine icon, and philanthropist. On a summer afternoon she still takes the time to whisk her young grandchildren around the latest exhibit at the Metropolitan Museum of Art in New York City. "That's how I smell the roses," shares Loida. "Taking time out. Being with the family." It's just days before a gala in memory of the man who passed away eighteen years ago and whom she has never forgotten: the man who told her, "Always take time to smell the roses"—the man she loved so dearly, her late husband, Reginald F. Lewis. The first African American to create a billion-dollar business empire, over twenty years ago.

The annual Reginald F. Lewis Foundation gala, launched by Loida, honors successful African American entrepreneurs under the age of fifty. Honorees include Eugene A. Profit, the CEO of Profit Investment Management, entertainer Sean Combs, and Don Peebles, a real estate magnate.

The story of Reginald Lewis is an inspiring American story. Loida says,

He wasn't born with a silver spoon in his mouth. His mother, Carolyn Lewis, as a single mother raised him from age five and when he was ten years old, his mother remarried to Jean Fugget. During his time with his mother's parents, who raised eight children of their own and adopted two nieces into the family in a small house on Dallas Street in Baltimore, Maryland, he learned the values of hard work, settings goals, and tenacity of purpose. His grandmother taught him the value of saving money.

Reginald received a football scholarship to Virginia State University in 1961. In 1965, the Rockefeller Foundation funded a summer school program at Harvard Law School to introduce a select number of black students to legal studies. Reginald lobbied for his acceptance and got in. He made such an impression that he was invited to attend Harvard Law School that fall—the only person in the 148-year history of the school to be admitted before applying.[4]

Loida met her husband-to-be on a blind date in New York in 1968. She was on a round-the-world trip, as a gift from her father for having earned a law degree from the University of the Philippines College of Law and was admitted to the Philippine bar that year. She was waiting for her sister Imelda, then a student at Columbia University, to finish her masters of arts studies. In seven months, Reginald and Loida were married in 1969 in Manila. In 1972, Loida established a monthly magazine for the Filipino-American community and served as the magazine's publisher until it merged with another publication in 1980. Their first daughter, Leslie, was born in 1973 and their second daughter, Christina, was born in 1980.

Loida was the first Asian American to pass the American bar without having been educated in the United States, a feat she accomplished in 1974. Loida became an attorney with the Immigration and Naturalization Service after she successfully sued the government for discrimination; she stayed at the job until 1988, when the family moved to Paris. During that period, she also wrote the book *How to Get a Green Card,* which reached the bestseller list in its genre and is still in print today, published by Nolo Press.

Meanwhile, after practicing corporate law for a respected Wall Street firm, Reginald was busy setting up Wall Street's first African American law firm. Driven by the desire to do his own deals, Reginald set up TLC Group, L.P., in 1983. He acquired Beatrice International in December 1987 and re-branded his company TLC Beatrice International Holdings, Inc. The $985 million leveraged buyout created the largest African American–owned company in the United States; the deal was also the largest offshore leveraged buyout ever by an American company. As Chairman and CEO, Reginald moved quickly to reposition the company, pay down the debt, and vastly increase the company's worth. With revenues of $1.5 billion, TLC Beatrice made it to the Fortune 500 and was first on the Black Enterprise List of top 100 African American–owned businesses for several years. Tragically, Lewis died from brain cancer in 1993.

At the time of his death, Reginald had started writing his autobiography, called *Why Should White Guys Have All the Fun?*—a book that Loida was determined to finish. "I didn't want his work of a lifetime to just vanish. And his life story would inspire young people to set their goals high and not lose hope," she recalls. Reginald used to tell audiences around the country, "Keep going, no matter what," and that's exactly what Loida did. "I just focused on the challenge of the moment: the challenge of finishing his book. The challenge of running his company so that I accomplished his game plan. The challenge of raising our two girls as both mother and father to them." In the dedication page, she wrote: "This book is dedicated to the memory of Reginald F. Lewis, my husband, lover, counselor, best friend, role model, and devoted father to our children, Leslie Lourdes and Christina Savilla." The book was completed with the help of writer Blair S. Walker, who conducted hundreds of interviews with Lewis's family, friends, colleagues, business partners, associates, and employees. Because Reginald was the most accomplished African American businessman in the world at the time, Loida's efforts to preserve his legacy were not just of personal value, but also of vital historical importance. "It was important for me when he died his story be told," Loida says.

In addition to finishing his autobiography, Loida was faced with the daunting task of dealing with his company. It was not doing well without Reginald at the helm. "By the end of the year after his death, I saw that the company's earnings were going south," says Loida.

So I said, this company was his life in the sense that TLC Beatrice was the first African American–owned company valued for nearly one billion dollars. So for it to fail, it would be terrible. I couldn't stand that. And after interviewing potential CEOs, all of whom were Caucasians and they were asking so much money to run the company, I just told myself, 'I'd better run it myself.' So that if it fails, I'd blame myself. And if I succeeded, it was because I've surrounded myself with people who are better than I was and who would be able to advise me wisely, and that's what I did. I also knew when he bought Beatrice Foods International his goal was not to perpetuate his name, but to create wealth for the shareholders. His thesis, for which he got an honors grade at Harvard Law School, was that in order to create wealth, you have to do it through mergers and acquisitions.

Loida shocked Wall Street as she took on the role of CEO. She made headlines for getting rid of the corporate jet and slashing the fat. She says,

I think as women we are very practical, with a common sense that is not ego-based. Giving up the jet was so logical. We were running out of cash. And the jet was eating up three million dollars a year of our revenue. I also sold the limousines. And we had thirty thousand square feet of space, but I had fired nearly fifty percent of our executives. So why did we need that space? So in one year I cut our expenses by seventy percent. We had a twenty-two-million-dollar loss the year Mr. Lewis died. After I took over, for the first year, we made a one-million-dollar net profit and the next year, a five-million-dollar net profit. Then a fifteen-million net profit in 1996. Then a nineteen-million net profit in 1997, and in the fifth year we started selling the different businesses. When we sold the supermarket chain in France, we paid all our corporate debt so we had zero debt and we still had the ice cream businesses in Spain, the potato chips company in Ireland, the bottling companies in Belgium and Thailand. The last company was sold in 2000. And the internal rate of return for our shareholders was thirty-five percent.

TLC Beatrice International Holdings, Inc., was liquidated, but Loida still kept the name TLC Beatrice because it was so closely identified with her husband. She went on to invest in start-up ventures in China and in the Philippines. Loida says,

> Unfortunately, those two businesses were total failures. So what did I learn from that? With Beatrice, Reginald had bought a company that had been around for forty years, so it had an existing structure. They knew how to make money and run a profitable company. With a start-up, you have to be there twenty-four hours a day, seven days a week, or close to that. You have to watch it like a hawk! You have to attend to it and be totally focused. I failed miserably and I lost all my investments. I liquidated my China and Philippines businesses at a big loss. I learned that I don't have the attention span, the intensity, or, frankly, the patience anymore to run a business full-time. So now I'm raising funds for the charities that I choose, enjoying my grandchildren and my freedom.

Loida has honored her husband's memory through the Reginald F. Lewis Foundation, founded by her husband in 1987, of which Loida succeeded him as the chair. The foundation made a $5 million donation to the Maryland Museum of African American History and Culture, which now bears his name. It is the largest African American museum on the East Coast. There is the Reginald F. Lewis Kappa Alpha Psi, Inc., Alpha Phi Chapter, Alumni-Endowed Scholarship Fund at Virginia State University, his alma mater, which recently named the business school after him; the Reginald F. Lewis International Law Center at Harvard Law School; the Reginald F. Lewis High School of Business and Law, a Baltimore City public school. She also started the Lewis College ten years ago in honor of Mr. Lewis in Sorsogon Province in the Philippines, where she was born.

In addition to honoring her husband's legacy, Loida has honored her own heritage by becoming involved with the Filipino and Asian American community and by participating in national politics in the Philippines. In 1974, together with other Asian Americans, she was cofounder of the Asian American Legal Defense and Education Fund (AALDEF). In 1997, together with Alex Esclamado, she cofounded the National Federation of Filipino American Associations, called the NAFFAA, and served as its president for four years. In 2010, being a dual citizen, an

American and a Filipina, she campaigned heavily for the current president of the Philippines, Benigno Simeon Aquino III. She also helped set up a watchdog group in the United States after the Philippine elections, U.S. Pinoys for Good Governance, to monitor happenings in her home country and to advocate political action when necessary. Her sister Imelda plays an active role in national politics as well and is now a member of President Aquino's cabinet as Secretary of Commission on Filipinos Overseas.

Loida has accomplished a tremendous amount in her life, and credits an ability to be focused with helping her achieve her goals. "Focus, and be clear on your objectives," she advises,

> because if you're not clear, the people around you will also not be clear. Communicate what you want to accomplish and then follow up. As a Filipino woman who grew up in the Philippines, I feel that women do not have to be like men, cursing, raising their voices, throwing tantrums, or being coarse. Keep your femininity but be very clear on your objectives. Listen to the people around you, your customers, your employees. Understand what they are telling you or not telling you. And know when you have to make an unpopular decision, like laying off your executives and your administrative staff. If somebody can't wing it, you've got to let him or her go, whether you're running a business or you're running a nonprofit.

Loida Lewis doesn't feel you consciously need to start creating a legacy; rather, you should recognize your talents and what makes you happy or gives you fulfillment and follow your inner guidance.

> I would advise women to look within themselves. Take time out to develop a habit of being quiet. Every morning I try to do the Zen practice of counting one's breath, which is really just being quiet. I am a woman of faith; I believe that God is with us. So during those quiet times, I get clarity of mind, clarity of thinking. It is very helpful when I arrive at a fork in the road and have to decide, "Should I do this?" "Should I do that?" It's only when you are quiet that you can listen to something within you. For me, there's God within me and if you listen, you will

hear Him, and He will show you which is the right path to take. And for those who do not believe in God, there is inner wisdom within us. But we should just take time to be quiet, to pray, to listen, and then it will be quite clear which is the right path to take.

LOIDA'S ADVICE FOR ENJOYING YOUR LEGACY

- Pick your passion. There are many worthy causes; find one that really means something to you.
- Believe that everything will work out in the end. Even when tragedy strikes, if you proceed carefully and with inner guidance, you will succeed.
- Trust yourself. As a woman, you are capable of accomplishing great things without a great deal of fuss, as long as your eyes are on the goal.
- Seek inner wisdom. Before you act, go inside your inner self and connect to your spiritual source. You will know what to do. To be sure that it is the right path for you, seek confirmation with one or two people whose wisdom you trust.

Katrina Peebles

If you are a busy corporate executive working in a successful company with your husband and raising two small children, how do you combine your business interests, corporate activities, and motherhood and still make time to give back to the broader community? Meet Katrina Peebles and you are first struck by her height, then her bright blond hair and blue eyes, and before a few seconds pass—her dynamism. There is a creative energy that almost walks with her. This energy has been a driving force behind her passion for her family, for real estate, cancer research, historic preservation, community involvement and political fund-raising for two decades. Katrina is an active woman with many passions who finds time to express them all.

Katrina's marriage to real estate magnate R. Donahue Peebles, best known as "Don," is a partnership of two dynamic individuals. Today the Peebles own large real estate developments in Washington, D.C.; Las Vegas;

and Miami—including a multibillion-dollar portfolio of luxury hotels, high-rise residential buildings and high-end commercial properties. Among many other accomplishments in her field, Mrs. Peebles spearheaded the development of the Peebles real estate tax assessment appeal business, which went on to become the most successful real estate tax appeal firm in the District of Columbia. In describing her working relationship with Don, Katrina says, "we play different roles but financially our interests are aligned. I have interests in our real estate projects and when they bear fruit, I make money, too. I'm good at marketing. I can come up with really out-of-the-box marketing ideas that will get your attention, but large real estate projects that are needed that will be visionary and make millions, potentially billions of dollars? Don's incredible at that."

Don Peebles was the recipient of the 2009 Reginald F. Lewis Award for successful African American entrepreneurs under fifty. He told the audience at the gala,

> It is because of Reginald Lewis that I wrote my book, *The Peebles Principles,* and that I am now running a multimillion-dollar company. The partnership of Reginald and Loida taught me what marriage is all about. They also taught me the power of entrepreneurship. My father was an auto mechanic, my mother a secretary, and my grandfather a doorman at a Marriott Hotel for forty-one years. . . . Twenty-five years later, I own a Marriott Hotel a few miles from where he worked. And so I am honored to accept the Reginald F. Lewis Award for Entrepreneurship because I am where I am because of what I learned from Reginald and Loida.

Katrina credits her interest in philanthropy and giving back to the larger community to the lessons she learned from her family.

> I learned a tremendous amount about philanthropy and the legacy of passing philanthropy on to your children from my parents. They got up and they tried hard and they worked hard. And those are the values they instilled in their children, and the value of giving back. You're an able-bodied person, and you have more advantages because you have a good brain, and someone will help you go to college, if you do well. And, therefore, it's your obligation to give back, and that's a form of legacy.

My grandparents did it. My parents did it. I will do it, and I'm teaching my children to do it.

Katrina painfully lost her mother to cancer, and drew strength from her mother's example of grace at the cancer center.

I remember my mom at the cancer center. I'd go with my mom and my dad. And she'd look around at the cancer center, and she'd say, "You know, Katrina, there are people here who are alone. Let's go talk to them. Let's go be with them." And, that's legacy, but not thinking, "Oh, how sad. I have stage IV pancreatic cancer, and I'm going to die, but what can I do to make somebody else feel better?" They always said if you're feeling sorry for yourself, go do something for someone who has it worse than you. And it's great advice, and I've passed it on to my children. And every now and again when I feel a little down in the mouth, I give myself a swift kick in the tush, and I say, "You know what? What do you have to feel sorry for yourself for? Go do something for someone else," because this is sad. You miss your mom. Whatever it might be. There are people who've lost their entire families. You'll learn a lot from this. This is grace under pressure, and I do think there's something that's not particular to women, but I do think that women can epitomize it.

Katrina is highly focused on her children and works hard to pass on her values to them. She also extends her love to children who don't have the same advantages as her children do.

I've put my children first. So it's been a bit of a balance, and the hardest decisions I've had to make are when I've had to leave my children for a day or two. I always thought there should be a test for parenthood, but there isn't. There's one for driving but not for parenthood. The children don't ask to come here, and if their parents don't care for them, then we as human beings of the earth should because their early experiences really will help them be able to create good legacy or not.

As the mother of two multiracial children, Katrina is determined that her children grow up to appreciate the legacy of all their ancestors. When she was in the hospital, she refused to check one or another box for ethnicity for her children. She then spearheaded a movement in the schools they attended to allow children to check multiple boxes for their ancestry. She makes sure they understand all the strength of the many cultures that are part of their heritage: Scottish, Austrian, African American, and Native American. Katrina says, "When I became a parent, I thought I wanted to make sure that my children were very proud of their multiracial heritage, so I did several things. One, I would read to them about African American history and great African Americans but also Africa, and great Native Americans. I didn't forget the Scotsmen or the Austrians either. I think if they saw *The Sound of Music* one more time, they were probably going to break the TV."

Katrina is also aware of the challenges of being a mother to very privileged children. She works hard to keep her children in touch with the challenges of those less fortunate. Katrina's father was a doctor at Stanford University School of Medicine.

As a family we had the opportunity to go to places in Central and South America, small Guatemalan and Indian villages where people literally lived in a piece of tin held up by a piece of wood. And there was a rivulet of muddy water. The survival rate for children was very low. And when I'd asked my dad, "How did they die?" he tried to explain to me when I was seven that basically they couldn't stop going to the bathroom. They would be basically dying from diarrhea, which is so curable. So from an early age, I understood how lucky I was. And my children have grown up, because my husband and I have been very successful, with more than either of us grew up with. So we've been very cognizant of trying to ensure that they don't feel they are better or even different because of any socioeconomic level.

To help her daughter Chloe understand the world she lives in, where she comes from, and how to give responsibly, Katrina started a fun project they call Chloe's Closet.

We take my clothes and sell them online, and Chloe figures out when we make some money which charitable organizations she would like to give the money to, and I try and choose ones that I know about, so that I know that the money that she and I have raised together will end up helping someone. So far we've done a lot with Smile Train. So I try and teach Chloe, Mom's old clothes make it possible for someone in another country to not only live, but be a part of a family and a community, and that's part of legacy building. I'm teaching them those things by doing. I'm exposing them by doing. So that's legacy building.

Chloe came up with the clothes tag. It's bright pink on one side and zebra on the other. She writes a little note and puts a dragonfly sticker on it and writes out the money amount. A map on her wall shows where all of Mommy's clothes have gone. And because I'm small in my size, we're very popular in Japan, Australia, Scotland, and Texas. It helps her with her geography, and she realizes the things that are sitting around in your closet can change someone' else's life.

The Peebles envision Chloe's closet will also support educational efforts and scholarships for female high school graduates. Katrina is proud that her son has also absorbed the family lessons of being sensitive to others. She recounts,

I had my son work on a construction project, ripping up carpet and putting a roof on. And I saw him in the kitchen one day making a sandwich. He's not a very good cook. And I said, "I'm paying you to work on this roof. Why don't you go get a piece of pizza or something that you like for lunch?" And he said, "The people I work with have families and kids and they can't afford to get lunch. How would it seem if I went and got an expensive piece of pizza when they can't do that?" And I said, "This is a very good learning experience. You learned something very important."

Katrina combines all her passions when it comes to philanthropy. She works with children, supports cancer research, and has worked hard at the historic preservation of the buildings that the Peebles real estate business acquires. She is a member of Honey-Shine and a former copresident of the Women's Cancer League. She is cofounder of the Recreation Wish List with former Washington D.C., First Lady, Cora Barry, which raised hundreds of thousands of dollars for the renovation of the District of Columbia

Department of Parks and Recreation facilities. She is a former Member of Miami Beach's Chamber of Commerce Board of Governors and was awarded the Key to the City of Miami and the City of Miami Beach. She is a former vice president and current board member of the Vizcayans. Katrina was appointed to the President's Advisory Committee on the Arts in 2011.

One of her favorite projects was the historic restoration of the Bath Club. It is South Florida's oldest private beach club. Established in 1926, the Peebles turned the club into an award-winning project combining the historic structure with luxurious tower residences overlooking the Atlantic Ocean. Reflecting on the project, Katrina shares,

> A building has a lot to do with legacy because this building will certainly last longer than I will. It was a good collaboration. We brought something to the table. I remember pointing the club out to my dad as we drove by and I said "Look! This is the building that we built! And it's got the colors of the sand and the blue ocean." We actually serve tea, which nobody in Miami Beach serves. You feel really proud of it because it was the very best you could do. Sometimes it was done under extraordinarily hard situations. It was a highly competitive process. We collaborated together, knowing it would be a five-star property, and it has turned out great.

In addition to working on charitable causes, the Peebles are very involved in politics as Democratic party supporters. Katrina and her husband, Don, have hosted more than one hundred fund-raisers for major candidates, including two U.S. presidents: President Bill Clinton, and President Barack Obama. Katrina was newly engaged and just twenty-six years old in 1992, when she and her husband hosted the presidential hopeful, Arkansas Governor Bill Clinton, at their home in Washington, D.C. They went on to serve as sponsors of the Clinton Inaugural. In May 2008, the Peebles hosted an intimate fund-raiser for President Barack Obama at the Bath Club, and Don Peebles is a member of the National Finance Committee for the Obama administration.

Katrina advises women who are considering their legacy to embrace all their passions and to allow their emotions to enliven their philanthropy.

KATRINA'S ADVICE FOR ENJOYING YOUR LEGACY

- *Envision, envision, envision* and don't waste time. "I envisioned myself speaking Spanish, and now I can, and still I make mistakes, which I expect because learning a language starting at forty is not easy. But I'm proud to say that my daughter is also fluent."

- *Pick something you like.* "I love to decorate. I love to do interiors. I stay up at night thinking about how I can make an interior better or get someone's attention on the Internet or sell it to a pharmaceutical company. And I don't consider it work. It entertains my brain hugely."

- *Ask questions.* "Don't be afraid to say you don't know, even in the middle of an interview, if somebody asks a question and you're not precisely sure what that word means. It doesn't mean that you're not smart. It just means that you care enough about the person's question that you want to get it just right."

- *Don't be afraid to make mistakes.* "Have a vision and reach very high, and it's not because you think you're going to land just a little low. You know that expression 'Reach for the stars. You'll land on the moon'? That's not what I mean. I mean reach for the stars and see yourself on the star. It may morph a little bit. Your inner child may say, 'Oh, gosh. When I was twenty, I thought I wanted to be on that star, but it's changed, and now I really would like to be on Saturn.'"

- *Think a good deal of yourself.* "Don't expect other people to be your pumper club. Some people need bicycle pumps around them. Respect yourself and believe in your abilities."

- *Talk about things that are important.* "If you hang around turkeys, you're never going to fly like an eagle."

- *Take the high road and go forward with kindness.* "You'll never regret your actions."

Doris Buffett

Many of us can look back on our childhood and remember more than a little pain. Some of us are able to take those painful experiences and transform them into a wellspring of giving that energizes us and brings us true joy. The true master can then share her expertise and knowledge with others, creating an army of effective givers.

We were truly inspired by the jubilant energy we heard in the voice of Doris Buffett, a wonderful philanthropist known as the Sunshine Lady. Doris is the elder sister of one of the wealthiest men in the world, Warren Buffett. She is using an inheritance of over $110 million dollars in Berkshire Hathaway stock shares to deeply impact people's lives through her foundation.[5] Doris says, "Even when I didn't have money, I was doing things that I could because I was aware of suffering. I had a rough childhood, I had always wanted a fairy godmother to come into my life. Nobody ever showed up. This way, I could be that fairy godmother."

From a tender age, Doris Buffett experienced what it's like to be an innocent victim and have your spirit broken and your opportunities limited by those closest to you. She took the brunt of abuse from a mother who now is believed to have suffered postpartum depression. While Doris had a loving relationship with her beloved father, Howard Buffett, a Republican congressman, her mother, Leila Buffett, constantly belittled Doris, continuously making her out to be stupid and exploding in tirades that would last hours.

While Warren and her sister, Bertie, went off to college, Doris never got that opportunity. Warren Buffett said in Doris's biography, *The Sunshine Lady,* that he often felt the urge to protect his older sister. "But I never did, because I was afraid of becoming the target myself." He even ran away to escape his mother's abusive explosions.

There were plenty of grains of sand to follow to add to Doris's oyster. Over her lifetime, Doris has had four failed marriages, two battles with cancer, challenging relationships with her own children, battled with depression, and nearly lost her house in the 1987 market crash. Out of all that pain grew one really magnificent pearl and a whole lot of sunshine.

"When people are really struggling and trying to do the right thing and they've had bad luck, that's when we can help," says the Sunshine Lady. Warren likes to say of his sister that when it comes to giving, "I'm wholesale, my sister's retail." Warren Buffett announced in 2006 that he is giving 85 percent—or nearly $40 billion—of his Berkshire stock to charity and around $31 billion of that gift will go directly to the Gates Foundation in annual increments.

Warren and Doris talk together frequently about their charitable work, which has created a strong bond between them. Doris says,

> we have a personal relationship and treasure it. He sees things really big. After the announcement of his gift to the Gates Foundation, he began to receive thousands of letters from people who needed financial help due not to bad choices, but to bad luck. He asked me to respond to these good but invisible people. We have processed over fourteen thousand letters. Warren financed our activities. We often send him the thank-you letters (and homemade gifts) we receive. We have a lot to talk about. He's very brotherly about the whole thing. He loved the book! It's nice to have a brother who likes you. We have fun together. This has been terrific for me.

The Sunshine Lady Foundation, a charity created by Doris in 1996, has distributed over $110 million in the last decade and counting. Doris Buffett believes in hand-ups, not handouts and says she hopes her last check will bounce. She is a totally hands-on philanthropist and has developed a very personal style of giving. She is very focused on affecting individuals who have experienced difficult times and are willing to help themselves. She is famous for sending checks directly to people hit hard. "The beauty of what I can do, I can send somebody that isn't in good health to the Mayo Clinic, or if somebody desperately needs a lawyer, we can do it instantaneously sometimes—because you have to." Doris has supported thousands of children to get an education or attend camp, sponsored young women in Afghanistan, paid for the public pool to entertain the youth in her local community, and created educational programs in the nation's prisons to successfully lower the rate of recidivism.

Her investing has inspired an army of Americans of all ages to become "sunbeams" in her movement; staff and volunteers communicating on the progress of the foundation's programs, and they often alert her when somebody needs another hand up. Sunbeams read hundreds of letters addressed to Doris Buffett and Warren Buffett filled with requests for help.

Doris Buffett is there, writing the checks, answering the phone, and working eight hours a day or more. And says she has found giving to be the most joyful thing in her life. "I'm not trying to build an empire. I'm trying to get this money out there while I'm alive," explains the eighty-three-year-old Doris. "Our ideal is to give a million a month, and that's hard to do intelligently. Our overhead runs about six percent. I like to work in this country close to home because I know who the players are. We keep records and know where all the money goes. Teenage pregnancy is a national problem, so let's work on it right here. Drop-out is another national problem, so we'll work on it here. I get the joy of seeing lives improve."

At the end of the day, the Sunshine Lady, like her famous brother, always gets down to business. Her mission focuses not on company performance but on the human condition.

> The number one tenet of what I do is to partner with the applicant, to work together to solve the problem. The personal touch is absolutely essential. We're selling hope and confidence and caring. It works. We're not giving money away, we're reinvesting money in people, and the payoff is that their lives are better. We have to stay in touch. And help them along the way because I want everyone to succeed. I don't want any failures, because failures are painful, and they can destroy a person if he has them over and over. In our collaboration, everybody wins. Hurrah!

Turning Survivors into Strivers

After running a shelter for battered women and discovering that some of the women in the shelter network around the country were interested in going on to get an education, Doris Buffett founded the Women's Independence Scholarship Program (WISP) in 1999. It has awarded more than $16 million in scholarships to over two thousand women across the United States.[6] "I remember the first woman who applied. Every morning when her husband went off to work, he took her shoes and the telephone," says Doris.

> She had little kids. Where are you going to? People have to realize many abused women are like hostages. Now, they're getting advice and support. A large percentage of women in our scholarship program have an average GPA of about 3.7. That's with little kids to take care of and a harassing ex-somebody. They of course start out thinking it's impossible because they've been told they're idiots all their lives by some guy.

Recently we had a woman that went on to the Wharton School of Finance. What do you think about that!

Doris receives hundreds of letters with stories of their children, too. "We have children growing up in a peaceful home. And consistently they admire their mother. Many of their moms become nurses and teachers and people who work in safe houses. They're giving back like crazy."

Learning by Giving: An Education

Doris has mastered how to give so effectively, and has seen such value in creating accountability in charity, that she has set up educational programs to teach the art and business of philanthropy. She likes to challenge philanthropists to produce effective and measurable results. She became upset when she saw ineffective giving programs. Doris says, "I know one foundation run by a son of the donor and his two kids. There were no outside people on the board, and I couldn't believe when I saw that he was paying himself $300,000 and his kids were getting close to $200,000 each in salary. We don't operate that way. We can account for every cent, whether it's my brother's donation or it's my money."

In 2003, a Boston College report showed that a $41 trillion wealth transfer would take place in the United States by the year 2052.[7] In that same year, the Sunshine Foundation launched, the Learning by Giving Program. "The goal of the Learning by Giving program is to support and promote the study of philanthropy at the undergraduate level nationwide in order to prepare, empower, and inspire young adults to become effective, knowledgeable, and skilled philanthropists and leaders in their communities."

"I've had a few good ideas and this was one of them," explains Doris.

Here we have all these kids going to college and I remember in the old days what the Communists used to do. They'd come into a college campus and they'd pick off four percent of the student body who were the smartest and most compassionate and recruit them. And I thought, well, maybe we can do the same thing with this. It started at Davidson. We had some junior sunbeams, down there at Davidson College and a professor who saw the potential value in such a class. It was a natural.

It's very simple: We give them ten thousand dollars in real money, and we say to them now you have to be philanthropists and go through all the steps. The only requirement we make is that you must give the money in your locality. You can't send it off to Bangkok or someplace like that. You have to make the site visit, you have to talk to their board, all those things you're supposed to do. They go into little teams and then they each pick an area they are interested in. Then they decide within their own group which is the best, and then the person who runs it comes to the class and tries to sell it to the class. Then they have impassioned discussions training to "sell" their choices to the rest of the class. The professors love to teach the class because the students are so engaged.

To date, the program has distributed over $175,000 to sixteen colleges and universities across the United States, including Georgetown, Cornell, NYU, Davidson, and University of California–Berkeley. The undergraduate philanthropy courses have funded more than fifty grants to improve quality of life in their local communities.

Doris Buffett calls herself a late bloomer, but she's certainly made up for "lost" time. This octogenarian who frequently works ten hours per day told us about a life-changing event that really resonated.

I went to a funeral in Morehead City, North Carolina, and the minister said of the deceased woman, "Well, she really loved to shop." I thought here's a tombstone, DORIS BUFFETT, and it says 1928 to 2050. I want to know that I made a difference. Life is very difficult and it's immense when you really know you've affected lives in a very positive manner. There are so many things that all of us can do. It's a challenge, of course, but the payoff in joy is better than the best day on the stock market.

In summer 2011, Doris endowed the program, and it was spun out of The Sunshine Lady Foundation to be run as a separate charity called the Learning by Giving Foundation. Her grandson, Alex Buffett Rozek, who is president and also sits on the board, runs the new foundation. He has worked for the program since its inception in 2003. Alex is carrying on her vision into the future alongside other family board members and leading experts in education, philanthropy, technology, and finance.

DORIS'S ADVICE FOR ENJOYING YOUR LEGACY

- Help those who need a hand up, not a handout.
- Become personally involved and know exactly where your money is going.
- Minimize overhead and send as much money as possible into good works.
- Be prepared to provide immediate relief in dire situations.
- Look at your philanthropy as an investment in someone's life and expect them to succeed.
- Keep in touch with those you help; your caring makes a big difference.
- Enjoy the true joy and energy that will come into your life as you help others.
- Think about the dash between your birth and death and what you want to be remembered for.

EPILOGUE

Wearing the Pearls with Pride

OUR SEVEN PEARLS OF FINANCIAL WISDOM encourage you to take action: to make financial choices that will enable you to live a powerful life overflowing with happiness and joy. We hope you are feeling wiser, stronger, smarter, and more prepared to face every stage in life with confidence. You should now feel comfortable enough to wear these pearls with pride.

Changing a longstanding pattern of behavior is a matter of daily practice. So save a pearl of wisdom to your smartphone; pin one upon the refrigerator; post one on the bathroom mirror; needlepoint your favorite pearl onto a pillow. Write a pearl on an adhesive note and stick it on the frame around your computer monitor. Absorb them, but above all, act on them.

We could have written a book filled exclusively with information and instructions, but we realized that you needed to hear from real women who share your experiences and your dreams and who can serve as successful role models. We want you to know that for every challenge you face, there are at least a thousand women who have walked the walk. Having inspirational women show you that it really *can* be done will encourage you to strive for your own highest level of mastery and achievement.

As we end this part of our journey together, we want you to know that you are in our hearts. We want to hear from you, too—we encourage you to contact us at www.thesevenpearls.com, and to tell us your own stories about how the pearls have affected you. This is the end of our book, but it is just the start of our friendship with you.

THE SEVEN PEARLS: A SHINING STRING OF FEMININE WISDOM FOR YOU

Remember what we have learned together:

A Woman Must Build Her Own Wealth
A Woman Should Require Good Finance in Her Romance
A Woman Must Nurture Her Prosperity in Motherhood
A Woman Must Exercise Her Power in Life
A Woman Under Pressure Must Act with Grace
A Woman's Dreams and Potential Are Ageless
A Woman's Legacy of Love Is Priceless

ACKNOWLEDGMENTS

One of the most exciting aspects of writing this book was the opportunity to meet and speak with some of the most fascinating, informative, and inspiring people in the world. We are deeply grateful to the many experts who agreed to be interviewed for our book. They shared their insight and their time willingly and passionately, often under extraordinary deadlines.

In each section, these wonderful experts are acknowledged in alphabetical order.

For the chapter on the first pearl: We would like to thank Jane Applegate, Marsha Firestone, Ana Harvey, Barbara Taibi, Cora Bett Thomas, Julie Weeks, and Jacki Zehner. Your work is enabling women to become dynamic successful business owners, who are creating jobs in America. We salute you for encouraging strategic decision-making, inspiring us to find the joy and lessons in new challenges and adventures as well as our successes. Thank you for being our great connectors.

For the chapter on the second pearl: We would like to thank Barbara Taylor-Bradford, Melinda Blanchard, Holly Dustin, Bettyann Glasser, Amber Kelleher-Andrews, Renee Siegel, and Vikki Ziegler. Your work and your own life stories show us how romantic love can thrive alongside a new business landscape for powerful women. Your dedicated care to protecting our hearts, our wealth, and our aspirations is remarkable. Thank you for helping us to understand the darker elements in our world while encouraging us to believe in true love, and walking the walk wisely yourselves.

For the chapter on the third pearl: We would like to thank Chemmy Alcott, Wendy Diamond, Ashley Dobbs, Sasha Eden, Dr. Rafaella Fabbri, Jolene Godfrey, Dr. James Grifo, Babette Haggerty, Fredda Herz-Brown, Erin Kennedy, Teresa Pollman, Dr. Eleonora Porcu, Ryan Pulliam, Robin Raskin, Dune Thorne, Marilyn Weiss, and Piper Weiss. As we tackle the motherhood juggle in its many forms, you have kept us on a course to wealth and security while demonstrating what an exciting and multidimensional journey is in our midst. Thank you for reminding us to love ourselves as we love others, and for reaffirming the prestigious enterprise of motherhood and family life.

For the chapter on the fourth pearl: We'd like to thank Sofia Adrogue, Miri Ben-Ari, Lauren Bush, Rita Cosby, Melinda Emerson, Moira Forbes, Cynthia Greenawalt-Carvajal, Martina Gordon, Lee Hanson, Beckie Klein, Nancy Mendelson, Kathy Reilly, Lauren Remington Platt, Linda Tarr-Whelan, and Bonnie Wurzbacher. We were the young girls who once watched *The Bionic Woman*. You've shown us in real life what can be done. Thank you helping us create a road map to understanding the power within us in all its forms, and for charting a course to our best destiny.

For the chapter on the fifth pearl: We would like to thank Lt. Erica Arteseros, Betsy Blumenthal, Mela Garber, Diane Giles, Helen Jonsen, Tania Neild, Tam St. Armand, Nancy Ward, and Anne Wojcicki. We are grateful for your groundbreaking work and experience in the business of saving and preparing human lives for the dark days. You never fail to demonstrate how to swim the rip tide armed and ready. Your courage is inspiring.

For the chapter on the sixth pearl: We'd like to thank Marie Dwyer-Bullock, Alyson Burns, Vera Gibbons, Beverly Mahone, Aleta St. James, Nancy Thompson, and Marian Wellman. Thank you for demonstrating that age is just a number. Prosperity and happiness are in abundance if we seek them all the days of our lives. We are grateful that you are showing the baby boomers and beyond how to do it right.

For the chapter on the seventh pearl: We'd like to thank Tina Albright, Doris Buffett, Mona Hanford, Loida Lewis, and Katrina Peebles. Thank you for inviting us to enter the most intimate heartfelt moments of your experience so we may flourish in our own lives and in the lives of others. We are so grateful you are setting America and the world on a course for growth, understanding, and giving.

We'd like to thank our literary agent Gene Brissie of James Peter Associates, who recognized the potential in our project, always answered all our endless questions, and never ceases to offer encouragement and counsel. We are grateful to our fantastic attorney Ken Weinrib of Franklin, Weinrib, Rudell and Vassallo. Thank you, Gene and Ken, for closing the deal and for your careful technical review and attention to detail in all our book affairs.

To the team at St. Martin's Press: Thank you for executing our vision for the book, and producing it with care and a deep sense of its style and content for women. We'd like to first acknowledge our editor, George Witte. We appreciate your poet's sensibilities and your respectful handling of our precious pearls. We'd also like to thank assistant editor Terra Layton. In addition, we are grateful for the assistance of the full St. Martin's Team including, in alphabetical order: publicist Stephanie Hargadon, social media coordinator Lauren Hesse, social media director Paul Hochman, proofreader Norma Hoffman, marketing executive Jeanne-Marie Hudson, and copyeditor Eli Torres.

Thank you to photographer Barry Morgenstein and his team, including the talented makeup artist Lisa Miller, for the beautiful photo used for the book cover.

Thanks to Mark Robohm and the team at Juicyorange for creating our wonderful website.

To our line editor, publishing expert, and dear friend Barbara Clark: We couldn't have done it without you. Thank you for seeing more in us than we could even see in ourselves at the time this book was born. You helped us clarify our vision and played a brilliant traffic cop to the end.

We'd like to thank our ace research support team including, in alphabetical order: Shawn Brady, Mavis Carr, Alicia Rancilio, and Elizabeth Robichaux Brown. We'd also like to thank our fantastic administrative support team, Kristen Steiner and Mei Po Wong.

We are grateful to the following individuals for helping us make the connections that were so vital to the book. They are acknowledged in alphabetical order: Robert Bradford, Tiffany Carr, Suzanne Currie, Sandy Elsass, Kim Fontenot, Anthony Gordon, Laura Hill, Frances Hooper, Tim Horner, Lauren Kelly, Greg Lee, Kym McNicholas, Anna Morris, Toni Nagy, David Nathan, Gloria Nelund, Mary Olsen, Don Peebles, Kendall Pryles,

Mariette Ravet, Josue Sejour, Nora Simpson, Mark Smith, Tim Speiss, Victoria Waldron and Elaine Wu.

We'd also like to thank the professionals who assisted us in connecting to our contributors, gathering content, and served as sounding boards and supporters of the book. They are, in alphabetical order: Alex and Heather Alcott, Joe Applegate, Claire Bailey, Shai Baitel, Tamara Bally, Lisa Barron, Blake Beatty, Katharine Blodget, Stephanie Borynak Clark, Morgan L. Brennan, Sally Butcher, Lawrence Caso, Terry Cater, Wendy Cohen, Lottie Cole, Simon Constable, Jennifer Starobin Davidson, Typhaine and Fred de Bure, Mary Ellen Egan, Cornelia Ercklentz, Anne Erni, Melissa Fisher, Samantha Foerster, Steve Forbes and the Forbes family, *Forbes* magazine, Forbes.com Video Network, Forbes Woman Bloggers, Emma Froelich-Shea, Gabriel Fysh, Jonathan Goldberg, Mike Grady, Kerima Greene, Mia Haugen, Lee Hawkins, Hilary Hayes, Jeff Hayzlett, Elizabeth Hewitt, Mike Hill, Lise Hilton, Peter Hilton, Vanessa Hope, Caroline Howard, Helen Kotchoubey, Carl Lavin, Paul Maidment, Lee Mason, Marcy McGinnis, Aileen Meehan, Debra Moore, John Perugini, Philip Revzin, David Rhodes, Nouriel Roubini, Joumana Saad, Fiona Siddall, Archie and Sabina Struthers, Virginia Tupker, and Jonathan Wald.

To our parents, Anne and Charles Pepper and Mollie and Daniel Webster, our families, and our friends: thank you for supporting us to the finish line, for inspiring us with your experience, and for celebrating with us throughout the journey. To our godchildren: we wish for you all the wisdom, love, strength, and success of the stories found within these pages.

Notes

Introduction
1. She-conomy.com, http://she-conomy.com (accessed July 27, 2011).
2. Aysegul Sahin, Joseph Song, and Bart Hobijn, "The Unemployment Gender Gap during the 2007 Recession," *Federal Reserve Bank Current Issues in Economics and Finance,* Volume 16, Number 2 (2010).

Chapter 1
1. American Express OPEN, "The American Express OPEN State of Women-Owned Businesses," (March 31, 2011): 2, http://www.womenable.com/pages.php?tabid=2&pageid=163&title=New+Numbers+on+WOBs (accessed June 3, 2011).
2. Alexandra Cawthorne, "The Straight Facts on Women in Poverty," October 2008.
3. American Express OPEN, "The American Express OPEN State of Women-Owned Business Report," 4.
4. U.S. Census Bureau, "Survey of Business Owners—Women-Owned Firms: 2007," http://www.census.gov/econ/sbo/get07sof.html?8 (accessed June 8, 2011).
5. Internal Revenue Service, "SOI Tax Stats—2004 Personal Wealth Tables," August 3, 2010, http://www.irs.gov/taxstats/article/0,,id=185880,00.html (accessed June 8, 2011).
6. Liz Weston, "Big Benefit of Being 50 and Self-employed?" *Los Angeles Times,* April 3, 2011.
7. The National Conference for Research on Women, Women in Fund Management Report, 9.
8. Hedge Fund Research, Inc., "Women-Owned Funds Universe," 2009.
9. Jeff Sommer, "How Men's Overconfidence Hurts Them as Investors," March 13, 2010, http://www.nytimes.com/2010/03/14/business/14mark.html (accessed June 8, 2011).

10. John Ameriks, Jill Marshall, and Liquian Ren/Vanguard, "Equity Abandonment in 2008–2009: Lower Among Balanced Fund Investors," (December 2009): 2.

11. Megan Frank and Susan Bishop, "Merrill Lynch Investment Managers (MLIM) Survey Finds: When It Comes to Investing, Gender a Strong Influence on Behavior," Hindsight 2 Insight 1 (April 18, 2005): 1.

12. Alexandra Niessen and Stefan Ruenzi, "Sex Matters: Gender and Mutual Funds," (November 2005): 36.

13. The National Council for Research on Women, Women in Fund Management Report, 9.

14. Family Wealth Alliance, "Seventh Annual Multifamily Office Summary—Executive Summary," 1.

15. Merrill Lynch Wealth Management, "World Wealth Report 2010," State of the World's Wealth, 17.

16. Merrill Lynch Wealth Management, "World Wealth Report," 17.

17. The Family Wealth Alliance, "Seventh Annual Multifamily Office Study," http://www.fwalliance.com/store/exec-summary-7th-annual-mfo.pdf.

18. Harris Interactive, Inc., "2010 Consumer Financial Literacy Survey Final Report," (April 2010): 3.

Chapter 2

1. Pew Research Center, "Women, Men, and the New Economics of Marriage," January 19, 2010, http://pewsocialtrends.org/files/2010/10/new-economics-of-marriage.pdf.

2. U.S. Census Bureau, "Unmarried and Single Americans Week: Sept. 19–25, 2010," Facts for Features, July 19, 2010, http://www.census.gov/newsroom/releases/archives/facts_for_features_special_editions/cb10-ff18.html.

3. Ben Woolsey and Matt Schulz, "Credit Card Statistics, Industry Facts, Debt Statistics," http://www.creditcards.com/credit-card-news/credit-card-industry-facts-personal-debt-statistics-1276.php (accessed June 9, 2011).

4. Match.com, "The Real Cost of Dating in America: Don't Bank on Assumptions," http://blog.match.com/2011/04/14/the-real-cost-of-dating-in-america/ (accessed June 9, 2011).

5. Match.com, "The Rules of Engagement: Dating in America," http://blog.match.com/2011/03/28/dating-in-america/ (accessed June 9, 2011).

6. Alice C. Chen, "In Search of a Soul Mate," San Francisco Chronicle, http://www.kelleher-international.com/editorials/san_chron.html (accessed June 9, 2011).

7. National Institutes of Mental Health, "Antisocial Personality Disorder," http://www.nimh.nih.gov/statistics/1Antisocial.shtml (accessed June 9, 2011).

8. Ibid.

9. Mary Quist-Newins, "Women and Money: Research reveals unmet opportunities and risks," April 20, 2010, http://www.thewealthchannel.com/articles/Women-and-Money-Research-reveals-unmet-opportunities-and-risks/ (accessed June 9, 2011).

10. Costs of Addiction, "The Economics of Addiction," http://www.drug-rehabs.com/addiction_costofaddiction.htm (accessed June 9, 2011).

11. Patrick F. Fagan, "The Effects of Pornography on Individuals, Marriage, Family, and Community," *Research Synthesis* (December 2009): 9.

12. Online Gambling, http://www.bonus.to/online-gambling.htm (accessed June 9, 2011).

13. Casinos and Other Legal Gambling, *Michigan in Brief,* 7th edition, 64.

14. Data confirming average gambling debt of males is between fifty-five thousand and ninety thousand dollars and that the problem gambler's average divorce rate is almost double that of a nongambler found at http://www.overcominggambling .com/facts.html#Statistics.

15. Gambling Court, "Statistics," http://www.gamblingcourt.org/infoStatistics.php (accessed June 9, 2011).

16. "Economic Effects of Divorce on Women," http://www.livestrong.com/article/ 123507-economic-effects-divorce-women/.

17. Pew Research Center, "Women, Men, and the new Economics of Marriage" (January 19, 2010): 1, 15.

18. Belinda Luscombe, "Workplace Salaries: At Last, Women on Top," *Time,* September 1, 2010, http://www.time.com/time/business/article/0,8599,2015274,00.html (accessed June 8, 2011).

19. Leah Hoffman, "Matrimony: To Have and to Hold On To," November 7, 2006, http://www.forbes.com/2006/11/07/divorce-costs-legal-biz-cx_lh_1107le galdivorce.html (accessed June 8, 2011).

20. "Economic Effects of Divorce on Women," http://www.livestrong.com/article /123507-economic-effects-divorce-women/ (2nd reference).

21. Janet H. Johnson, "Women's Legal Rights in Egypt," Fathom Archive, 2002.

Chapter 3

1. "Parental Leave Law and Your Child," http://labor-employment-law.lawyers.com /family-medical-leave-act/Parental-Leave-Law-and-Your-Child.html (accessed June 29, 2011).

2. Sue Shellenberger, "Downsizing Maternity Leave: Employers Cut Pay, Time Off," *Wall Street Journal,* June 11, 2008, http://online.wsj.com/article/SB12131379175 1362341.html (accessed June 28, 2011).

3. "The Cost of Raising a Child," United Press International, June 18, 2010, http:// www.upi.com/Top_News/US/2010/06/18/The-cost-of-raising-a-child-222360 /UPI-39221276914536/ (accessed June 29, 2011).

4. Advanced Fertility Services, http://www.infertilityny.com/costs.html (accessed June 29, 2011).

5. 2002 National Survey of Family Growth, "Fertility, Family Planning, and Reproductive Health of U.S. Women," http://www.cdc.gov/nchs/data/series/sr_23/sr23_ 025.pdf (accessed June 29, 2011).

6. Sabrina Tavernise, "Census Data Shows Changes in Childbearing Patterns," *New York Times,* May 10, 2011, http://www.nytimes.com/2011/05/10/us/10birth.html ?_r=2 (accessed June 28, 2011).

7. Jeanie Lerche Davis, "Fertility Treatment Less Successful after Age 35," June 18,

2004, http://www.webmd.com/infertility-and-reproduction/news/20040618/fertility -treatment-less-successful-after-35 (accessed June 29, 2011).

8. Camilla Webster, "Why Women Are Freezing Their Eggs," *Forbes,* April 13, 2010, http://www.forbes.com/2010/04/13/family-planning-pregnancy-fertility-infer tility-forbes-woman-health-older-moms.html (accessed June 29, 2011).

9. "Pregnancy after 35," May 2009, http://www.marchofdimes.com/pregnancy /trying_after35.html (accessed June 29, 2011).

10. Rachel Lehmann-Haupt, "Why I Froze My Eggs," *Newsweek,* May 2, 2009, http://www.newsweek.com/2009/05/01/why-i-froze-my-eggs.html (accessed June 29, 2011).

11. Camilla Webster, "Why Women Are Freezing Their Eggs."

12. Source: Dr. Grifo in interview with Camilla Webster 2011.

13. Debra Aho Williamson, "Moms Who Blog: A Marketing Powerhouse," October 2010, http://www.emarketer.com/Report.aspx?code=emarketer_2000723 (accessed June 28, 2011).

14. Debra Aho Williamson, "Moms Who Blog: A Marketing Powerhouse."

15. John Sobel, "HOW: Technology, Traffic and Revenue—Day 3 SOTB 2010," November 5, 2010, http://technorati.com/blogging/article/how-technology-traffic-and-reve nue-day/ (accessed June 28, 2011).

16. "BlogHer—Advertisers," http://www.blogher.com/advertise (accessed June 28, 2011).

17. "BlogHer Ads Affiliation Agreement," http://www.abdpbt.com/personalfinance /the-blogherads-affiliation-agreement/ (accessed June 28, 2011).

18. "BlogHer Advertising Information," http://www.blogher.com/files/BlogHerAd vertisingInformation.pdf (accessed July 29, 2011).

19. Tatiana Morales, "Mom Rocks: Tina Knowles," December 5, 2007, http:// www.cbsnews.com/stories/2004/05/07/earlyshow/contributors/melindamurphy/ main616148.shtml (accessed June 28, 2011).

20. Carolyn Pope Edwards, Susan M. Sheridan, and Lisa L. Knocke, "Parental Engagement and School-Readiness: Parent-Child Relationships in Early Learning," 2008, http://cyfs.unl.edu/docs/Publications&Presentations/Parental%20Engage ment%20and%20School%20Readiness.pdf.

21. Sara Kershaw, "In Studies of Virtual Teams, Nature Wins Again," September 3, 2008, *New York Times,* http://www.nytimes.com/2008/09/04/garden/04twins .html?fta=y&pagewanted=all (accessed June 28, 2011).

22. Sara Kershaw, "In Studies of Virtual Teams, Nature Wins Again."

23. Anthony P. Carnevale, Nicole Smith, and Jeff Strohl, "Help Wanted: Projections of Jobs and Education Requirements through 2018," June 2010, http://www9 .georgetown.edu/grad/gppi/hpi/cew/pdfs/fullreport.pdf.

24. National Stepfamily Resource Center, "Step Family Fact Sheet," http://www .stepfamilies.info/stepfamily-fact-sheet.php (accessed July 27, 2011).

25. Pew Research Center, "Women, Men, and the New Economics of Marriage," January 19, 2010, http://pewsocialtrends.org/files/2010/10/new-economics-of-marriage .pdf.

26. National Stepfamily Resource Center, "Step Family Fact Sheet," http://www.step families.info/stepfamily-fact-sheet.php (accessed July 27, 2011).

27. Marilyn Coleman and Lawrence H. Ganong, "Financial Management in Step-families," *Lifestyles: Family and Economic Issues,* Fall 1989.

28. American Pet Products Association, "Industry Statistics 7 Trends," http://www .americanpetproducts.org/press_industrytrends.asp (accessed June 28, 2011).

29. Ibid.

30. Ibid.

31. Ibid.

32. K9K Cancer Walks, "Canine Cancer Information," http://www.caninek.org/Can cer.html (accessed June 28, 2011).

33. Ranch and Coast, "Traveling with VIPs (Very Important Pets)," October 29, 2010, http://www.ranchandcoast.com/DETOUR/27/DESTINATIONS/2464/TRAV ELING-WITH-VIPS/PAGE/7/ (accessed June 28, 2011).

34. Babette Haggerty's School for Dogs, "Basic Group Obedience," http://www .haggertydog.com/basic.html (accessed June 28, 2011).

Chapter 4

1. Dictionary.com, http://dictionary.reference.com/browse/branding (accessed July 15, 2011).

2. Kashmir Hill, "Feds Okay Start-up That Monitors Employees' Internet and Social Media Footprints," *Forbes,* June 15, 2011, http://blogs.forbes.com/kashmirhill/2011 /06/15/start-up-that-monitors-employees-internet-and-social-media-footprints -gets-gov-approval (accessed July 15, 2011).

3. Catalyst, "The Bottom Line: Corporate Performance and Women's Representa-tion on Boards."

4. Catalyst, "The Bottom Line."

5. 2001 Ion Report, "How Change Happens: The 7th Annual Status Report of Women Directors and Executive Officers of Public Companies in Fourteen Regions of the United States," March 2011.

6. Ibid.

7. Ibid.

8. Ibid.

9. Giving USA 2011, "The Annual Report on Philanthropy 2010."

10. The Nonprofit Sector in Brief, "Public Charities, Giving, and Volunteering, 2010."

11. Sarah Anzia and Christopher Berry, "The Jackie (and Jill) Robinson Effect: Why Do Congresswomen Outperform Congressmen?" May 24, 2010.

12. Sarah Anzia and Christopher Berry, "The Jackie (and Jill) Robinson Effect."

Chapter 5

1. David U. Himmelstein, Deborah Thorne, Elizabeth Warren, and Steffie Wool-handler, "Medical Bankruptcy in the United States, 2007: Results of a National Study," *The American Journal of Medicine,* August 2009.

2. Matthew Bennett, "Average Insolvency Rates Rise Fourfold within 5 Years of Diagnosis," *Star Global Tribune,* June 30, 2011.

3. Usha Ranji and Alina Salganico, "Women's Health Care Chartbook: Key Findings from the May 2011 Kaiser Women's Health Survey."

4. Ibid.

5. Sara R. Collins, Michelle M. Doty, Ruth Robertson, and Tracy Garber, "Help on the Horizon," the Commonwealth Fund, March 2011.

6. Ibid.

7. Empire BlueCross BlueShield, "TraditionPlus Hospital Program," July 5, 2005.

8. Ibid.

9. Jim Angstadt, "Most Americans 'Live to Work,' But Don't Prepare for Illness or Injury That Could Put Their Income at Risk," April 29, 2010.

10. Social Security Administration, "Fact Sheet on the Old-Age, Survivors, and Disability Insurance Program," June 28, 2011.

11. Jim Angstadt, "Most Americans 'Live to Work.' "

12. Ibid.

13. Shared Hope International, "The National Report on Domestic Minor Sex Trafficking: America's Prostituted Children," May 2009.

14. Mike Celizic, "Teen Recalls Horror of Abduction into Sexual Slavery," *Today,* November 3, 2008.

15. Kids Fighting Chance, "Kidnapping Statistics," http://kidsfightingchance.com /stats.php (accessed July 25, 2011).

16. Timothy Weinstein, "The Financial Cost of Child Abduction," http://bringsean home.org/?page_id=64 (accessed July 25, 2011).

17. Bring Sean Home Foundation, http://bringseanhome.org (accessed July 25, 2011).

18. Trey Wilder and Brett Lipton, "Top 10 Kidnap-Rated Countries with Ransom Stats," April 3, 2008.

19. Ibid.

20. Environmental Protection, "Harris Poll: Most Americans Think Devastating Natural Disasters Are Increasing," July 8, 2011, http://eponline.com/articles /2011/07/08/poll-most-americans-think-devastating-natural-disasters-are-in creasing.aspx (accessed July 25, 2011).

21. The World Bank, "Second Technical Advisory Group (TAG) meeting," February, 5–9, 2001.

22. FEMA: Federal Emergency Management Agency, http://www.fema.gov (accessed July 25, 2011).

23. FEMA, "Personal and Family Preparedness Checklist."

24. Ibid.

25. National Climatic Data Center, "Billion Dollar U.S. Weather Disasters," http:// www.ncdc.noaa.gov/oa/reports/billionz.html (accessed July 25, 2011).

26. FEMA, "Protect Your Property or Business from Disaster," http://www.fema .gov/business/protect.shtm (accessed July 25, 2011).

27. Ready.gov, "Continuity of Operations Plan," http://www.ready.gov/business/plan /planning.html (accessed July 25, 2011).

28. "About CERT," http://www.citizencorps.gov/cert/about.shtm (accessed July 25, 2011).

29. Cinnamon S. Bloss, Nicholas J. Schork, and Eric J. Topol, "Effect of Direct-to-Consumer Genomewide Profiling to Assess Disease Risk," *New England Journal of Medicine*, February 10, 2011, http://www.nejm.org/doi/pdf/10.1056/NEJ Moa1011893 (accessed July 25, 2011).

30. Thomas Goetz, "Sergey Brin's Search for a Parkinson's Cure," June 22, 2010, http://www.wired.com/magazine/2010/06/ff_sergeys_search/all/1 (accessed July 25, 2011).

31. Victoria Barrett, "Genetic Giving," June 2, 2011, http://www.forbes.com/sites/victoriabarret/2011/06/02/genetic-giving/ (accessed July 25, 2011).

32. Kristina Allers, Gero Hutter, Jorg Hofmann, Christoph Loddenkemper, Kathrin Rieger, Eckhard Thiel, and Thomas Schneider, "Evidence for the cure of HIV infection by CCR5Δ32/Δ32 stem cell transplantation," March 10, 2011, http://bloodjournal.hematologylibrary.org/content/117/10/2791.longtemp2k (accessed July 25, 2011).

Chapter 6

1. William J. Cromie, "Why Women Live Longer than Men."

2. Chavon Sutton, "43% Have Less Than $10k for Retirement," CNNMoney, March 9, 2010.

3. Carol Fleck, "Running Out of Money Worse Than Death," AARP *Bulletin*, July 1, 2010.

4. Richard Kiy and Anne McEnany, "Health Care and Americans Retiring in Mexico," May 2010.

5. Donna Fuscald, "8 Great Places to Retire Abroad," Kiplinger, June 29, 2011.

6. David McKeegan, "What You Should Know about U.S. Taxes While Living Abroad," http://www.liveabroad.com/articles/taxes.html (accessed July 25, 2011).

7. AARP.org, "Nursing Homes: Cost and Coverage," http://assets.aarp.org/external_sites/caregiving/options/nursing_home_costs.html (accessed July 26, 2011).

8. AARP.org, "Nursing Homes: Cost and Coverage."

9. Jim Angstadt, "Most Americans 'Live to Work.' But Don't Prepare for Illness or Injury That Could Put Their Income at Risk," April 29, 2010.

10. Social Security Administration, "Fact Sheet on the Old-Age, Survivors, and Disability Insurance Program," June 28, 2011.

11. AARP.org, "Home and Community Preferences of the 45+ Population http://assets.aarp.org/rgcenter/general/home-community-services-10.pdf (accessed July 27, 2011).

12. Ibid.

13. Ibid.

14. The Cohousing Association of the United States, "Developing Senior Cohousing," http://www.cohousing.org/2010/program/developingsenior (accessed July 27, 2011).

15. Ibid.

Chapter 7

1. "How to Succeed in Family Business," *The Wall Street Journal,* June 12, 2008.
2. Capgemini, Merrill Lynch World Wealth Report 2010.
3. Capgemini, Merrill Lynch World Wealth Report: 10th Anniversary, 1997–2006.
4. Reginald. F. Lewis, "Biography," http://www.reginaldflewis.com/biography-2.php (accessed July 26, 2011).
5. Katherine Calos, "Billionaire's Sister Helps Those Down on Their Luck," December 19, 2010, http://www.sunshinelady.org/?p=987 (accessed July 26, 2011).
6. Women's Independence Scholarship Program, Inc. (WISP, Inc.), http://www.wispinc.org/About/tabid/54/Default.aspx (accessed July 26, 2011).
7. John J. Havens and Paul G. Schervish, "Why the $41 Trillion Wealth Transfer Estimate Is Still Valid: A Review of Challenges and Questions," *The Journal of Gift Planning,* June 6, 2003.

INDEX

.